FASTER THAN THE SUN

Faster than the Sun

PETER TWISS

With a Foreword by Lord Brabazon of Tara

GRUB STREET · LONDON

Published by Grub Street
4 Rainham Close
London SW11 6SS

First published in hardback 1963
Second edition first published 2000
This edition, expanded and updated, first published 2005

Copyright © 2005 Grub Street, London
Text copyright © Peter Twiss

British Library Cataloguing in Publication Data
Twiss, Peter
Faster than the sun: the compelling story of a record-breaking test pilot
　　1. Twiss, Peter 2. Test pilots – Great Britain – Biography
　　3. High-speed aeronautics
　　I. Title
　　629.1'3'092

ISBN 1-904943-36-5

Typeset by Pearl Graphics, Hemel Hempstead

Printed and bound in Great Britain by
Biddles Ltd, King's Lynn

To my Mother

CONTENTS

Acknowledgements	6
Foreword	7
Introduction	8
1. I FIND A WORLD BEATER	11
2. A BOY WITH NO THOUGHT OF FLYING	20
3. WE KNOW WE CAN DO IT	23
4. THE UNWILLING SCHOLAR	31
5. OBSTRUCTION AND RED TAPE	34
6. A CHECKERED PATTERN OF SCHOOLDAYS	39
7. WE PLAN FOR A RECORD	43
8. TEST PILOT BY ACCIDENT	54
9. CLOAK-AND-DAGGER	59
10. WARTIME LANDMARKS	67
11. TIMING THE RECORD	72
12. READY TO GO	85
13. WE BEAT THE RECORD – AND FAIL	87
14. PRIVATE LIVES AND PUBLIC IMAGES	92
15. OUR LAST CHANCE	95
16. SWEATING IT OUT	102
17. ONE SWALLOW…	112
18. AND THE PRESS SAID…	115
19. THE YEARS AFTER	125
20. WAS IT FOR NOTHING?	129
21. ENGLAND IS BARRED TO US	137
22. ON THE SHELF	146
23. SEABORNE NOT AIRBORNE	152
EPILOGUE	159
MY WARTIME YEARS	174
Appendix I	198
Appendix II	204
Appendix III	206
Index	211

ACKNOWLEDGEMENTS

1 would like to make it clear that the views expressed in this book and the comments on the events described are entirely my own.

I am indebted to all those in the aviation world, particularly those in the Fairey organisation past and present who, amongst other things, built the Delta and gave me the opportunity to fly it. Unfortunately it is impossible to mention everyone concerned by name in a personal account such as this; I hope that those omitted will take the will for the deed.

P. T.

FOREWORD

by LORD BRABAZON of TARA

I have always admired the cool, calculated courage of the test pilot. Anybody who knows the dangers ahead and yet faces them day after day is in a class by himself, compared with he who on the spur of the moment does something remarkable under the stress of emergency.

I don't know why I was disinclined at first to read Peter Twiss's book, but it was very silly for the reason that after getting into it I could not put it down.

The story of the Delta, and the speed record by it of over 1,000 m.p.h., is told in an arresting way.

No one, till they have read this book, can have any idea of the technical difficulties of timing such an experiment. Almost does one get the impression from Peter Twiss that the actual timing was more difficult than the flying, but the accuracy of his patterns through the air 40,000 feet up, having for measurement purposes to fly through imaginary "hoops" in order to get the record officially established, must be read to be appreciated.

In a book of this sort there must come through the pages the character of the writer, and I find this wholly agreeable.

His acknowledgement of debt to the team that made it all possible and especially his tribute to Gordon Slade, who gave up his undoubted right to fly the record trip in order to help the Author over a very difficult technical stile, are typical of the generosity of this man.

The actual story of the breaking of the record after so many failures, not because the speed was not enough, but because of failure in the variety and difficult organisation of the timing, glues one to the book.

Having really got into the book I should have welcomed more details of his interesting experiment on "sonic" bangs at low altitudes, about which we know so little, but the book is a feast and this is a selfish criticism.

I am sure the work will be a great success and read by thousands, for it deserves it, both in the writing and as an epic.

Also it is my earnest wish that in Peter Twiss's new venture on calmer waters he will find interest, success and contentment. He deserves it.

INTRODUCTION

Flying an aeroplane is one thing. Writing the story of my life is quite another. You know where to start with an aeroplane. It is all cut and dried for you. There are no two ways of doing things. You get into the cockpit and, provided you do the right things in the right order, you've started. But where the hell do you start your own life's story?

I was born on the twenty-third of July, 1921, in the usual way.

Perfectly true. But almost every flying book I've ever read started off, I was born on the . . . and I have been bored stiff skipping the pages until the chap got to where it really mattered: in the air. It's as bad as being shown the family picture album; being told when the poor soul first said Mama, or when he first discovered he could stand on his own fat two legs and promptly fell out of the cot on his head, or when he bit the neck of the gripewater bottle off with his first tooth. But that time he came in to land with half the brass of the services watching and ended up in a cloud of dust and the most expensive noise he'd ever heard because he'd forgotten to put his undercart down – that's something.

If I told you my life story from the beginning, you'd find that it was a duller, even more ordinary life story than your own, and you'd wonder why I'd ever bothered to write it at all. False modesty? How can I honestly say my life has been quite ordinary? I was a test pilot? I was the first man in history to fly at a thousand miles an hour? These are the things that make it harder for me, because they set me apart from you. You think there must be something extraordinary about me. Well, judge for yourself. I had the perfectly conventional childhood of the son of a serving army officer, seeing rather less of his parents than children whose fathers were not serving army officers. I had a perfectly conventional middle-class education, except that I was more idle than most. It was quite by chance that I became a pilot at all. I was probably as wicked an unruly little bastard as any small boy in the country. It was the Boy Scouts that gave me a sense of direction and stopped me growing up into an unruly big bastard. My Scout troop at school was easily the most formative influence for good in my early years.

Doesn't sound like the test pilot in embryo you'd imagined?

I warned you it was all very ordinary. And there's worse to come. I wasn't all that interested in aeroplanes as a small boy except in an offhand sort of way. My abiding passion was nature study, bird watching and, later, bird photography. Above all, when I left school, I wanted to be a game warden. It never occurred to me that all sorts of qualifications were needed. I thought all I had to do was to leave school and apply to be one. I didn't know they needed good school-leaving qualifications and a university degree. If I had, I might have worked a bit harder. Very well, I could set my sights lower. I'd become a gamekeeper, or even an assistant gamekeeper. I wrote away to various farms and estates offering them my services. Nobody wanted an assistant gamekeeper. Instead, my ambitions as a nature lover died in the dust of Aldgate. Round about the time of Munich I found myself in the human ant-heap of the City of London instead. City gent, aged eighteen. Morning train by rush-hour to Aldgate East. Brooke Bonds. An apprentice tea-taster. Eighteen shillings a week, and the only nature I could see around me was far from my liking. It didn't last long. There were some people who had a farm near Salisbury, friends of my mother. They were short-handed, wanted a general help around the farm.

If it hadn't happened that the farm was on the route to the air station at Ford, in Sussex, I'd probably still be there. There was a signpost which I somehow confused with the airfield itself. I thought it would be nice to fly from there, imagining that the airfield was only just around the corner from the farm and I could have the best of both worlds. Even at that, the first time I tried to join up, they turned me down.

Hardly the story of the hell-bent young aviator with his eyes fixed on the sky that you'd expected? Until then, the only time I ever had my eyes on the sky with any positive intent was when I was watching the falcons that I trained at Sherborne School, thereby getting excused from playing cricket which bored me to distraction.

But surely now, there must be more than this. What about the world speed record? Ah, yes. It is this you want to be told about, just as this is really the only thing I want to tell. But how?

Saturday, 10th March, 1956. As the tiny Fairey Delta 2 and I roared across the measured course seven and a half miles up above the official timekeepers on the Sussex coast below, I knew we had succeeded.

This is true. But this is also the kind of thing you can only write about other people. When you write it about yourself it becomes impossibly, self-consciously egotistical. It sounds immediately like the classic wartime line-shoot: There was I, a ball of flame, 30,000 feet up, and upside down with the cockpit hood jammed, and what did I do. . . .

I've read stories that start like that. Not by pilots, though, because pilots don't think like that. It always makes me thoroughly uncomfortable. Even more so if I had to look at the printed page and realise that all those capital I's were me. Anyway, I didn't feel like that. It wasn't like that at all. It was a personal highlight, the world speed record run, of course. But every one of us has a highlight of some sort or another in his life. The ordinary man who found himself in the Dieppe raid or dropped in at Arnhem; the man who gets sudden and unexpected promotion in his firm; the man next door who raised a larger chrysanthemum than anyone had ever grown before. Or the boy who grew up to miss his vocation as a game warden and ended up by flying into four figures for the first time; and who now has two acres of garden and a very ordinary job directly under the strip of sky where all this happened.

I'll swear this to you. It was a hell of a sight easier to fly the record than it is to tell you about it in this book. At least I knew how to fly the Delta 2. How to get this story off the ground, let alone get it down again in one piece, is quite another matter. This is primarily the story of the Fairey Delta 2, from the moment I first took her off the ground to the time we beat the record against what seemed at times impossible odds of fortune, frustration, and failure even in the moments of success. Somewhere amongst all this, I hope enough of myself will emerge to convince you that I am still essentially the same person I was before it all happened; and that if you found that person standing beside you in the local, as very well you might, you wouldn't give him a second glance.

The major chapters, then, tell the story of the Fairey Delta project in a pretty straightforward chronological order. The shorter chapters in between fill in some of the personal background and can safely be skipped by the reader hasty to get on with the matter in hand. They have, perhaps, a certain curiosity value, in that they illustrate how oddly destiny can play a man's hand for him, creating the moment for the man if not always the man for the moment.

Thirty-six years after the original book was printed, I was approached by Grub Street regarding a reprint to include certain incidents in my later life from the 1960s to the Millennium. The story of the Fairey Delta 2 is still the main focus, however, with the speed record the primary feature.

The FD2 WG 774 lives on, now in the Fleet Air Arm Museum, Yeovilton, Somerset in the Concorde section in its modified form as the Bristol 221. The original aircraft has "lost" its looks! The "Ogee" wing, which was superimposed onto the FD2 Delta shape, added to many other modifications and significantly changed the appearance of the

FD2. However, it did sterling work and many of the Concorde wind tunnel theories were given full scale trials. After the record days were over and I had stopped serious flying, there were numerous interesting periods and incidents in my life which made the years race by. My reintroduction to flying, after 25 years, soaring and gliding, is something I should have done before.

Not content with me updating the original edition, in 2004, John Davies of Grub Street suggested that it would be welcomed by his loyal readership if I was to write in more detail about my wartime career. Again, this has not been an easy task but I have managed to revisit those momentous years and my thoughts are now revealed in the final chapter of the book. Further, there is now an extra section of photographs in the book from that time.

Peter Twiss
Titchfield 2005

1

I FIND A WORLD BEATER

I can remember, even more vividly than the speed record itself, the moment when I first knew that we could be the first people in the world to fly at more than a thousand miles an hour. It was on a bright October day in 1955. It was a day to remember in more ways than one, because this was the first time the Delta had flown for nearly a year. The last time I had flown this highly original aeroplane it had crashed on Boscombe Down with me in the cockpit. For a few moments then it had been a very open question as to whether the Delta or indeed myself would live to fly again, let alone beat the speed record.

It is not in the nature of a test pilot's temperament to brood neurotically on past events. If nothing ever went wrong with a new aircraft there would be no need for test pilots. It is our job to expect the unexpected, and we try to play the game as safely and with as much intelligent prediction as possible. There is never any harking back to past misfortunes. Once we know why it happened we can put it right, and from then on that at least is one potential failure we do not have to worry about any more.

Nevertheless, on this bright October morning, waiting to start the development programme again and to carry on from where we had been forced to interrupt it, I was very conscious of that November day a year before when for a time everything hung in the balance. I could even remember the date quite clearly: November 17th, 1954. . . .

It had been a good flying day with the crispness of late autumn already in the air, and, driving into White Waltham from my home, the autumnal colours of the countryside and somewhere the smell of burning leaves told me that soon we would be on to our winter schedules with its necessarily curtailed test flying.

On that morning, though, the weather had been fine and exhilarating, and the Delta was still new enough for the prospect of another day's test flying to be exciting. It never occurred to me that it might be exciting in the wrong way. We had made the maiden flight six weeks previously, and from the very first take-off she had handled beautifully. We had been able to push ahead with our programme much faster than anyone had anticipated.

At White Waltham I picked up the old de Havilland Rapide which we used as a communications aircraft providing a shuttle service between White Waltham, which was the home station, and Boscombe Down where the actual tests were being carried out.

I went to get the schedule for the day's testing, and then across to the Delta, standing ready and, even with her nose drooped in the landing position, looking very beautiful and flyable. The "droop-snoot", as it was called, was a device dreamt up by the design team in order to give the pilot better visibility for landing and take-off. It made the aircraft look as if someone had broken its nose, but, as soon as she was in flight, the "droop-snoot" was drawn back by hydraulic jacks into line with the rest of the fuselage, so that with its sword-pointed nose, slim fuselage, and Delta wings, it looked, and was, one of the most beautiful aircraft ever designed and one which always seemed to me to be so aesthetically right that it could not fail to succeed.

Design is essentially a team function these days; the time has long since passed when the major features of a new aircraft could be attributed to a single individual. However, Leslie Appleton must be mentioned here as the leader of the basic design team who bore the main responsibility for the Delta. The ingenious idea of the "droop-snoot" was the brain child of Charlie Chaplin, for many years Fairey's chief designer. Robert Lickley was chief engineer throughout the Delta's flying days.

In those early days, we were still treating her very gently. As is the common practice with all test development flight schedules, we were making haste slowly. The Delta was designed purely as a research aeroplane to study flying conditions at transonic speeds, i.e., just under and just over the speed of sound. Certainly it was never designed with a world speed record in mind. The whole development programme was a thoroughly hard-working one with day-to-day routine testing and without any such eccentric thoughts.

My first flight that day was the twelfth we had made, and we had followed this almost immediately after with flight number thirteen. Both had been entirely without incident. By now it was mid-morning and, remembering the threat of coming winter in the air that morning, we added one more flight to the day's schedule. Anxious as we were to press on with development as hard as we could while good flying weather still lasted, we removed a small sealing strip between the airframe and the engine which was threatening to become detached, because we were afraid it might be taken into the impeller during flight. Little did we imagine that, by making this very minor modification, we were storing up disaster for ourselves.

At that time we were gradually increasing the speed of the aircraft on each test, working up to the first time we would put her through the so-called sound barrier. We had not yet flown her supersonically but, on this particular day, we were very close to it, carrying out flutter tests at speeds of Mach 0.9, or just on the fringe of the speed of sound.

I had waited until she was refuelled and then got into the cockpit, carried out the routine cockpit check, which, with all the various test instruments involved was quite an extensive routine, and started up. Everything was absolutely normal, as it had been in the two previous tests, and I taxied out to the end of runway 24, pointed the Delta westwards down the runway and made the various routine checks that always have to be done before take-off. Again, everything was absolutely normal. I released the brakes and raced down the runway on the take-off run.

I suppose that somewhere at the back of his mind, every test pilot has a heightened sense of perception, which makes him aware quite unknown to himself of any deviation from the normal sounds and dial readings and vibrations in the curious solitary environment of the cockpit. However, in the flight, it isn't the things that might happen that occupy his mind but the things which are happening; on routine test flights such as these, the pilot's mind is far too occupied with the multitudinous observations he has to make during the flight to think of anything else.

The more I flew the Delta the more I liked it. This was a pleasant, relaxed flight, and if I thought of anything at all apart from the job on hand it had probably been about getting home and the people who were coming in that evening. It was still perfect flying weather with only a little fluffy cumulus cloud scattered around. I was listening to the R/T while I climbed up to 30,000 ft. where we were due to level-off to make the flutter tests. Everything had been going very smoothly, and with the wonderful feeling of flying an aircraft which you felt instinctively was with you all the way.

Then, as I levelled off at 30,000 ft., I glanced at the fuel gauge during a routine check of the instruments. I could not believe my eyes. As I watched, I saw the needle swing right round anti-clockwise from "full" to "empty" – all in the space of a few seconds.

I don't remember being particularly worried at that stage. I knew that we could not suddenly have lost all our fuel, as the instrument readings seemed to suggest, and I was inclined to put it down to some temperamental quirk on the part of the fuel gauge itself. Certainly there had been no other signs that the aircraft was not performing perfectly.

As this was part of the outward trip, I had still been making distance between myself and the base at Boscombe Down, so, as a precaution, I called up the ground controller on the R/T and asked for a home bearing just in case the meter reading spelt trouble and I had to get back in a hurry. They gave me the bearing and I noted it mentally, and really, I think, quite casually, never dreaming for a moment that I was going to need it.

Within a few seconds the fuel pressure warning light had come on, confirming that the fuel gauge was giving a correct reading. This was beyond my understanding, as I knew from all the indications in the cockpit that we had plenty of fuel for the flight. A few ridiculous thoughts went through my mind about what happens to test pilots who run out of fuel, when the inevitable happened. Surely and inescapably the engine was losing speed. With a curious kind of fascination I watched the engine rev. counter unwind.

This left me at 30,000 ft., still flying away from Boscombe Down, but with no engine. The Delta was now a glider and a pretty fast one at that. Almost automatically I turned to the bearing I had got from Boscombe Down and pointed the nose down slightly to keep flying speed.

Then it was time to do some thinking. The main question was: "Can I get back to Boscombe safely in one piece or will it be wiser to eject?"

I had sufficient height to use the ejector seat, there was no doubt of that, but there could be several other snags. One of these was that the aircraft was fitted with power controls and no manual reversion. This meant that the controls would only work if there was sufficient hydraulic pressure. Unlike other aircraft, if there was a hydraulic failure, there was no way in which you could switch over the controls so that you could work them directly from the pilot's stick. As it was, the stick simply controlled a lot of valves which operated the flying controls through hydraulic jacks. If the hydraulic pressure failed I was helpless to maintain control. What I had to decide, pretty quickly, was whether, with the engine dead, there was sufficient hydraulic pressure left to get me back. We had previously done several calculations on the ground and these gave me confidence that I stood a fair chance of getting back, but that it would be best to keep all movements of the controls to an absolute minimum since, every time 1 used any of the controls, this meant using up some more of the small reserve of hydraulic pressure that remained.

There was, of course, the fact that I was flying a most valuable aircraft, and I naturally wanted to save it if I could. And one other thing which is often overlooked in cases like these, was that I was sitting in a comfortable cockpit. Because there seemed a chance of getting back, I was naturally reluctant to exchange the familiar cockpit for what would be, for me, the unknown experience of using an ejector seat and being blown into a cold outside world.

All this takes some time to explain on paper, but these thoughts ran through my head in a few seconds and I decided to take the aircraft home. I called Boscombe Down and told them I was in trouble and coming back. I asked them to guide me down because, from where I was, looking diagonally down through the clouds, I could not see the airfield and I could not afford to make a number of corrective control movements to line up with the runway.

Throughout the flight I had been talking into the ground recorder which made a record of everything I said, giving a running commentary on what control movements I had made and what effects they had. I did this so that, whatever happened, there would be a record of the flight. With an emergency like this, the recorder assumes an even greater importance; so much so that, while I was receiving homing directions from Boscombe Down, I still continued to talk into the recorder so that there might be some chance of tracing the trouble if I did not get back.

Looking down, I saw that I was over Newbury, in Berkshire, and height was falling off rapidly. By this time it is no exaggeration to say that I was feeling uncomfortable. In order to save what hydraulic power was left I decided not to use the dive brakes. Another snag was that the so-called "droopsnoot" could not be operated, once again because it needed hydraulic power to do so. Now the whole idea of this drooped nose was to give the pilot some sort of sight of the runway on which he was to land. Without it he was blind because the Delta assumes a position, as it comes in to land at its normal approach speed of 150 m.p.h., in which its nose points up in the air to a much greater extent than with ordinary aeroplanes. Normally this would mean that the pilot was looking directly up into the sky at the very moment when he wanted to see the runway. The hinged-nose section overcame this by lowering the pilot section of the aeroplane to increase runway visibility. I remember wondering vaguely what it would be like landing without seeing the runway at all, or, alternatively, coming in at over 200 m.p.h. By this time I was sweating considerably both from efforts of concentration and a certain amount of apprehension. The radio directions were still coming in and then, at 2,000 to 3,000 ft., I broke cloud. I was relieved to see the runway nicely in position about six or seven miles ahead. It was reassuring to find that I was in fact lined up with that long concrete strip, especially as I was now committed to a landing.

The runway came nearer much faster than I would have liked, and then I received the last transmission from Control:

"You are cleared straight in on 24 – you will be slightly down wind. Best of luck," came the voice in my earphones.

By then I was a mile and a half from the runway with plenty of height still in hand and much too much excess speed. Without the brakes there was very little I could do about this. I decided that it was time to try to get the wheels down.

On the Delta there is a safety device which prevents the main undercarriage locks coming down before the nose-wheel is down. I selected the "undercarriage down" control, and waited to see what would happen. The nose-wheel came down fully but, as I had half expected, there was insufficient hydraulic pressure left even to unlock the main wheels. It would have to be a "wheels up" landing at about a two-hundred-miles-an-hour touchdown. Curiously enough this was not my chief worry. What I had been afraid of all along was that the hydraulic pressure would fall so low that I would not be able to operate the flying controls. In this case the aircraft would have been out of control altogether. Now to my relief I found that we were coming over the runway with still enough hydraulic power left to operate all the flying controls necessary to get us down in one piece.

I was doing 230 to 240 m.p.h. as I crossed the threshold of the airfield and held the Delta off for a landing. Immediately, the Delta took up her high-angle landing aspect and, without being able to use the "droop-snoot", the long reassuring runway disappeared from view behind the tilted nose and I found myself looking helplessly at the sky.

The first thing I felt was the tail scraping the runway and making a most expensive-sounding noise. Reports from Maurice Child, our flight-development engineer who was watching the whole performance, told of sheets of sparks from the rear fuselage. The front of the aircraft pitched down on to the extended nose-wheel so that, without our main wheels down, the aircraft was skidding along the runway still with her nose stuck right up in the air.

Then I was careering down the runway with the aeroplane supported by the tail at the rear and the nose-wheel at the front. My speed was still over 120 knots. This had its advantages in that it gave sufficient flying stability to keep the wings level.

After that there was nothing I could do. My part in the flight was now over. The Delta 2 was on her own and I was merely an unwilling passenger. Instinctively, I operated the rudder and brakes, but neither could be effective because the wheels were safely tucked away.

We raced down the runway like this for $1\frac{1}{4}$ miles. The speed seemed to take an eternity to dissipate. Then, at about 110 knots, the stability began to go and the Delta veered off to port. I thought she was going to hit the Control Tower. Sitting completely impotently in the cockpit I had the ghastly sensation of careering round a corner at high speed – completely out of control.

We had left the runway some time ago and, on the grass, the speed dropped more rapidly. At 70 m.p.h. the starboard wing stuck in the ground and I was afraid that, with her narrow wing span, the Delta would tip over. I had another worry, too. I was very much afraid that, with all the bumps and shocks which were going on, the ejector seat would go off and I would find myself in the unfortunate position of being ejected at ground level.

We were still making thirty to forty knots when I jettisoned the hood. I was out of that cockpit almost before the aircraft had stopped moving.

From the time that the engine had stopped at 30,000 ft. to the time I had jumped from the cockpit was no more than six minutes. But even looking back at it now, it seemed like an eternity.

The ambulances and fire engines were there waiting, but were not needed. The Delta did not catch fire, and, although I was considerably shaken and had twisted my back during the aeroplane's crazy journey at the end of the landing run, I was otherwise unhurt.

Having made the ejector seat safe, I checked the wing fuel tanks. They were full. The engine had been starved by a curious fault in the fuel system which no one could have foreseen and which was the direct result of air pressures inside the fuselage set up during high-speed flying. Who could have foreseen that the harmless, unwanted piece of rubber seal we had removed could have caused so much trouble? It took us several weeks to find out that this simple action had resulted in air pressure building up around the rubber fuel tank in the fuselage until, in the end, it had collapsed. The second thing I did was to persuade the doctor that I was still in one piece and make rapidly for the local pub, where I restored as quickly as possible the fluid I had lost in the most concentrated five minutes of perspiration I have ever experienced.

Now, on this October morning, very nearly a year later, I lifted the Delta off the runway once again, to continue where we had left off.

I had liked the Delta well enough before, but now, as I climbed up to 30,000 ft., I liked her even more. During the period when we had been repairing the aircraft, the team had taken the opportunity to make several small modifications, and it seemed to me now that the aircraft was flying better than she had ever flown before. The intention on these resumed flights was to continue with flutter tests, which had been so rudely interrupted the previous November, at just under the speed of sound. We went supersonic a few flights later. Furthermore it was done so easily. The remarkable thing was that there was nothing, apart from a flick on the needles of the instruments, to tell me that I had gone through the sound barrier at all. There was absolutely none of the turbulence or vibration or eccentric behaviour which pilots had always noticed with previous aircraft going through this very critical speed. The Delta was the first aircraft to be designed specifically to fly supersonically and, as if determined to prove that she knew it, she just slipped through when I wasn't looking. If ever the Delta had had to justify herself to me after her crash, this wonderful little aircraft did so that morning when she flew as gently as a bird into the hard supersonic October sky. From that moment, I knew we had a world-beater.

2

A BOY WITH NO THOUGHT OF FLYING

I was awarded the Queen's Commendation for bringing us both back on that occasion, dented but otherwise unbowed.

But the honest truth is that I brought the Delta back as much as a matter of self-preservation as anything else.

That was only one of many times during my life that destiny created the moment for the man; even, perhaps, occasionally created the man for the moment. But there was certainly nothing in my early years to suggest that here the child was father to the man.

There is, in fact, very little about my early years that I can remember, except being in trouble. I took my first breath on July 23rd, 1921, in a Sussex village called Lindfield, near Haywards Heath, where my grandmother lived. My grandfather was an admiral. My grandmother, therefore, was an admiral's wife and, later, an admiral's widow in comparatively reduced circumstances because the admiral's pension died with the admiral. At the time I was born they lived in what I was later to appreciate as a very pleasant Georgian mansion, Lindfield House.

But I'd been taken out to Burma and Malaya, Mandalay, and back again before my infant wits had developed any record of the scene, my father being stationed out there at the time on attachment to the Burmese Regiment. I'm not quite certain why I was born in England at all in view of these circumstances, except that there seemed to be a curious custom at that time whereby wives of serving officers carrying their unborn sons were expected to return to the scene of the crime to give them birth, presumably to ensure that they should receive the inestimable benefit of yelling their first lungful on true English soil, with the sun making rays like the Union Jack through the haze of British atmosphere. Or perhaps my mother just wanted to come back.

No mention of my mother would be complete without at least a brief tribute to the efforts she made throughout my childhood to hold the family together, often under very difficult circumstances. Firstly, with my father serving abroad, our home life was necessarily being interrupted continually. Later, much of the burden of educating two teenage boys fell on her shoulders alone, and involved considerable personal sacrifices to which I have probably never paid ample tribute. She gave rather more than her all and, like most boys everywhere, we probably took it all very much too much for granted.

There is one glimmer of memory in those very early years, and it is only worth reporting because I very nearly fell out of a porthole into the Indian Ocean. I certainly couldn't have been more than about three, so I suppose it rates as my first conscious memory.

Where in all boyhood can I find even a hint of the man who was to bring the Delta back to a dead-stick landing thirty years on? The only things you remember at that age are the times you were in trouble. My brother, Paul, two and a half years older, and myself in the boat coming home from Mandalay. Finding one of those round cigarette tins that you get only on board ships and which seal-in fifty cigarettes, and some string in my mother's cabin. Dangling this thing out of the porthole to try and get it down to the sea on its piece of string. And throwing all the soap out of the window. My mother looking in, dressed for dinner, all splendidly arrayed, to see how her dear children were behaving – and in the cabin was her youngest, already well through the porthole, on the way to the Indian Ocean.

You need a sense of adventure, I suppose, to be a test pilot. But a sense of recklessness?

You have to be preternaturally inquisitive, too. You have to be interested in why things work and, when they don't work, why they don't. An innate inquisitiveness, together with a lot of cussedness and plain everyday luck on the occasion of that dead-stick landing, saved us months of time in the development of the Delta. Had we lost the aircraft, we would have lost our clues at the same time.

Certainly I can find the germ of this innate inquisitiveness as far back as I can remember. And, also, that curiously detached self-reliance – a rather solitary thing – that almost all test pilots have. Possibly it had something to do with the fact that, for various reasons, I never had much of a family life as a child, and was thrown back on my own resources a great deal. Even as a toddler – when we'd just got back to England, with my father quartered at the South Staffs barracks at Whittington, just outside Lichfield – I was never afraid of being lost; or of being alone. Like the day I set off for the kindergarten and never got there. On the way, I stopped at a place where the road was up and they were doing something to the gas mains or the electricity system. They had one of those splendid tents over a hole in the road. Fascinating to a small child.

There was a wonderful smell of that black bitumen or pitch, or whatever it is they use for sealing electric cables. Hours after I had been reported missing, they found me in this road-up tent, filled and happy with eggs and bacon cooked over the Primus by the men in the hole, quite oblivious that anyone might be wondering where I had got to – and quite unneedful of anyone except myself.

By and large, though, I believe I was a pretty typical small boy, horrible little beasts that they are – wicked, stubborn, independent, hungry, bone idle, and straight out of one scrap into another with the resiliency of a rubber ball.

It all adds up to the rather dull conclusion that any normal high-spirited boy could have grown up to do the things I did, had destiny only dealt him the sequence of events it dealt me. It was certainly no overweening ambition to be the fastest man in the world that got me into the cockpit of the Delta. Such thoughts never entered my head. It was the sequence of quite unrelated events that, quite accidentally, determined my destiny, not *vice versa*. Just in the same way as the Delta decided to break the world air-speed record. We didn't create the situation; the situation created us. All we did was what the Delta told us we had to do.

3

WE KNOW WE CAN DO IT

As I landed the Delta after her first supersonic flight, the short October day was already closing in. It was as if I, as well as the aircraft, had gone through a barrier that separated the present from the future, one that had taken us beyond the conception of high-speed flight as our experience had known it up till then and had led us through into the exhilaration of the unexplored future.

I was feeling immensely exhilarated, and I could sense that this exhilaration was shared by the rest of the team. This had nothing to do with the idea of attacking the world speed record at all, which was still only a partially germinated seed of an idea at the back of my mind, not yet fully appreciated nor consciously grasped. Our excitement that day was due possibly in part to some subconscious relief that, in our first flights after the crash, the Delta had gone through a full day's flying with no coincidental misfortune. One knows that, in testing, these coincidental misfortunes don't happen, or very, very seldom, but test pilots and designers alike, no matter what their appearance to the outside world may be, tend to be somewhat withdrawn and introverted people whose actions and emotions are not always dictated solely by logic. Deep down inside all of us are all the taboos and symbols and superstitions of a million years. It is superstition that makes some of us carry useless talismans on flights to ward off evil actions which we know won't happen anyway; just as it is superstition that makes others amongst us experience a sense of elation at the end of a successful flight following a bad one.

However, the main reason for our elation this time was simply that the design of the Delta had shown us in the most impressive way that we were very much better than we knew. I cannot, at this stage, remember the details of our discussions on that occasion, nor can I even be certain of all the people who were there. Certainly one of them was Fairey's chief test pilot at that time, Gordon Slade, and he was almost certainly the first person to whom I mentioned that we might have a go at the record.

Gordon Slade, as chief test pilot, was my immediate boss, and a very good boss he was, too, quite apart from being a brilliant pilot. But he could be unnerving on first acquaintance, this tough group-captain. Uncompromising and a strong disciplinarian, he could be short on tolerance and was the kind of man who got things done without undue regard for other people's feelings.

One very soon found a very firm and generous friend underneath this somewhat forbidding exterior, and a tremendous sense of fun. The latter could be boisterous. There had been an occasion soon after I joined Fairey's, when Gordon and I had sat through a pompous and very stuffy dinner at the Midland Hotel, Manchester, following a conference between the firm and the Ministry of Supply. Someone made a paper aeroplane out of the menu, and across the room it went. This gave Gordon the idea that he could do better. Suddenly an absolutely vast prototype sailed out of Gordon's hands, carrying a cargo of all the cutlery he could lay his hands on. In a shocked silence, we watched it fly straight at its intended target, finally disgorging its load in the laps of the senior members of the conference. I shall remember him above all for a quite fantastic generosity of character.

The Ministry of Supply, who had given us the contract to develop the Delta, would certainly have had a restless night in a few high places had they known what was going through our minds that afternoon – and this time it was no paper dart. They were to know, but not until some time later and even then it shook them to their foundations. Ministries, as we shall see, are more likely to throw a bureaucratic spanner into the works than creative imagination, when faced with a project which is not in the book of rules and which requires vision rather than a visible filing system.

The more the impact of the Delta's performance that day sank in, the more astonished we were. That evening, Gordon Slade and myself made a few mental calculations and realised that, although we had not been the first aircraft to go supersonic on the level, instead of having to make a power dive to do it, we had done it quite effortlessly, using only a fraction of the available power in the Rolls-Royce Avon engine. And even with this considered, we still had a vast potential of unexploited power in the re-heat system, which we had not yet touched. On the present schedule of routine testing, it would be some weeks yet before we would even consider using the afterburner. Up till then the idea of a record bid had been so far from my mind that I didn't even know exactly what the present record was, though I knew it was something round about 820 m.p.h. (The standing record was, of course, 822.26 m.p.h., and it was held by the American test pilot, Col. H. "Dude" Haynes, flying a North American F-100C Super Sabre.) I had to look it up before I could be sure about it. Now, as I thought about it, I became more and more convinced that not only could we go well above "Dude" Haynes's figure, but that we could be the first in the world to reach four figures. To me, there was a magic in these four figures – 1,000 miles per hour – which held a fascination that no ordinary record figure could ever hold.

Looking back on it, it now seems a curiously inverted situation that the pressure for a record bid should come from a couple of test pilots instead of as a directive from some elevated governmental department, eager to see Britain regain her falling prestige in the aircraft industry. In point of fact, the suggestion would never have come from ministerial sources and, had we not pushed it ourselves, it is very unlikely that it ever would have taken place, and it is almost certain that the American hold on the record would have remained unbroken. As it was, by far the hardest part of the whole project was persuading the Ministry that this was a thing we ought to do.

As far as I am aware, no one at this stage ever sat down and wrote a memo saying "This is what we should do". The germ of the idea was planted solidly that day. And the project grew casually, like an unwanted weed. Suddenly, it seemed almost impossible to have a conversation with anyone in the Fairey organisation without the topic somehow cropping up. In the next few weeks, of course, everyone in the organisation, as well as those at Boscombe Down and White Waltham, knew that we had gone supersonic much more easily than we had anticipated. I imagine that the idea must have arisen spontaneously in quite a number of different people's minds. This was after all to be expected. Whether you are flying aircraft, or training for a four-minute mile, or anything else, as soon as you discover that you can go faster than you thought, your mind immediately asks – "Faster than what?" Immediately, as part of human nature, you seek competition, something to prove yourself against. Thus it was that around Fairey's in the days following this flight, although previously you never heard any mention whatever of either the existing or any future air-speed record, suddenly the place was full of it. People who had only a fringe interest would suddenly show unexpected knowledge of record statistics and regulations. Others for no apparent reason would suddenly ask their colleagues or neighbours, out of the blue, what the present speed record was. But no one mentioned the magic figure of one thousand miles an hour. At that stage, I think I was probably the only person who was quite convinced that it could be done, with the possible exception of Gordon. It became an obsession with me, although I had very little real hope that we would ever get permission to try; and I was certainly not being driven forward by any sense of personal self-glorification for I quite naturally assumed that, although I would play my part in any such project, it would be Gordon Slade as my chief test pilot who would make any actual record flight. It was simply that I knew the Delta could do it. I knew the Americans were on the fringe of doing it, and I believed that we should get there first. But how I was going to achieve this objective I had not the slightest idea. I remember standing in one of the office passages at Hayes a little while later and catching one of the directors as he came out from a conference. It has been said that all the significant conferences of the world have taken place, not in the conference hall, but in corridors so that, geographically, this one can take its place with the best. I caught him in the corridor as he passed with some of his co-directors. He made some remark in passing about the Delta and this gave me the opportunity I was waiting for. I asked him, " What would you say if we had a go at the world speed record?"

I wish I could report honestly that this remark had the effect which, for the sake of the dramatic integrity of this narrative, I feel it should have had, but the true facts are that it went off like a damp and only partially heard squib. Whether I had mistimed it or not I don't know, but it is quite certain that no one treated it with any seriousness at all. As they passed on their way to a boardroom lunch, I was left alone in the corridor with the impression that I had simply made a vaguely humorous throw-away remark. I felt very much like the man who starts to tell a funny story and then suddenly forgets the end and discovers that his audience has gone.

But at least, to myself at any rate, the fact that the matter had now been broached, even in this highly unsatisfactory and somewhat unorthodox way, at executive level, gave the thing body and substance whereas, up till then, it had only been a fluffy thought with blurred edges wandering round from mind to mind without any clear definition or purpose.

From then on, it became a personal quest. Myself, Gordon Slade, and members of the design and flight-development team, notably Maurice Child, who at that time was chief development engineer, could be seen at all hours of the day and night poring over figures on scraps of paper. Maurice Child and I had neighbouring offices and, when the calculations got beyond my modest capabilities, it was in his office that you would find me using his considerable mathematical resources to prove the point. This burning of midnight oil over abstruse mathematical equations, as if we were performing some secret rite with cabalistic signs of mathematical mysticism to invoke success, was not simply a matter of conjuring up our particular gods. These calculations more than anything else convinced the board that all was possible. Even so, we still found it hard to believe that the Delta could give us the fantastic performance that all our experience led us to believe it could. At times it seemed so improbable, that we felt certain something must be missing from our calculations. And so, now that we were committed to pushing this thing forward just as far and as hard as we could, we crept away into quiet corners and did sums and still more sums, rather more carefully-worked-out sums than we had done before, just to make certain we weren't in fact simply making clowns of ourselves. Behind my own mind at this time was very much the same feeling one had had at school when, having completed a calculation, one was suddenly conscious of the mathematics master poring over it from behind one's shoulder in an atmosphere of ominous silence. At any moment, I expected one or the other of us suddenly to say, "Oh look, we're all being complete fools – look, you have forgotten to add here or to subtract there," or to do something else that was equally ridiculous. But try as we would, we could not refute our figures. On the contrary, the more we extrapolated the performance figures from those we already had and the greater detail in which we considered them, the better the prognostication appeared.

These were trying times for the whole of the team, for we still had to carry out our day-to-day routine development tests on the Delta according to the original contract schedule and, indeed, all the manifold daily administrative detail as well, as if there was nothing else whatever in the air. And all the time the tension was increasing because we knew the vital need for urgency if the thing was ever going to be done at all. Every day that passed made it less likely that we would succeed, because we had unquestionable information about the Americans and knew that they had at least two aircraft capable of exceeding the existing speed record and, if need be, of being pushed up to the four-figure mark. They had limitless resources compared with ourselves, an entire continent from which to choose a location ideally suitable from the climatic point of view, and an already established routine and technical equipment to measure a high-altitude run to the satisfaction of the controlling body. We had none of these things, and if the Americans succeeded in jumping the gun on us, the record, as far as we could see, would be out of our reach for ever. This was quite probably the last chance that we in Britain would ever have to prove that, in spite of all the critics could say about the British aircraft industry and in spite of our pitifully small financial resources for such projects, we could still design and build aeroplanes to beat the best in the world.

The situation was one of extreme frustration, because there was no simple straightforward way of giving the project the impetus it so urgently needed. Sir Richard Fairey, of course, is part of the history of aviation. For this very reason, the firm had a curiously feudal composition, which I suppose must be considered somewhat of an anachronism in the twentieth century but which was nevertheless the basis of its strength in its heyday. It was not so much a family firm as a benevolent autarchy ruled over by the formidable figure of Sir Richard himself. In fact, by lobbying the various directors of the board, we were well aware that we were achieving little else than battering our heads against a buffer which was placed there deliberately to prevent such onslaughts against the inner sanctum itself.

This is not to say that good relations did not exist between the staff and those at the top of the firm. On the contrary, it was one of the finest firms imaginable to work for and I for one would not wish to work for any other. We all had personal friends amongst the members of the board. In particular, Richard Fairey, the son, was one of my closest friends. But we all stood somewhat in awe of Sir Richard himself. However, the son might not necessarily be the best person to put the suggestion forward and to get the answer we needed from the father. In any case the problem could not be solved by a simple yes or no. The Delta, although we always thought of it as our own, did not belong to us. It belonged to the Ministry of Supply. It had never been scheduled to go out after records. At no time had that been its intended purpose. Whatever decision was made, the routine development programmes took priority and would still have to continue with an absolute minimum of interruption. Certainly therefore not even Sir Richard could make a decision that we'd just go out and have a run on our own. There was inevitably the wearying and time-consuming process of political lobbying, masses of formal minutes, decisions withheld, decisions put forward, decisions put back. I had little doubt myself that we would receive little or no help from the Ministry and in fact, as we shall see, they very nearly scotched it altogether eventually. Without government aid in some form or another, which was unlikely, to what extent would the firm feel justified in becoming involved in the considerable expenditure of mounting a record bid?

Only one person could make decisions such as these. Sir Richard himself. And he certainly did not possess the kind of personality that would encourage you to approach without thinking for a very long time about it first. He was a very awe-inspiring individual, both physically and mentally, and anyone who wished to get his ear was acutely conscious that he was addressing 6' 7" of aristocratic aeronautical history.

Our chance came, as these things so often do, outside the office. Sir Richard often held shooting parties on his Stockbridge estate, to which I was invited. On this particular occasion, as far as I can recall, there were no flying people at the party at all with the exception of myself and Richard, the remainder of the guests being family, friends, and business acquaintances.

I think it was Richard who suggested that I should have a word with his father during the party.

Richard was a truly tremendous personality who, with his fantastic zest for living, and physically, towered above those around him. He had immense kindness and endless courage. Shipwrecked during the war, he lost both his legs after appalling suffering from exposure and frostbite. Now, with these injuries already aggravating hereditary hypertension and knowing that, still only in his thirties, he was doomed, he still lived his life at a pace that would have killed many a healthier man. He was a born pilot and lived for flying and all that went with it. Above all, he had tremendous understanding. A natural leader, his motives were sometimes capable of being misunderstood, but he was a first-class executive director. He had been something of a playboy in his early youth and, unfortunately, the reputation stuck with him to the end. Those who knew him well, as I did, saw beneath the veneer of the playboy. His whole life was dedicated to the aircraft industry, particularly the aviation firm his father had built. He died almost immediately after Fairey Aviation were sold to Westland's. It was a tragic death which the industry could ill afford.

I must confess that I did not relish the idea of approaching his father, but it was now or never. It was at lunch that he gave me the cue I had been waiting for. He was talking about progress in the air, and about speed, and was explaining to the party with obvious personal pride what a marvellous aircraft the little Delta was.

I had spoken before I realised what I was saying. As he finished, I asked him, "I suppose, Sir Richard, you haven't considered that we might have a go at the speed record?" His reaction was entirely characteristic. He immediately said, "Yes." It was sharp and short and definitive. And then, very properly because he was the head of the firm, he added, "Yes, of course I have. And I think we ought to have a go at it." He said it again. And then changed the subject.

As far as I was concerned, that was all he needed to say. I had got the message through. What Sir Richard said commanded attention and appropriate action, and it would be a brave man who ever spoke to him out of turn. I did mention it once again to him later on that day. All he added was, "We must think about this more seriously. I shall have to talk to the directors about it." The seed was sown and I knew now that it would germinate.

In the days that followed, nothing appeared to happen as a result. I, for one, was not in the least worried. In my years of service as a test pilot under Sir Richard Fairey, I had come to understand that words were not bandied about uselessly. He had accepted the proposition. There was nothing more needed to be said. The next thing we would know would be action. But even the full 6' 7" of Sir Richard Fairey couldn't get action out of the Ministry.

4

THE UNWILLING SCHOLAR

Here, perhaps, is the first glimmer of how even the apparently most unrelated factors in that haphazard sequence of events that made up my life had a significant bearing one upon the other; so that in the end it could happen no other way than accident – or destiny – had determined for me.

I don't believe in predestination. Neither did I ever read my fortune in the tea-leaves. If I had, there would have been ample opportunity while I was at Brooke Bond's as an apprentice tea-taster to do so in the firm's time.

Some people map their lives out ahead of them. They have ambition, personal drive, they develop their own destiny. As I would have done if I'd been a game warden, probably. Others, certainly myself, don't find the reason for their actions, if indeed there is any, until years later.

It may seem odd, and perhaps a little boastful, that I, an ordinary run-of-the-mill test pilot on the payroll, whose chief duties during the ten years I'd been with Fairey's had been routine testing of Gannet aeroplanes, should have the confidence of Sir Richard to such an extent that I was *persona grata* at shooting parties attended mainly by business tycoons. It must make me sound like one of those chaps who, still in their twenties, already have their name on some door marked Managing Director, already waiting for them to burst through their cocoon and fly in, a fully-fledged Big Business butterfly.

Of course it wasn't like that at all. It simply so happened that during all my boyhood years of nature study roaming the countryside, I had covered many an acre of land rough-shooting on my own, and was a fairish shot. And when you have a shooting party, whether you are the head of an aviation company or anything else, it is natural to want a few people around you who can shoot, too. I was just another gun.

But if I hadn't had this tremendous love of the countryside as a boy, I wouldn't have had any interest in shooting. And I wouldn't have had the entrée, even for this humble reason, to Sir Richard Fairey's house parties. And I never would have had the chance to pop the Delta question at him, at the psychological moment of truth when he was receiving loud and clear.

Glancing back, I see that I have come out very much the hero of the piece who alone bearded the awesome chief in his lair and got the authority for the record bid. This is one of the difficulties of writing in the first person – and I certainly don't feel competent to write in any other way. You forge ahead saying, I did this, or I did that, forgetting that the reader doesn't know, as one knows oneself, that all this time there were a lot of other people doing and saying things as well.

I played my part in pushing the project through, but it was only a minor part politically. The only major rôle I could perform was to analyse the possibilities of the aircraft from day-to-day experience of it and give my facts to the boys in the board-room as extra ammo.

The whole of the Delta team was in this thing together. It was impossible at any stage to say that any single individual was the originator of the idea. It just so happened that I could use a sporting gun and that, in this unexpected way, it served a more useful purpose, putting the Delta up in the sky, than shooting Sir Richard's pheasants out of it.

Of course, there is the stranger fact that, had I not had these boyhood interests and had they not been frustrated when I tried to carry them forward into an adult career, it is very likely that I never would have flown at all. And that, if I had not found inspiration in a Scout troop at a time when it was vitally necessary for something to give me a positive bearing, these interests would without doubt have been forgotten in the pursuit of much more disreputable ends.

I think that, by the time I went to Sherborne preparatory school, I must have been getting well on the way towards being beyond parental control. And it could so easily have happened that way instead of the other.

I had been to various preliminary schools already, for various reasons. First there was the kindergarten in Lichfield. Then the primary section of the high school. And then my mother went abroad again – to West Africa – and my brother, Paul, and I were packed off to our first boarding schools. Then the trouble started. There was no longer a home to go back to in the holidays so, come holiday time, down we went to Sussex, to grandma's. Poor grandma.

The next term I was sent to Parkfield, just outside Cuckfield. I think I was beaten the first day I got there. If not, I certainly had several beatings in the first week. Eventually my mother, in desperation, took me away after about two and a half years, and I was sent down to Sherborne preparatory school. My brother was already at the senior school there.

By this time, looking back on it, I have no doubt that I was a fully-fledged problem child. It obviously couldn't have gone on much longer without either something drastic happening or else something equally drastic being done to prevent it.

It's difficult to say why I was so terribly unruly. My brother wasn't very much better. In the holidays we used to get up to the most frightful sort of hooliganism, and there used to be tremendous wars between the village boys and ourselves. This was real war. Air guns were used. It was very dangerous and heaven only knows why there weren't any serious casualties.

It would be convenient to blame it on unsettled home conditions. We had no disciplinary influences from anyone. Certainly we had none from my grandmother, who indulged us outrageously. I think she was sorry for us. She knew something at that time which I didn't yet know. My parents' marriage was breaking up.

In truth though, I think I simply had the kind of personality which could have developed into something bad just as easily as something good. And it's very much the luck of the draw.

At least this will show you that if ever the popular image of a test pilot had a counterpart in real life – which I very much doubt, having met most of them – it certainly wasn't me. There was none of this obviously-born-to-do-something-big-from childhood aura around me – none of this bright head prefect and leader of the school and born-to-be-a-leader-of-men kind of thing. I did manage to avoid being expelled, but that was about all. The only quality that emerged during this phase of childhood lawlessness that could possibly have been any help whatever in my future career was a self-reliance that allowed me to face danger without unreasonable fear, and without running home crying if I got hit. For there was no one to run home to.

5

OBSTRUCTION AND RED TAPE

The Ministry of Supply was being seriously disturbed by a cuckoo in its paper nest. The cuckoo was of course the Delta, and it only needed the first tentative approach to Whitehall to start off urgent and agitated ministerial twitterings at the very idea of flying a Ministry contract aeroplane around on such frivolous projects as world speed record bids. The answer was a categorical no.

It is very difficult, even now when it is possible to look back on it objectively, to understand the reasons for official policy at that stage.

Even the responsible press, in reporting and commenting on the record achievement, were obviously misled as to the part the Ministry really played in the matter. In a special supplement of *The Aeroplane* the editorial leading article said:

> "The secret of the Fairey F.D.2 had been well kept for a long time. The Fairey team, the directors of the company and the officials at the Ministry of Supply who had drawn up the specification and placed the contracts for the two machines were but seeing the triumphant achievement of what they had set out to do some seven years previously. This foresight should not be overlooked; for if the time has seemed long, it is encouraging to know that officials and designers alike had faced up to the task of building truly supersonic aircraft a long time back."

By this, and many similar comments in the daily press, it was clearly implied that the initiative of the Ministry was in the forefront of promoting the record bid. This was, at best, a very misleading half-truth. When the Delta project was started in 1949, the Fairey Aviation Company took the initiative because, although the design study was made in close co-operation with the Ministry of Supply, it was not until considerably later that the Ministry issued an official specification, and it was later still that Fairey's received a Ministry contract. It was specifically for the design of a research aircraft capable of flying at high supersonic speeds, covering the design and construction of two such aircraft specifically to investigate flying problems at transonic and supersonic speeds, much less about which was known at that time than now. Even then, the project was held up, at a stage when both the Americans and Russians were forging ahead with a very much accelerated rate of progress, by the Ministry itself, who clamped a super-priority on the Fairey Gannet, with the result that the Delta project had to be shelved indefinitely. It was, in fact, not until September 1952 that drawings were issued to the shops and work on building the F.D.2 really got under way.

Secondly, of course, the press statements are misleading in that, until that day in October when I had slipped through the sonic barrier, the idea of making a record bid had never entered anybody's head at all. The record could therefore hardly be said to be the result of foresight in any shape or form.

A statement to the press from the Ministry of Supply at this period speaks for itself:

> "For some time in the late 1940's this country had fallen behind in supersonic speed and research into supersonic speed, and we have had quite a good deal of ground to catch up. With our resources smaller than those of America or Russia it is difficult to catch up. What gives me heart in this matter is the way in which we are setting about closing that gap and making up the time we lost. We mean to go on pushing ahead our search for knowledge in supersonic flight."

This statement can be slightly misleading. By itself, it is a reasonably fair statement. By placing the contracts for the Delta in the first place, the Ministry had clearly shown some interest in, rather tardily perhaps, trying to catch up with the rest of the world in supersonic research. And, to be fair, it must be admitted that the Ministry itself had to face considerable opposition in the government. There seemed to be a general feeling that the high-speed fighter was now out-dated, even though, of course, the military themselves knew the position perfectly well and had an outstanding requirement for just the kind of aircraft which could conceivably have been developed from the Delta. However, taking the Ministry's statement in relation to the record bid itself, one might be excused for believing that the major credit for the whole project was due to long and far-sighted ministerial imagination.

Two Fairey directors carried most of the brunt of this initial battle to get permission for the bid from the Ministry: Mr. G. W. Hall, who was assistant managing director at the time of the project, and Mr. R. L. Lickley, who was the company's chief engineer.

It is not my intention to suggest that the Ministry took undue credit for the record after it had been achieved with any deliberate intention to falsify history in their own favour. It is perfectly understandable that, at such times and in the national interests, it would have been damaging to the tremendous upsurge of national prestige which we had obtained as a result of the record, if it had been shown to have been produced by a country divided against itself and with no positive policy to pursue and capitalise on the success that had been achieved. However, it seems to me only right and proper that, at this later stage, the correct sequence of events should be made known.

It was the drive and the determination of the Fairey team and the Fairey team only, that made the record possible. With individual exceptions, the whole attitude of the Ministry was rather one of resentment that a contractor should see fit to take a development project awarded by the Ministry and use his own initiative to put it to ends which the Ministry had not envisaged. There may have been a certain amount of professional jealousy involved here. Or it may simply have been the normal process of bureaucratic machinery at work, unable to make a snap decision and incompetent to put any decision into action except in quintuplicate. More likely than not the attitude was the result of ministerial diplomacy. Knowing that it was far from having the full backing of the government for any supersonic research project such as the Delta, it would have been understandable if they had stood aside from the record bid officially, so that they could not be accused of wasting public funds if it failed; and yet give the project its unofficial blessing.

But this was exactly what they did not do. At the beginning, not only were they unwilling to take any official part, they were equally adamant that they should have no unofficial association with it whatsoever. Not only did we get no support from them even in an informal way, but there was positive obstruction. We were told that we must not interfere with the official flight-test and development programme. The few who did support us in the Ministry, notably Mr. R. A. Shaw, the Ministry of Supply project officer on the Delta programme, found their own hands tied by the same officialdom.

From the point of view of the Fairey organisation, this was very serious indeed. There was certainly no time to haggle, or the record would have been pushed out of reach by the Americans by the time the talking had finished. Furthermore, there was the question of financing the bid itself, and Fairey's, quite understandably, considered this as a national concern in which the country should bear some of the expense. Secondly, quite obviously, it did not wish to risk offending the Ministry, on which it depended for future work. This is not to deny the obvious fact that, of course, there was a certain amount of self-interest involved at Fairey's as well. For some time, it had been considered that a larger-scale Delta was a military possibility, because it was the kind of design which could be built on larger scales and yet retain its theoretical and practical design capabilities. This by no means always applies to aircraft and, very often, for no apparent scientific reason, a scaled-up version will fail even although a smaller development version has performed extremely well. This "scaleability", we felt, was one of the strong virtues of the Delta commercially. We felt that, out of the Delta, we might very well be able to produce the supersonic fighter which we knew that the military wanted. By bringing it dramatically into the public eye, by the world's speed record, we hoped that we might be able to help the case of the military who kept on telling the Ministry that this was the type of fighter aircraft they needed, only to be told by the Ministry that it wasn't. We would have liked to have obtained a development contract for such an aircraft, naturally enough, for it would have been a very valuable contract. Perhaps this also may have been a factor in the Ministry's attitude towards the record bid. Perhaps they felt that, if we succeeded, we might put them in a position of giving us a development contract for a type of aircraft which, in spite of all specialist advice from the Services, they were determined to prove that the Services did not need.

In the end, after persistent lobbying and a lengthy process of attrition, we did obtain grudging ministerial permission to go ahead. But, far from financing the project, at one time it even looked as if we would have to hire the aeroplane which we had built ourselves, to make the bid; and then pay them for the privilege of using it to beat the world. Eventually, an arrangement was made whereby Fairey's took the Delta on a loan agreement from the Ministry for the period of the record bid. Certainly we had to carry our own insurance on it, which was by far the major cost. And, furthermore, we also had to pay for the hire of the specialist camera equipment and team from the R.A.E. Farnborough, who timed the record runs.

The whole situation was difficult enough to understand then, and I find it just as incomprehensible now, looking back on it as an objective outsider. The Ministry did, in the end, give us a number of minor facilities free of charge. But the vast majority of the cost of the run was financed by Fairey's. And little good did it do them. By then the aircraft manufacturer was faced with a monopoly purchaser, the Ministry of

Supply. No matter how much we may have pushed up British prestige in the record bid, we did not push up our own prestige sufficiently for the Ministry to give us the following contracts which could have kept us in existence. Within a matter of months of the record bid the writing was on the wall. It was later to prove to be the swan-song of one of the world's historic aviation pioneering firms, even though they have remained active in many other industrial fields.

However, at this stage, we were not worried about the future. It was the present that occupied the whole of our time. The game was on and, for the moment, the future could take care of itself.

6

A CHECKERED PATTERN OF SCHOOLDAYS

We were not worried about the future. The game was on and the future could take care of itself. Yes, I suppose that is a pretty fair reflection of my philosophy of life from childhood upwards, if such an irresponsible approach could be called a philosophy at all.

I'm afraid it debunks another popular myth about the test pilot. These are the dedicated men of the air. Dicing daily with death while the brave little woman sits at home waiting for the telephone to ring. I don't think I've ever been dedicated to anything, in that sense. Nor, probably, has any other test pilot. A good test pilot has to be too detached to be a completely dedicated man. There is always part of him separated from the things he's doing, watching, observing everything that is going on, from outside, himself included. It sometimes makes him difficult to live with. It isn't that he's broody. He just isn't there.

If I'm interested in anything, I'm capable of becoming completely absorbed by it. That's as far as dedication goes. I was interested in test flying. But, now that it's finished, I can become just as absorbed selling boats. I think it would probably be true to say that one has no permanent allegiance, as a dedicated man has.

Is this a desirable thing? For a test pilot, I think, yes; although the popular image wouldn't agree with me. For the individual himself? I'm not so sure. Probably those involved in my married life would say it wasn't. There have been crash landings. For the child that became the man? Looking back, I can see now what a terribly explosive mixture this capacity for enormous enthusiasm without direction was.

I've only met one truly dedicated man in my life. And thank goodness I met him when I did. The master at Sherborne preparatory school who ran the Scout troop. His name was E. W. Thompson, known throughout the Scout movement as Mingan, and he had an uncanny understanding of what goes on inside a small boy's head, even the wilfully undisciplined head that sat so uncomfortably on my unwilling shoulders. It was his life's work, running this troop, apart from being a good maths master. His life was making the Scout movement do the things it can do so well when someone like himself gets the reins. The pity is there are more reins than there are such drivers.

Sherborne preparatory must have been awaiting my arrival with some trepidation, as indeed I was too, because I assumed they would have received a report from my last school. But as soon as I came under this man's influence, my outlook was transformed. In a sense, I suppose he took the place of my father, whom I very seldom saw. He had the most extraordinary facility for making everything he wanted you to do interesting. He always had some plot or play or ploy for the week or the day or the season or the term, which was always full of interest.

Even better than the things we did in term time were the things we did in the holidays. Very enterprising they were, too. There was an annual camp, which had a lot in common with the Outward Bound courses, although the latter hadn't yet been thought of. The first year, we walked all the way along the Dorset coast, carrying our personal kit and pulling the rest on a trailer behind – all the way from Weymouth to Bournemouth – about seventy miles. The next year we went on a similar sort of trek except that we went right round the Lizard.

The excitement of these holiday adventures – for, to me, they were adventure of a high order – and the companionship, the sense of belonging within a group, are difficult to recapture even during the war in Naval fighter squadrons – even test flying. It went with childhood. It probably meant more to me than to most boys because it took the place of real family holidays. There were some years when my mother was home, but there were many when, through no fault of her own, she wasn't.

If this remarkable man had happened to read this, he'd be very surprised to hear that the Delta world speed record certainly owes as much to him as it does to me. For, had it not been for him. I wouldn't have been there at all. Goodness knows where I would have been.

If Sherborne preparatory wrought a reasonably social animal out of the unpromising raw material of my early boyhood, Sherborne School itself, where I went when I was fourteen, certainly tempered it in a pretty ruthless way.

There was a very good play about public school life called *The Guinea Pig*. There was a terrifying housemaster, and an even more terrifying horde of adolescent males intent on destroying any individual who didn't conform to their self-made rules. Many of those who saw it thought it must have been exaggerated. It wasn't. Warren Chetham Strode, who wrote it, was at Sherborne. I was in Parry-Jones's House, and he was about the most terrifying thing I ever met through the whole of my boyhood – except the horde bent on the destruction of non-conformity.

There were a number of outrageously sadistic practices ready to confront the new boy on his first day. Altogether it was something of a cold douche for me, coming from a very kindly preparatory school where I'd had a lot of friends and a pretty free and easy time altogether. The whole system put the fear of God into me. Not that it did me any harm. But I can still remember the sinking feeling in the stomach, felt even more strongly when one is young, when I found myself at last out in the open, as it were, without childhood's protection any more, in what seemed to me at the time the most terrifying crowd of boys and habits.

Particularly, there was the Boxing Party. Each house was divided up into a Day Room, where all the small boys were, the senior room full of what seemed to me to be perfectly enormous boys, and studies where the most exalted had their being. The Boxing Party was a phenomenon of the Day Room, and consisted of about half a dozen senior boys. Every evening there was prep. And every day for fifteen minutes there was another sit-down when you had to read or else sit absolutely still and pretend to read. During the period, the Boxing Party operated. In this fifteen minutes of fear and silence each day, you sat and waited to see whether it was you they wanted.

It was here that you atoned compulsorily for any misdemeanours stored up against you, not in the eyes of any of the prefects or the housemaster, but in the eyes of the Boxing Party. Their rule was absolute. You couldn't ask what you had done.

In the corner of the Day Room was a large box where all the orange peel and other junk of the Day Room ended up, and which was emptied only once a week. During the fifteen-minute silent period, the Boxing Party would rush around the room putting the fear of God into everybody because nothing was said in advance, you never had any warning, you never knew whether it was going to be you or not. You simply held your breath wondering what you'd done without knowing it and what they'd got to hold against you. Then they'd all stop behind one boy, who'd sit there trembling and knowing he mustn't make a noise, mustn't break the silence. Then they'd grab the one next to him instead, perhaps. It wasn't you after all. They'd turn back – grab you instead.

Once in their hands, there was nothing to do but wait for it. You weren't allowed to resist or to ask why. You were dragged away with two of them holding each arm, and swung unceremoniously into the box. Swung into it from about six feet away. If you were particularly unfortunate and there was someone else to be boxed as well and you were the first, the odds were that he'd be boxed on top of you.

Why the hell no one ever broke any limbs I just don't know. It was a

barbarously sadistic custom which everyone knew went on and which
no one in authority lifted a finger to stop. I had more than my fair share
of it, not being of the naturally conforming type.

I believe they did clamp down on it a little later. Not surprisingly.
These days, someone would take legal action against someone else the
first time they tried it.

Taking the rough with the smooth I didn't really mind all that much.
I don't think all these things did us very much harm. Certainly it didn't
do me any lasting damage. Might even have brought me to heel instead
of being the complete rebel I'd started out to be. All in all, I think I
really quite enjoyed my schooldays. I certainly enjoyed the years at
Sherborne preparatory. I didn't enjoy Parkfield where I was trying to
resist authority all the time and refusing to conform. And I enjoyed the
last year of Sherborne School tremendously.

This was my last fling as a naturalist – training falcons. We'd perch
these falcons on our shoulders and go to the fields around about on our
bicycles. It was a halcyon end to a period which could never return.
There was Munich. Then there was the war. And now there was the
Delta.

7

WE PLAN FOR A RECORD

I was not personally involved in the political aspects of the record bid at this organisational stage and, like the majority of those engaged on the project, most of the time had not the least idea of what was going on. In fact, by far the majority of my time was still taken up on the development programme of the super-priority naval Gannet, and there wasn't really much time in working hours to think of anything else. As from time to time one met various directors who were engaged in these negotiations, one would search their faces for any hopeful clue or would try and find the double entendre in what they were saying, hoping that behind the tone of voice there might somewhere be, unspoken, the news that we were waiting for. It was rather like waiting for a surgeon to give you his diagnosis after he had examined you and then, when he had given it to you, wondering whether in fact he was keeping anything back. It was a period of gleaning the rumours and picking up at second hand any scraps of information that might have been overheard.

For all that, there was not really much time for idle speculation. From the moment Sir Richard Fairey had decided we all felt fairly certain that the record bid would go through, but we also knew how infuriating the delaying tactics of the Ministry could be, and my one fear was that we would be too late. We were certainly too busy to let it affect our concentration. I was flying the Delta whenever the Gannet programme would allow me to. And, as far as the record bid was concerned, this period was very much the theoretical phase in which Maurice Child, the chief flight-development engineer, who had an office adjacent to mine, Robert Lickley, and Gordon Slade and myself, were consolidating the vast sums and jottings that we had been doing in the previous months. This was completely an unofficial exercise – the results never appeared in any official report, nor was it on the agenda. Between ourselves we worked out the whole project on paper, and then worked it out again and again until we were convinced that there was no loophole left. We could see that four-figure symbol at the end of every equation – a thousand miles an hour.

These calculations were no longer concerned with whether or not the aircraft was capable of flying at 1,000 m.p.h. We knew it was. Since that first supersonic flight on 28th October, 1955, the accumulation of flying data proceeded rapidly. It was quite common to carry out as many as four flights in a day. This was not actually as heavy a flying schedule as might appear, because the flight endurance of this particular aircraft, being strictly a research type, was very low. The average length of any single flight was twenty minutes.

It must have been well towards the end of 1955, or even at the beginning of January in 1956, that we knew formally that all obstructions had been cleared for the bid. By this time we had made well over a hundred flights with the Delta. Up until the first supersonic flight that October, we had of course never flown the aircraft with the re-heat system switched on. In those early stages following that flight, all supersonic flying had been done using the engine less re-heat. Even at that, we found the power quite sufficient to take the aircraft up to about Mach 1.1. When, to complete the schedule on flutter tests, we wanted to go up higher to Mach 1.2, I found that I could achieve it without difficulty by a slight dive. Thus we could approach very close to the existing speed record without using the additional boost of the re-heat system at all. It remained to be seen what would happen when we switched the re-heat on.

This, of course, in common with any flight-test development schedule, only happened after the most extensive ground testing had been carried out.

Very briefly, a re-heat system consists of an arrangement whereby fuel in enormous quantities is pumped into the jet pipe. This fuel is ignited and burns, providing, in effect, a second propulsive jet effort over and above that provided by the normal action of the engine. It can only be used for a very short period due to fuel reserves but the additional power is tremendous. We calculated that, on the Delta, at 38,000 ft., which was approximately the altitude at which we did the record, the effect of switching on the re-heat system would be to very nearly double the available power of the aircraft. The way we looked at it was that, knowing that we were very close to the existing record as it was, we had all the additional power of the re-heat to get us beyond it. There was no doubt that this was a very impressive margin indeed.

The first day that I flew the Delta with re-heat in operation is one that I shall not forget. At that time, re-heat was put on or off by what was virtually an "On-Off" selector switch in the cockpit. There was nothing in between. Either you were on full boost or the re-heat was not on at all. This meant that as soon as I turned the selector on I would effectually be doubling the power instantaneously. The acceleration had to be felt to be believed. I don't know what it represented in terms of "g", but it was reminiscent of the days I had had in the Services operating on Sea-Hurricane Squadrons in which the adapted Hurricane was catapulted by rocket off merchant vessels. It was a breath-taking experience and I had the unpleasant sensation of sitting in the middle of a vast surge of power which neither I nor anyone else in the world could control. One lost much of this sensation with experience, but nevertheless I noted in my flight reports at the time that the amount of instantaneous power available was in fact an embarrassment to accurate flight testing because it made it very difficult to operate within the close test limits required.

Quite early on I had an experience which will illustrate quite well what I mean. In making flutter tests, we always respected very fully the axiom of any test pilot who was to stay alive, to "make haste slowly". Only after the most exhaustive series of flutter tests at one speed would we progress to the next, and then only by a very small increase. Thus the tests were carried up to the higher speeds in a great number of test runs, step by step. Under no circumstances did we exceed the speed in flight at which the last cleared series of tests had been made. However, at the stage of testing we were now reaching, it was necessary to light the re-heat system during the subsonic climb up to the altitude at which we wanted to carry out the tests. This resulted in what felt like, at the time, a meteoric climb to altitude. But it was not the effect of this that worried me. The first time I climbed under re-heat I found it almost impossible, even though we were climbing steeply, to prevent the aircraft going well past the Mach number and air speed at which satisfactory flutter tests had already been covered. The truth of this fantastic situation was that, even though we were testing at supersonic speeds by then, we could not keep the Delta slow enough even in the climb! Eventually this additional surge of power did in fact become such an embarrassment for testing, and so difficult to handle, that we had to make provisions for introducing it under more gradual control.

By now I was consistently flying faster than the existing speed record of 822 m.p.h. which Col. Haynes had set up in the Super Sabre.

Our problems at this time were mainly concerned with how a high altitude speed record was laid on in practice. Until now, we had been concerning ourselves almost exclusively with whether or not the aircraft could achieve what I believed it could. The run itself had been taken very largely for granted. Now, beginning to look at even a few of the practical details, we began to realise just how little we knew about it and, also, how much more difficult and complicated the technicalities surrounding a run were than the actual physical process of piloting the aircraft across a measured 15-kilometre course.

To begin with, a suitable place for the record had to be found. Then we had to decide at what height the record had to be flown. We did not know whether we had accurate enough instrumentation. No one in this country, as far as we knew, had attempted to measure speed to the accuracy required by the governing bodies. We had to calculate whether, in its existing condition, the Delta could in fact carry enough fuel to make the record possible. In the end, as we shall see in a later chapter, the whole thing was vastly more complicated than even we ourselves could possibly have imagined. We had to make arrangements to use special R.A.F. radar units; and a special and hitherto completely untried method of measuring the actual speed was given its baptism of fire without the opportunity for any previous practice whatsoever. All in all, including those indirectly involved, about one thousand people must have been actively engaged at any instant while the record bid was in progress.

One of the problems I remember Maurice Child and myself discussing at great length was this question of measuring the actual speed. In particular, we would have liked to have found out how the Americans had measured Haynes's record flight to the satisfaction of the controlling bodies, and how they substantiated their claims. I could get no information about this at all and, to this day, I still don't know how they did it. The whole thing was done under secrecy and there was no way of finding out at all. Presumably the Americans got around this on grounds of security. I am not suggesting for a moment that there was anything dubious in the American bid, nor that the method used was not entirely reliable. From my own point of view, however, it has never seemed to me to be very satisfactory to rely on unpublished measurement techniques. And this belief was reinforced particularly when, as we shall see later, we ran into formidable instrumentation troubles in getting an acceptable run ourselves. Our own experiences were to show only too clearly the immense difficulties involved and, in fact, we very nearly missed the bid because of a mere instrumental technicality; indeed, we thought we had been disallowed. Our policy was that the principle of measurement should be made known just as soon as possible after the record run, and in fact we gave complete details of our methods, in conjunction with R.A.E. Farnborough who developed them, just as soon as we could get around to publishing them. The methods themselves are, I think, of considerable interest and will be described in detail later. All of us felt strongly on this point of principle because, without in any way disputing the American record, we did feel that using a security cover created a dangerous precedent in which the way could be laid open for achieving record runs under conditions in which adequate official scrutiny might be impossible. However, at this particular stage, only two months before the record was made, it was purely an academic exercise to discuss high-sounding principles, because we ourselves had not the least idea how the job was going to be done, or even whether it was possible to do it.

Methodically, we laid down a schedule, working on each individual problem until we had found a solution, in a logical sequence, taking first things first, and gradually building up the whole technical and organisational structure. This, as can be imagined, was a terribly complex business. As far as I recall, it did not devolve on any one particular individual, but was a function of the very fine type of team work which existed during the whole of the Delta development and record-breaking programme. Our primary problem, and one which really we only solved to our own satisfaction a few days before the first attempt, was to co-ordinate the whole course of the flight to conserve fuel as much as possible during the climb, the approaches, and the return to the airfield, leaving the vast majority of the fuel to be burnt up at explosive rate during those frantic few seconds of the 15-kilometre run in each direction. The following examples will give some idea of the fantastic fuel consumption and how uncomfortably close our margin was. Altogether, the Delta carried about 290 gallons of usable fuel, the design being such that the majority of this was carried in the wings from where it was automatically transferred to a collector tank in the fuselage during the flight. Of this, no less than 140 gallons, or nearly 50 per cent of all the fuel we could carry, was burnt up in the few minutes of acceleration and during the 15-kilometre runs in each direction. Some 25 per cent, or about 60 gallons, were consumed in climbing to the 38,000 ft. of the altitude at which the run was made. Another 10 per cent was used turning round after the first run over the course in order to get into position for the second run. This accounted for about another 22 gallons. Thus, even on our most sanguine plans, it was inevitable that at the end of the run we would be left with certainly not more than 15 gallons in our tanks, or no more than an average touring car would carry for a weekend trip to the country. It was not altogether a comfortable feeling to realise that, at the end of each record run, I would be some thirty miles from base at 38,000 ft., and with virtually only the drops at the bottom of the tank to get me safely back there. There was always an unpleasant possibility that, if there was any miscalculation, I might find myself landing the Delta on its nose wheel for the second time.

This, however, was the least of our worries, because it really needed very little fuel to get back and there was a safety device fitted in the aircraft which automatically cut off the re-heat the instant that the wing tanks were empty and insufficient margin was left in the collector tank itself. The importance of this is obvious when you realise that re-heat doubled the fuel consumption. What was worrying us was that if this cut-off operated, it would mean that the run had failed, because the re-heat would have cut during the actual second run. All in all we had to fly something between 150 and 200 miles on each record attempt, from take-off to landing. It is interesting to note that, when, after the record, we flew the Delta 300 miles across the North Sea to Norway for some special testing, we actually used less fuel than we consumed during the few minutes it took us to make the double run over the course. Once the re-heat was switched on, it was equivalent to someone at the head of a weir opening the flood gates.

Nobody pretended to be happy about the situation, because it left far too little a margin for error. Unfortunately we had no alternative. We considered all sorts of possibilities, such as fitting drop tanks, which would give us additional fuel to bring us up to altitude and which could then be jettisoned, and all sorts of other ideas were put forward. We simply had to accept the fact that they were all impracticable because no additional fuel could be provided without making a greater or lesser modification to the aircraft, and we simply did not have the time. Even if we had been able to make the time somehow, it still could not have been done. Costly though it was, the whole project was being mounted on a shoe-string compared, for instance, with American standards, and we did not dare to involve ourselves in additional expense for modifications which were not strictly associated with the contract development programme. Secondly, officially and from the ministerial viewpoint, the record bid was still only the No. 2 Priority job, one which was not allowed to disrupt normal flight testing, and one for which official permission had been given only very grudgingly and after considerable heartache. We might well have lost the permission we had fought so hard to obtain had we then been discovered making special modifications specifically for the record bid. It all added up to the fact that there wasn't time to do anything except to fly the aircraft as it was and make the best of it. Had there been time, I am quite certain we would not have cut it so fine.

The fact that we had so very little fuel margin raised a whole host of technical problems which would not have been necessary had we had the full facilities to mount the record in a more ideal way. Once the site for the record had been determined, the whole flight had to be plotted out and adhered to almost foot by foot. The whole thing had to be calculated theoretically down to the last detail without any possibility of error, because shortage of time once again allowed us to do no practising whatever, and the first time we met the actual conditions in practice would be on the first officially-timed run. These calculations were tremendously complicated, because so many variables were involved. Only the actual length of the course and the height were predetermined by the record regulations. For the rest, we could climb up to altitude any way we liked, approach the course any way we liked, and turn between runs any way we liked. This gave endless different possibilities, but it is obvious that any and every one of them would alter the reading on the fuel gauge at the end of the run. It was rather like working out a football pools coupon with mathematics instead of with a pin. Amongst all these possible permutations, which was the best combination, the one that would use the least possible fuel getting there and back and leave us the maximum to drive us over the course? Would it be best to make a quick steep climb, or to take longer about it and climb at a more shallow angle? Should we attempt to make a tight climb at the turn, and risk losing accuracy in hitting the exact point on the approach run, or should we take a wider turn and possibly use more fuel?

It is a remarkable tribute to the flight-development engineer on the team that he plotted a flight course completely in theory which we followed exactly in the actual flight with precisely the answer he had anticipated.

At this stage, one problem was only solved at the expense of producing another even more intractable one. No sooner had we determined our optimum flight plan than we had to set about finding ways and means of implementing it. Taking off from the base at Boscombe Down, you had to time the climb absolutely right to end up at the predetermined spot on the approach where re-heat would be switched on and the acceleration would start. Flying at high speed over a total area of something like a thousand square miles of sky, we nevertheless had to be absolutely certain of starting this acceleration at precisely the right second. If I misjudged it and switched on the re-heat too early for the first run, it would mean that we would run out of fuel on the acceleration for the return trip. Altogether re-heat was on for $4\frac{1}{2}$ minutes during each record attempt, that is $2\frac{1}{4}$ minutes for each run including the approach acceleration; our margin of error was so small that I had rather less than ten seconds – or considerably less than it takes you to read this sentence – to play with. If, at the end of a run, the fuel gauge showed that we had more than our safe fuel reserve – usually not more than twenty gallons – left, it would be a sure indication that that

particular bid had failed because, at one stage or another, 1 had switched
on the re-heat a second or so too late and consequently had not got all
the acceleration that was possible. We were pushing to the limit, at
pinpoint accuracy, relying entirely on directions given by people on the
ground $7\frac{1}{4}$ miles below. For a time the problem seemed completely
insuperable. In everyday terms it was rather like asking someone to aim
a rifle at a supersonic bird, and be certain he could knock the pip out of
an ace of spades it was carrying in its mouth, every time.

Even when we found answers that would give us this kind of
accuracy, our worries were by no means over. For where and when any
direction from the ground was given was of course completely tied in
with various directions that had been given by several other people in
earlier phases of the flight. There was therefore also a tremendous
problem of co-ordination, so that not only did everybody achieve the
impossible in terms of accuracy at exactly the right split second, but that
everyone else should be informed that he had done so. This involved a
maze of communications which the G.P.O. solved in the most
remarkable way, as if it was the sort of thing they did every day without
thinking twice about it.

All these, difficult though they were, were only preliminary
problems. I have purposely not yet mentioned the most difficult
problem of the lot – that is, how to get a tiny little aeroplane with a 28-
ft. wing span, travelling at over fifteen miles a minute, on to an invisible
hairline over seven miles up in the sky, and keep it there not only
straight and level but without deviation to left or right and without
changing height. Never mind, we will come to this presently. It was no
good worrying too much about this until at least we were sure that we
had all the other snags of the flight ironed out.

It was obviously quite impossible for the pilot to know the exact
geographical pin-point at which to switch on the re-heat. If anybody
imagines that I sat in the cockpit with my eyes glued on to a stopwatch
and doing a sort of personal countdown, nine, eight, seven, six, five,
four, three, two, now re-heat on, as if I were conducting a one-man
missile launching, I am afraid that I must disillusion him. I relied on a
verbal signal from Squadron-Leader Tommy Thompson at the radar
station. Another vital signal was, in the end, automated as it were, by
transmitting a signal in the form of a pulse automatically from the
ground as I passed over a given spot on the run-in. This automatically
put a mark on my sealed height recorder at the beginning of the course
in each direction.

Of course it should be remembered here that I would be making
something like a thirty-mile sweep around to come into the line of the

runs, and it had to be certain that I would be lined up correctly, not only so that I would receive the signals but also because, if I deviated, I would be out of visual range of the special camera equipment which was tracking the record itself. This again was no mean problem. We received invaluable help from the R.A.F. units which were lent to us for the whole period of the bid and which were wonderfully co-operative. The R.A.F. also lent us one of their radar experts, Squadron-Leader Tommy Thompson, mentioned previously, who was in charge of the units and who lived with us for the whole of this preparation period patiently learning our problems and translating them into terms of radar. He was the most tremendous help to us, and, with Gordon Slade, did the actual control during the majority of the runs.

In the end we found that even radar could not give us the accuracy which we knew we had to have if we were going to have a chance of success. By using radar stations at either end of the course, the ground units could quite easily pick up the Delta at the point where the acceleration started, and thus put the operators working the recording cameras on to it. But there were limits. It should be remembered that throughout this bid, working on a Cinderella budget as we were, we were having to compromise with whatever equipment kind friends in the Services and elsewhere could provide for us. In America, I am quite certain that, under the same circumstances, a budget many times greater than our complete allowance for the whole of the project, and even possibly approaching a cost equivalent to that of the development of the Delta itself, would have been put aside for the design of special recording and automatic tracking devices. It is obviously desirable, for instance, if a camera recorder is going to be used which, naturally enough, has to get an image of the aircraft in its sights if there is going to be anything on the recording film at all, to use some automatic tracking and lock-on arrangement so that the camera automatically finds the aircraft and then follows it as it moves overhead. We had none of this. Keeping the Delta in camera was purely a function of the skill and swift reaction of the operator who, peering through a telescopic viewfinder, had to pick up the Delta visually and make certain, while he was swinging his camera round, that he never let it disappear.

To give him a chance of doing this, it was imperative that he should be able to find the Delta visually at the very beginning of the acceleration period. Here, within limits, the radar fix could help him. But these radar stations were not the special tracking and positioning devices we would ideally have liked to have. They were perfectly ordinary Service radar stations and, as such, were never designed to give an accurate pinpoint in space. What they are designed for, and what they can do to a very fine accuracy, is to get two aeroplanes together in the air regardless of geographic position.

Certainly we had no time to collect a bundle of boffins around us and devise some elegant solution to this problem. What with all the wonders of modern science, we were forced to the regrettable conclusion, even though we made every possible excuse to avert our thoughts from it until it became inescapable, that the whole of the record attempt would have to depend on that fully established and well-proved instrument, the human eye – and only a single eye at that, peering through a high-magnification telescope with virtually no area of field at all. Were we asking the impossible? To get some idea of the problem, stand on the ground and try to pick up a fly flying along at a thousand feet! This, in proportion, was what we were asking the timing-camera operators to do with the aircraft at 38,000 ft. In fact, the task we were setting the radar units and the camera observers between them was to position an aircraft with absolute pinpoint accuracy over a spot in space geographically initially some sixty miles away. Both from the point of view of getting the aeroplane in camera, and also to ensure that it was in the right position to start the acceleration run, it was absolutely imperative that they should be able to spot the aircraft from the ground, at an angle of about 30° coming towards them at fifteen miles a minute.

We had realised from the outset how difficult this was going to be, and a sense of almost neurotic urgency began to creep in as day after day went by without finding a practicable answer. We had not dared allow too long for our preparatory period. We had in fact only allowed ourselves two months, a ridiculously short period which, quite obviously, we only accepted at the time in the nature of "fools rushing in where angels fear to tread". Had we known at that stage what we know now, it is quite on the cards that we would have been too discouraged to continue. We spent weeks thrashing it out, and the more the time went by the quicker it seemed to pass, like those calendars you see in film sequences with the pages being blown off with ever-increasing acceleration, taking the years away from you helplessly in front of your eyes. And all the time the obvious answer was staring us in the face and we were becoming too complicated to see it.

There was not much intelligence required to appreciate that there was no satisfactory way in which we could mark the aircraft itself, for it was quite invisible to the naked eye and only just visible to those who had the correct apparatus to look for it. It would be necessary to arrange for the aircraft to leave a trail behind it. My first idea was to use smoke, in exactly the same way as the R.A.F. Black Arrows burn smoke to leave trails behind them in exhibition formation flying, and advertising aeronauts write messages about the latest consumer product in the sky. There were several ways we could burn smoke; either in the intake, in the exhaust, or by carrying smoke canisters.

It was an unintelligent idea. If we had thought about it a little more, we might have known from the beginning that burning smoke was no answer. If you let one of these smoke canisters go off when you are on the ground, you would think that you were making enough smoke to leave a trail from here to eternity. This is simply because all the smoke is in one place. On the actual run, far from being in one place we constantly expected to have to spread our smoke over a distance of probably some fifty miles, if you include the approach, and make it concentrated enough to be able to be spotted by the naked eye anything up to sixty miles away. The prospect of making a smoke trail went into the waste-paper basket along with the other stillborn ideas when someone, a little brighter than the rest of us, decided to make a calculation to find out how much smoke-making fuel would be required, and came up with the disconcerting answer that, in order to leave a recognisable mark, we would have to carry more smoke-making material than actual fuel to power the engine. It takes a lot of smoke to leave its mark, we discovered, when you want to lay it at over 1,000 m.p.h.

As it was, all I had to do was to look up into the clear sky over Boscombe Down to see a better solution. It was a sight almost as familiar to me as breathing. Way up in the sub-zero sky, two aircraft were leaving pellucidly clear condensation trails like giants playing with a piece of chalk. We would fly the Delta at an altitude where it was certain to leave a condensation trail.

The theoretical phase was over. Now we had all the answers we needed, to know how the record bid could be made, recorded, and approved, without using any equipment that was not already in existence. We gave ourselves a five-minute break, and got on with the next phase. This, as it turned out, was going to have equally intractable problems of its own. The job now was to put theory into practice. Until now, security had been no problem, because only a handful of us at Fairey's knew what was going on. But now we had to involve units widespread over the country, with possibly as many as a thousand individuals directly, or indirectly, involved, a single word from any one of whom, at home or in the local or overheard at the wrong moment, could break our secret wide open and give a free gift to American Intelligence. Our task now was to tell this polyglot population of people, drawn by chance events into a world record bid without knowing it, exactly what we wanted them to do without letting them have the least idea of why we wanted them to do it.

8

TEST PILOT BY ACCIDENT

All the time I've been writing this, I've been trying to equate the seemingly mature and well-integrated test-flying personality that stares at me out of the page, with the indecisive and still somewhat anti-social adolescent from which, apparently, it grew.

If it doesn't get across to you how such an unpromising grub managed to come out of the chrysalis stage with such a noteworthy pair of wings, I'm not surprised. I find it pretty difficult to get across to myself.

I've never been forced to look into myself like this before. I've always taken the sequence of my life very much for granted. Like almost everyone else's life, I suppose, it's been very much as if one was wandering cross-country in a landscape known in only the most general terms, with only the haziest of purpose. One is aware that one must keep going forward, but that's about all. You turn a corner, and it shuts off what has gone before. It's past now and it isn't important any more. You come to a fork in the road and you take the left-hand one for no particular reason. You never really wonder why you took the left, or where the road to the right would have taken you instead. You don't worry about what's round the next corner either. That's in the future. The present is all you have to live in. Above all, you never see the landscape as a whole. You see the spot you're standing on, there and then.

One drifted from the first few years of childhood into school – drifted from boyhood into adolescence – drifted into a job and out of it again. And then there was the war, so one drifted into the Naval air service, and learnt to fly, and collected a few decorations. And then, because you'd got quite a lot of flying hours in your log-book and had had the chance to fly more types than most, when the war finished you learnt to be a civilian test pilot. And so now you'd drifted into the curious situation where you were waiting to take the Delta over the measured course, to be the first man ever to fly through a thousand miles an hour.

Now, instead of knowing only the given spot I'm standing on in this landscape at any given moment, I find I have to try and see it as a whole. It is rather like what happens when you fly above a stretch of country that you knew well enough when you walked over it on the ground. Now there it is, stretched out below you. The whole of it. But it has changed. It is unfamiliar. You can get lost before you know. You fly on a general bearing until you spot a landmark you recognise. Then the rest of the landscape around it becomes familiar although you had forgotten it.

Perhaps everyone ought to write a book about himself and then tear it up, as I've been tempted to do with this one a dozen times. It gives you a different slant on yourself – makes you wonder how much of what happened to you was really in your own hands – makes you search out real landmarks.

When I really try and look back through my life, I find that memory is so often a liar. This is something I've come strongly to suspect since I started writing this book. For instance, I've always taken it for granted that my life has been a pretty happy one. My memories even now don't tell me otherwise. Could my childhood really have been as happy as I remember it? I doubt it. . . .

For one thing, I must at times have been more lonely than most, more thrown back on my own resources. Quite early on, while I was still at Sherborne preparatory school, my parents' marriage was breaking up. I'd never seen a great deal of my parents anyway because they were abroad so much, but this situation obviously made matters more complicated still. The only one in the family I was really close to was my brother. But once I went to boarding school I didn't see so much of him either. He was 2½ years older than I and, instead of going to Sherborne preparatory school so that we could have been there together, he was sent to a separate school down on the Solent, at a place called Stubbington, only just round the corner from where I live and work now. I don't remember questioning it at the time, but it must have been a serious wrench. Children take things for granted. Looking back on it. one sees perhaps more than mere coincidence in the fact that my brother's preparatory school was situated geographically only a stone's throw from one of the forts on Portsdown Hill, where my stepfather, as he was to become, was stationed.

It did mean that this very close companionship between my brother and me was broken up. Except at holidays, we never saw a great deal of each other because, although we were together at Sherborne School, a gap of two and a half years at that age means you might just as well be a continent apart. Soon after I got there, he left to go on to Sandhurst. He was the professional pilot and, of the two of us, it should have been he who made the flying headlines. As a professional soldier, he transferred out of the army into the R.A.F. and went into a Mosquito squadron. But he was killed two days before the invasion in 1944, during an intruder mission. At the same time I was also doing intruder ops. A life thrown away before it had ever had a chance. He was a great companion, easy-going and with loads of charm. Very good-looking and a great success with the girls from an early age, he married in 1941.

It's extraordinary how this terrain around the Solent seems to keep coming back as a landmark in my life, each time in quite a different setting with no association apparent between them. It was here, also, that I had my first significant meeting with an aeroplane. It was in 1931, when I was ten. My future stepfather comes into this too. He had contacts of some sort with the Schneider Trophy team. I was taken down to Calshot and introduced to G. H. Stainforth, who, after the trophy races, broke the then existing world speed record at 407 m.p.h. They actually let me climb up on the float of that wonderful forerunner of the Spitfire, the Supermarine S.6B – a tremendous thrill for a small boy. Yet, oddly enough, I can remember very little about it now, although I can remember the scene at Calshot very clearly. The waters where I now boat regularly are the very waters where they used to take off.

But I do remember around that time, certainly quite early on, having a blazing physical standup row with my future stepfather. He used to be about quite a lot. With some justification, I can see now, realising how completely undisciplined I was, he used to try and help my poor mother by inflicting much needed discipline upon me. It was badly needed, but he was the wrong person to do it. I was very "anti" any such practice, particularly at the receiving end from someone I regarded as a stranger and whom I suppose I resented anyway.

Not that I remember actively hating him because my parents' marriage had broken up. I was too much of a child to realise what was going on in those early days. Later, in my teens, when my mother went out to India, and the divorce had gone through, and she re-married out there, I realised that was what she wanted, and consequently I accepted it. But I was never very close to him at all. And I had long since lost contact with my father too.

That was towards the end of my time at Sherborne. I remember that I went down with pneumonia, and that was the next time I saw either of my parents. I came through it but I was very weak, as one is after such things. They got in touch with my father. He arrived at the school and took me pretty nearly straight out of bed down to the Poores' farm outside Salisbury.

That was about 1937, when I was sixteen. I didn't see my father from that day until we met at the Farnborough show in 1959, twenty-two years later. I don't recall that this worried me much at the time, but I suppose it must have done. If it didn't, I certainly couldn't have been as ordinary a child as I thought I was until now.

That bout of pneumonia was something of a blessing in disguise because, through it, I got to know the Poores very well indeed, and their farm. This was certainly a landmark. They became one of the significant influences in my young life. On that occasion, I was put straight to bed on arrival, and there was a somewhat protracted convalescence. But it was the Poores who, a little later, rescued me from drifting from that job at Brooke Bond's into permanent chair-bound misery, and brought me back into the country again to farm with them. Until the sight of the aircraft flying, and just across the fields a signpost which said Ford, decided for me where my next landmark was to be. In the air. For all the wrong reasons, as I've already explained. Simply because I imagined I would naturally be stationed there, near the people and the farm I loved. My decision was conditioned as much by a coincidental, and largely imaginary, geographical situation as by any ardent desire to fly.

The Poores were a delightfully happy family. Mrs. Poore was a widow who was a real friend to young people of all ages, and she kept open house at the farm. Apart from her kindness to me, I remember her particularly for her complete and absolute refusal to come to terms with anything mechanical. She had been a great horsewoman in her day, and still was in mine. Even when I knew her, she avoided the horseless carriage like the plague and went everywhere in a pony and trap. I did try to teach her to drive the car on the farm, with disastrous results. We were going quite well, through a wood (on a private road, thank goodness) when, with the crest of a hill in front of her, the time came to put on the brakes. Taking firm hold of the reins, she pulled hard on the steering wheel and shouted, Whoa! Whoa! The bushes at the bottom of the hill still probably bear our imprint to this day.

It could be that if the pattern of my life hadn't been such that the stability and the family environment of the Poores' farm became something unique in my young experience, because of the lack of it in my own family upbringing, I wouldn't have been naive enough to imagine I could keep close to it by joining up.

Until now I've always believed that I joined the Naval air force for the same reason thousands of other pilots volunteered. There was the threat of certain war and everybody was joining up, and I was absolutely ripe for it. Impressionable, and, until I took root at the farm, in an unsatisfying sort of job. Trying to look at myself in the round, I'm not

now so sure. It could be that, at the back of my mind, the idea of a
Service squadron offered me something of the companionship, the sense
of belonging in a group, that had never been a highlight of my family
life. It could have been nothing more nor less than the Boy Scout troop
again, only in a more mature form.

It all seems a long way away from the period we are considering now,
with the Delta already making vapour trails over that very spit of land
where, a war and two and a half decades ago, a small boy had stood
excitedly on the float of Stainforth's Schneider Trophy aeroplane.

9

CLOAK-AND-DAGGER

It was now late in January 1956 with the security shutters clamped down and double locked, closing us in on ourselves just as unpleasantly as the long winter nights themselves. At this stage it seemed impossible to imagine that, in only a few weeks' time, the Delta would break through this self-imposed shell of silence that isolated us from contact with the outside living world. The January skies themselves were blanketed deeply and darkly, making the whole project seem even more remote and with a curious sense of unreality that had a certain closed-in, dream-like quality. We were enclosed in an invisible shell of security, a vacuum in which existence and intercourse with the outside world had ceased. While we looked at the low January clouds and invented lie after lie to cover up our true intentions and withdrew more and more from contact with the world we knew outside, the moment of wide, clear skies and the Delta streaking its con-trail across the vast openness of space for the world to see became more and more difficult to visualise in real terms. It bore so little relation to our present isolated world that one's perception lost touch with it.

Curiously enough, in the whole of the project right up to the day that the record was actually flown, it is the strange unreal atmosphere of secrecy that remains most strongly in my mind. The amateur phase of jotting calculations down on scraps of paper, the informal huddles in Maurice Child's office, were over. We were now a full-scale operation: Operation "Metrical". The code name had been invented for us by the Royal Air Force. It was like being back in the Services, giving fighter cover in a Seafire Squadron to Operation Torch, the North African landing, and intruder operations over Europe with the code names of D-Day coming up.

Practically all of us engaged in Operation Metrical, being in the aircraft industry, had spent the war years on terms of intimate familiarity with secrecy, our lives and actions surrounded by the blanket of top secret security. But in peace time it was oddly different, because it was existing in parallel with our normal mundane domestic lives. The background of the war, where you were quite used to doing things you couldn't talk about, was really very different because, most of the time, you were amongst people who were in the secret, too, and you had long lost any but occasional contact with the civilian world. But here, I would leave after a day of plotting and planning, and I would immediately be in another world where my secrets made me a stranger, driving home in the evening and keeping the problems that were going round in my own mind, the real part of myself at that time, withdrawn and a stranger even to my own family. Security was so restrictive that they thought we were still on routine flight testing until I told them the day I left to make the first record run.

None of us had the least doubt about the necessity for these measures. We were quite certain that if anyone started talking and bragging about it at all, even letting slip a hint of what we were doing, the Americans would take the tip; and we were equally certain that, particularly with their climatic advantages, if even the slightest rumour of what we were about got to their ears, they would have a go themselves before we were ready. It was this ever-present danger that kept our intelligence on a hairspring the whole time, no matter what we felt sometimes emotionally.

At this stage, probably no more than a hundred people knew altogether. Outside the Fairey team itself, a handful of senior officers in the R.A.F. and in the Royal Navy were given the whole story. The Royal Aero Club also had to be put in the know, as they were the only people who had a clear understanding of the rules, but we left it as late as we possibly could and only told them about a month beforehand. Even then, only the two or three of them who had to be official witnesses were told.

The security blanket was terribly time-consuming, because one had to spend hours using roundabout methods to get something essential laid on, when a direct explanation could have achieved it in a few minutes. It had its own problems quite apart from the personal ones, and created tremendous difficulties and complications inside the firm itself as well as outside. Even within the firm, surprisingly few knew anything about it. We copied very closely the highly successful American "The Need to Know" philosophy of security. It is simple, ruthless, and effective. No matter how closely involved in the project a man may be, or how close a personal friend, at the bottom or the top of his own particular hierarchy, you simply ask yourself, does he need to know in order to play his immediate part. Seniority or intimacy with the aircraft had nothing to do with it. If he didn't need to know, you didn't tell him. We took this so far that even the fitters and the team who had been working on the Delta since the moment it had made its first flight were not let into the secret. The only reason they would have had to know was if it had been necessary to give them an incentive for all the additional hours they were now having to put in. But there wasn't a single individual ever on the Delta team who did not believe that he himself had a personal stake in the Delta as an aircraft design, and who would not have gladly given up any hours of the night or day necessary to tend to it. These were dedicated craftsmen who needed no incentive.

All the same, we felt a little guilty about not telling them, and we passed the buck to Freddy Parker, who was the engineering manager, to break the news to the team only forty-eight hours beforehand and try to make certain that they did not resent the fact that they had been excluded until then. There were, of course, some grudging feelings at all levels, perfectly understandably. It was difficult to know what to say when someone who had worked alongside you for years came up and said, "Well, I'm in the firm, too, and I've been involved in the Delta since the beginning, and at least you might have told me." But we couldn't.

This phase also had its amusing moments. I became an accomplished liar, and more adept than I could have supposed at inventing completely fictional situations. I must confess to a mildly malicious sense of amusement when I went down to the Chemical Warfare Division at Porton to see if they could find us a way of making satisfactory smoke trails. Here, at the gates of an establishment which is as closely guarded against the ravages of the outsider as a harem of top-level concubines, I had to talk my way in on a story which bore very little relation to the truth. All the time they must have been wondering why I had come to them, when there were plenty of well-known places where perfectly adequate devices were available for making smoke in large quantities. As they scratched their heads and wondered why we couldn't use ordinary canisters like everybody else, we could not tell them that the containers would have to fit into the tail parachute stowage because it was the only space available. But they co-operated wonderfully and eventually produced four containers, one for each run, filled with a chemical called Hexachloroethane which, when we burnt it on the ground to try, must have given the impression that we wanted to lay a smoke screen over the whole of the south coast. Within this top secret establishment, I was well aware, they were unwittingly being played at their own game. Not only was the ground enveloped in a smoke screen as we carried out our tests. They were innocently producing suggestion after suggestion to satisfy the apparently insatiable appetite of a chimera which was simply an absurd creation of my own imagination. I forget now what the cover story was, but it must have been a good one.

The search for suitably secure sites for the timing cameras, and so on, also had its moments. Our choice was necessarily restricted, because we had in fact very little freedom of choice as to where we would lay out the record course itself, and this, in turn, determined within fairly close limits where the various sites would be. However, as far as possible, we wanted to avoid any of these installations sticking up like a sore thumb in the middle of open country and attracting the curiosity of the general public; for it would only need something like this, together with a few supersonic bangs, and someone would be bound to put two and two together and break the story prematurely.

Our choice of locale for the record bid was limited by three main considerations. Geographically it had to be somewhere that was within very easy reach of Boscombe Down, because this was the base for all our routine tests on the normal development contract and we could not disrupt them. We did not dare to take any action that would make the record bid appear to be more than a part-time junket done out of working hours. The Ministry had given us permission, but it had never given us its approval. If we had preferred a site anywhere else than at Boscombe Down – and it is quite possible that there were potentially better sites available – it would have been more than the whole bid was worth to suggest moving base, and consequently interrupting the Ministry's development contract, merely for a world speed record bid. Ours was a Priority 2 record. Sometimes some of us thought it might even be Priority 3. Probably all those who read the headlines when the story broke took it for granted that the whole project was laid on at top level and that everything was done to make conditions as easy and as ideal as possible. On the contrary. This is one of the inevitable disadvantages of doing a record on the cheap, and it compares vividly with the ballyhoo, the magnificent facilities, and all the backing behind any American effort that can result in national prestige. One has only to think of the tremendous press facilities, rather more like a Roman circus than a serious scientific experiment, that recently accompanied their first successful launching of a man in a rocket flight. Everything was there from the brass bands downwards. And this was done well knowing that no matter how successful the flight would be, it was still a minor achievement compared with the Russian orbiting of Yuri Gagarin. The Americans know that when they have got something to shout about the thing to do is to shout hard, but when they have got something not quite so good then the thing is to shout harder still. I would still prefer to make records the way we do. But we would have liked to have had as much support from the Ministry as they get from their appropriate government departments.

We realised that unless we accepted this situation, it would have meant disrupting the whole normal programme to such an extent that it would virtually have stopped all development on the aeroplane for about five months. This was obviously a thing to be avoided for our own sakes, quite irrespective of any adverse reaction we might expect from the Ministry. Thus it was that we had decided quite early on that, whatever the actual course might be, we must be able to take off and land from Boscombe Down. Secondly, we were vitally dependent on getting good weather, and it was essential that we should select an area where statistically the probability of suitable record flying conditions would be at least as good as, and preferably better than, any other in the British Isles. The third consideration was that we had a great number of different people to bring together from a great number of different organisations, and it was necessary therefore to select an area which, if possible, would be convenient to them all for access. This applied particularly to the camera operators, the Royal Aero Club officials, and so on; and it would also be necessary to choose our site so that there were fairly easy and rapid facilities for taking instruments and recordings to Farnborough at the conclusion of each flight for official inspection.

It seemed obvious that the course would have to be coastal, because it was desirable that the pilot should be able to line up on it from 38,000 feet visually if need be, and to do this he would need some easy reference point. As luck would have it, the south coast within range of Boscombe Down is excellent from this point of view because, if one draws it very roughly, it is a straight line as seen from that height and remembering that, at the speed we would be travelling, such reference points would be about a hundred miles apart instead of the usual church steeples and so on which a pilot looks for at more normal speeds.

We also wanted a fairly level area, if possible, in order to save the Ordnance people a great deal of trouble and expense, because in order to meet the stringent height requirements for the record, the whole course would have to be accurately surveyed.

Once again this meant having to consult a great number of people who had not been brought into the picture before. We had to make the meteorologists and other experts at Farnborough put cold towels round their heads and turn out a phenomenal amount of statistical work for us. I seem to recall that we spun some outrageous yarn to the Met. Office at Farnborough as a cover, to the effect that we were carrying out a missile-testing programme.

Provisionally, we selected the flat stretch of coastal plain in the Chichester area. This was very nearly ideal from the point of view of ranging from Boscombe Down. Any point nearer would have given us no advantage because of the distances to be covered in climbing to the height at which the run was to be made, at an angle which would use the minimum amount of fuel. And, also, it gave the pilot the aiming point some fifty miles ahead so essential to help him to line up visually on the initial stages of the run. On paper, this looked ideal also, using Beachy Head and Southampton Water, or Fawley Oil Refinery, as landmarks. We found out later, however, that this was of little value because, although the coast line gave a general guide to the direction, the cockpit arrangement in the Delta is such that the pilot seeking landmarks ahead can see absolutely nothing downwards, so I could not pick up the landmarks anyway. Visual positioning became only of secondary importance, and we made up our minds that radar assistance was absolutely essential.

In general, though, luck was entirely with us. The meteorological statistics from Farnborough showed that a stretch between the Naval Air Station at Ford and Portsmouth had one of the best records on the south coast, and this was almost exactly the area we had been considering as best meeting all the other requirements. Any rate, we went down to have a look at it, making up one excuse after another if we met anyone showing any appreciable interest in what we were doing. Everything looked splendid and, to the relief of the Ordnance Survey people, it was nice and flat with no violent fluctuations in elevation at all.

Now, within this area, we had to make the most important siting decision of all – where the actual measured course would be. The decisive factor in this was that the two timing cameras, when pointed up at the sky absolutely vertically, had to range on the start and finish of the course. We decided to position the master camera site first, and then find the nearest suitable point over the minimum course length. The rules allowed us a range between fifteen and twenty-five kilometres, but, for reasons of fuel conservation, we wanted to keep it as close to fifteen kilometres as possible.

We put the first camera site actually within the Royal Navy Air Station at Ford; it was a friendly place and we knew the people well there. Quite apart from this, there were obvious advantages in siting on a Service establishment. We would be away from the prying eyes of everyone except Service personnel on the station, and they were quite used to seeing aeroplanes about and would be unlikely to ask too many questions. They were not let into the secret anyway – only the Station Commander was told in advance – but I suspect that, once we began making supersonic bangs all over the sky and they saw camera equipment tracking us, many of them must have guessed what we were about. There was, however, absolutely no leakage at all. As this was an operational airfield, it was obviously as near ideal as we could hope to get. The station facilities made it much simpler to tie-in the mass of operational communications that had to be centralised at this main site.

So we put our first pin in the map at Ford, and then, as it were, paced out fifteen kilometres, plus just enough margin to make sure we were on the right side of the rules, and put our second pin down on the second spot. The ideal point turned out to be the sewage farm at Chichester. We were absolutely delighted because we could not imagine that many people would go out walking in the early Spring to a sewage farm; but the second of the camera teams were perhaps not quite so happy, faced with a very unsavoury week sitting amongst these big rotating sewage filters. The old boy who ran the sewage farm, I remember, was delighted at this novel change from his daily routine, and the prospect of having a few social contacts normally sadly lacking in his unsalubrious area of work. We spun him some outrageously romantic tale too, although I can no longer remember what it was.

Existing radar stations were used so their siting provided no difficulties.

At this stage we had to bring the G.P.O. into the project in a big way because we could no longer avoid the problem of communications. Vitally important in particular was the provision of completely reliable communications between the two camera sites. The camera-timing mechanism on one hand had to be electrically connected with the camera-timing mechanism on the other. And, of course, there was also the question of all the other interconnections that had to be made available in the whole network that was now beginning rapidly to develop as the time got nearer. We went to the highest-ranking G.P.O. official to whom we could find access, and told him what it was all about. By this time our imaginative approach towards cover stories was beginning to wear a bit thin, and we were much relieved when he immediately fell into the spirit of the whole thing and invented some splendid cover stories of his own. They discarded the idea of running wire nearly fifteen miles overland as being too big an undertaking, and one which also raised questions of reliability. Instead the whole communication system was networked through the ordinary G.P.O. exchanges. It was obviously important to go through an absolute minimum of exchanges, both from the point of view of reliability, speed of operation, and security. In the end only a small number of village exchanges were involved. The whole plan was full of complexity, and the way it was done represented a considerable achievement. The G.P.O. were absolutely magnificent. From the day they took the project on, including running cable from the local exchanges to the actual sites themselves, testing out, and so on, it was done with the most incredible speed and efficiency. I will never forget going down to have a look at one of the camera sites one day, and not believing my own eyes. It seemed as if every telegraph pole and every bush for half a mile or more was swarming with men with little green vans hanging wires up. The picture has been so firmly imprinted on my memory that I still see it in my mind's eye quite clearly today. I have never seen such a sight before, and will be surprised if I ever see a comparable sight again. Without any fuss whatever, they had completed the whole job in a couple of days.

The main masses of the plan were now blocked in. I realise that, recording this on paper in retrospect and at a distance, it must look as if everything went smoothly and sweetly and according to plan. I cannot help but to have failed to evoke even a glimmering of the quite unreal atmosphere which was our environment at the time. It was an amalgam of all sorts of things: of optimism, of frustration, of tension, of a sensation that the whole of the project and one's self was becoming completely submerged in an overwhelming mass of unmanageable detail; fears and doubts, not about the actual flight itself, but a terrible physical disbelief that all these multitudinous details spread geographically from $7\frac{1}{4}$ miles up in the sky to a sewage farm in Chichester, and all the countless independent individuals involved, could all possibly, as in fact they did, become a single coordinated organism equipped to take co-ordinated instantaneous reflex actions during the split seconds which spelt success or failure for the bid. But above all there was the way that all of us watched the meteorological forecasts. And, ever increasingly as the day grew nearer, that curious hesitancy before you opened a paper or turned the radio on to the news, each time half expecting to see or hear the headline that could make the whole thing a waste of time – America makes a new world speed record. But we were lucky. And our security screen held. And on the other side of the Atlantic they sat quite happily working out the forecasts for the baseball leagues in the forthcoming season. We had a clear run ahead.

10

WARTIME LANDMARKS

Re-reading the last two chapters, I'm suddenly embarrassingly aware that, if this book had been written about someone I didn't know, I'd take the poor fellow as being something of a genius at the executive and organisational side, capable of doing dozens of quite different things simultaneously, and co-ordinating the lot. Quietly. Calmly. An ice-cool administrative brain.

If I were a tycoon of Big Business, I'd take the chap on right away as my Personal Assistant so that I could be sure there would be some-one competent to step into my shoes as soon as the time came. . . .

Well of course nothing could be further from the truth. And certainly no one has ever made me such an offer.

I'd never had any training in the administrative side of business at all. My war, thank goodness, was notably free of such things. It was a typical pilot's war, until 1944 when I was sent on a mission to America. Even then, it was my experience as a night-fighter pilot which was needed. There was very little administrative work; although I did find myself having to knock about with pretty high-up people at times in a curious atmosphere that was a strange combination of amateur diplomacy and commercial espionage. Not that I thought about it like that at the time.

I was only just eighteen when I first applied for the Fleet Air Arm, and was turned down. The war had already started by the time I found myself in the services. Naval Airman, 2nd class. The lowest of the low and suitably dressed in the square rig uniform and the bell bottoms of a sailor. There was no intention then of making flying a career. I joined H. O., that is for Hostilities Only. When it was all over, I was quite certain, I'd go back to the farm.

My early days in the Service were absolutely conventional. Square-bashing course. Elementary flying training under the R.A.F. First solo in a Tiger Moth. Then, much to my excitement, posted to Netheravon to train on Fairey Battles, my first experience of Fairey aircraft. My excitement was not so much due to the fact that I was now a fully-fledged pilot but that, miraculously, the posting took me back to within reasonable distance of the farm.

Then the Solent came back into the picture again. My first operational posting was to the Navy's fighter school at Eastleigh near Southampton; and then, almost immediately, to Yeovilton, in Somerset. The Battle of Britain was on. Our only direct connection with it was that the R.A.F. took our one and only Spitfire away from us. We grieved about this. It was one of the few Spitfires in the country and we made a pet of it because it made us feel important. Then I did a conversion course at Andover to twin-engined aircraft, only to find at the end of it that I was posted to the Orkneys, towing targets for other people to shoot at. In the winter there wasn't much of that either, because it was dark all day long. However, this period did give me the chance to fly a whole variety of different aeroplanes quite early on, including Blackburn Skuas, Rocs, Hawker Henleys, Blenheims, two or three American Marylands, and the famous Swordfish. Very useful groundbait for a future test pilot this variety was, too.

I was quite happy up there, except when they got me on to making the daily meteorological flight. On these days I had to take the Swordfish up to about 12,000 ft., which was getting on towards its ceiling, through a slow and dreary climb, irrespective of whether the weather was fine, black, snowing, or anything else. I found it a comfortless task to be given in an open aeroplane.

It came as something of a relief to go back on first-line duties – even though it turned out to be on the new CAM ships.

This was a new idea, to try to frighten the Focke-Wulf Condors off the North Atlantic shipping lanes. CAM stood for Catapult Armed Merchantman. The technique was developed at the Royal Aircraft Establishment, Farnborough. You sat in a Hurricane on a small ramp up in the overcrowded bows of the merchant vessel. Immediately behind you were a fistful of rockets. At the right moment, you opened the throttle wide, full boost, and the captain pushed a button. The rockets went off and, with your engine at full power, you were in the air almost within the length of the aeroplane.

It all sounds pretty exciting, but in fact there wasn't very much in the actual rocketing itself, except that the initial 'g' was quite high for those times. The most unnerving thing was to watch somebody else, and to see all the flame and stuff pouring out of the back and wondering whether the aircraft could ever get away without blowing up.

It was a pretty dreary and uncomfortable period for me, with little or no flying. There was altogether too much time to think about the ships that were being sunk around you in the convoy, without any chance of getting relief from it by personal action; you just had to sit around on deck without taking any active part, feeling very much like a sitting duck and wondering if it was your turn next. There could, at best, be only one take-off on each trip – and very possibly no landing – because, once the aircraft had been catapulted off, there was no way of recovering it. Then, in 1941, when I was twenty, I was posted to 804A Flight at Gibraltar. Still no action. I was transferred to 807 Squadron on the *Ark Royal*, flying Fairey Fulmars. The day the *Ark Royal* was sunk I was in the air and my kit hadn't yet joined the ship.

There followed a period at Gibraltar. The main thing I remember about it was that some of us, bored stiff with the Rock, managed to nip across the border and take a ship to Tangier for a long week-end. We nearly found ourselves in an international incident of some magnitude. And we nearly got lynched. It was quite incredible, looking back, that we ever went to Tangier at all. As an international free port it was uncommitted in the war and it was full of Germans. We didn't care a damn. A standard opening gambit was to find the most obvious-looking Prussian blonde and introduce ourselves as: Well, we know you're a spy, so let's get all the questions over first and then we can have fun. Espionage never gave us any trouble after that gambit.

But on this occasion, no sooner had we grabbed a taxi off the rank on the quayside than there was an ear-splitting roar and the rest of the taxi-rank vanished, together with the lives of about thirty Arabs. Someone had put a time-bomb in the mail bags. We'd travelled over in the same ship.

We were lucky to escape with our lives. And it wasn't all that healthy, quite apart from being only a few seconds away from the explosion itself. The locals were convinced the bomb had been planted by the British. We were British pilots. What were we doing in Tangier, anyhow? That night there were anti-British demonstrations. We were in a night-club and didn't notice them. The only end-result of the incident was that the British Consul found himself faced with a number of unexpected hotel bills because we had to wait for the officials to release the boat and, in the meanwhile, we ran out of funds. The whole thing was a curious facet of the war which, in a sense, made it all seem rather ridiculous. . . .

Very shortly afterwards, operations started again. The squadron had been transferred to the aircraft-carrier *Argus*, and our job was to escort convoys through the Mediterranean down to Bomb Alley, which lay between Sicily and the North African coast. On my first sortie we spotted some Italian CR. 42 fighters and doubtless they spotted us. The thing that sticks in my mind was the strange way they were behaving.

They were doing all sorts of curious aerobatics and carrying on more like a circus act than a serious operational threat. Perhaps it was just natural Italian ebullience. I shot one down. It was the first time I'd fired my guns in anger. The crew jumped out in their parachutes. Whether I had actually hit them or whether they jumped out because they were frightened, I've never to this day quite made up my mind.

The following day, whilst chasing an Italian BB20 reconnaisance aircraft who was having a look at the fleet, I got rather too close to him in my initial attack; he put a shot clean through my spinner into the propeller. The prop promptly flew into fully fine pitch, the windscreen was covered with oil, and I thought the engine was going to come off its seating. I was faced with the prospect of either ditching in the gathering dark or trying to get back to the ship. In the end we got back and landed on, covered in oil, much to the consternation of the people on deck who knew perfectly well I couldn't see a thing.

It was not an experience I wanted to repeat. But in fact, although I've never considered it until now, it may well have been one of the factors that conditioned my decision to bring the crippled Delta back that time I got the Queen's Commendation. I don't believe I could have thought it any more difficult than nursing the Fulmar back with no visibility and my eyes filled with oil.

It was now 1942, and the war was beginning to move for me. The squadron was kept fully occupied providing fighter protection for Malta-bound convoys. I got a D.S.C., which made a very nice twenty-first birthday present. However, it was a depressing business because there was really so little we could do to help these terribly hard-pressed convoys. On one of the last convoys we escorted, all but two of the ships were sunk and we lost five aircraft from the squadron.

Then, towards the end of the year, we returned to U.K. for reforming into a Seafire squadron. Then we went back to the Mediterranean to give support to Operation Torch, the North African landings. There was a Bar to my D.S.C., and then I went back to England to train at the nightfighter school at Drem. This was something quite new and, to me, quite fascinating. It was the beginning of airborne radar.

And from there I went to the Naval Air Station at Ford. Ford was an operational intruder airfield from which we flew at night to hover over German airfields at low level, waiting for them to take off so that we could shoot them down over their home base. But it was also an Operational Research Unit. All the time we were fitting new equipment, then flying on an operational sortie to try it out. This was the pattern, the very essence, of test flying. It was this that began to fascinate me more than the actual long-range intruder operations, although I had my fair share of both. Ford was a landmark because it was here I began to get the taste for test flying. This had nothing to do with high-speed flying, nor with the so-called glamour of test flying which the popular sporting press has pushed as a hero-image. I had always been good with my hands, and I was the kind of person who could keep a lot of detail comparatively tidily in his mind. The same sort of aptitudes that a radio ham and an office accountant might have. Or a test pilot. Now, here was an aspect of flying that had never entered my head before, an aspect where you could play about with ideas on the ground which you thought might work, and then take them up in the air and see what actually happened in practice.

Ford was a landmark in another important way too. Destiny once again found the moment for the man. My experience at Ford resulted in my name being put forward as one of four officers on a naval mission to America to investigate what they were doing in the same field.

It was during this period in America, in 1944, that I flew my first jet aircraft, just twelve years before the record attempt. The administrative experience I gained during this phase of the war also stood me in good stead when I found myself caught up in the massive organisational network of the world speed record bid. The preparatory detail work was enormous, and even though more of it fell on the shoulders of others in the Delta team than on mine, there was plenty of it for all. In retrospect, curiously enough, I don't remember finding it notably difficult, although it certainly gave us more headaches than any of us had ever bargained for.

11

TIMING THE RECORD

February had come and gone before we knew where we were, and the record bid was already on top of us. There was at times a frightening feeling that the whole system was unmanageable and out of control, and that time was bleeding to death in front of our eyes without us being able to do anything to stop it. The atmosphere at times was one of quiet desperation, like those science fiction novels where a strange mutation takes root and multiplies so quickly that it envelops everything and, when you cut it down, it immediately grows again twice as quickly and as strong.

We were still heavily engaged on the super-priority test-flying programme on the Gannet. Gordon Slade and I were having to deal with all the record preparations in such off-peak periods as we could find.

I must have chafed at all this detail organisational work at the time. It was just as important to us to see that the fitters preparing the site for the first camera team at the Ford Naval Air Station had sandwiches and somewhere to sleep as it was to take the aeroplane up on a supersonic test flight. A thousand and one little jobs. We may not have liked them at the time, but in the long view they were a godsend. No one had time to chew his nails.

It would certainly be ridiculous to suggest that we regarded the record bid as just another day's work, or that there was not a certain amount of nervous tension involved in it all. But we certainly did not dwell morbidly over prospects of the bid itself. Certainly I was not conscious that there was any overbearing stress and neither, I am certain, was Gordon Slade. The reason for this was doubtless not that we were particularly insensitive people ourselves so much as the fact that the detail planning never gave us a moment to think about it and, when we packed in at night and went home, we were so dog-tired that sleep came easily and the morning came too soon. Quite the most nerve-racking thing of all was ensuring that all this detail organisation worked because, for reasons which I hope I have already made clear, it needed only one minor detail in one small section to go infinitesimally wrong and, no matter how fast we flew, the run would be null and void. The total co-ordination was a tremendous problem and, to me at any rate, far more difficult and worrying than flying the thing.

The nearer the day approached, the more we felt the pressure of the organisation bearing down upon us from all sides as it slowly knit itself into a coherent existence capable of common logical action. By now the time had come when we realised that we were finally committed to making the attempt within the next few days, and it was no longer just something on paper in the future, and we began to spread the responsibility. Then, having done exactly what we had been saying in all the weeks previously that we wanted to do, having got this load of detail responsibility off our shoulders and delegated it to others, we felt uneasy instead of relieved. We knew how much still had to be done and how little time was left in which to do it, and we could not help feeling apprehensive. This, of course, does not imply that we did not have complete faith in everyone concerned. But the whole thing was so difficult. In a sense, the responsibility passed out of our hands. We felt that we were now delegating these responsibilities to people who were strangers to us, unknown people inasmuch as they were outside the close little security team we had been up till then. Quixotically, one anxiety replaced another. Having managed to get myself freed of a lot of detail responsibility, I immediately began wishing in a way that I hadn't been. Quite unreasonably. I suppose, looking back, all this does indicate that I was more tensed up than I knew. I think probably we all were.

I had been very much occupied in this later stage making sure that the height at which the flight was made would be recorded with absolute accuracy, and that I would be able to fly the aircraft within the limits required. I had never flown the Delta, or any other aircraft for that matter, at speeds even approaching these, to the limits of accuracy which the rules demanded. It had to be very carefully planned indeed and, even then, no one could be quite certain that it could be done because we had no time to practise.

It must be remembered that the international rules for very high speed flying at high altitudes were comparatively new, and no one had very much experience as to how they could best be applied. Even the Americans only had Haynes's run in the Super Sabre to give them experience, and they had never announced publicly either how they measured his record or indeed to what accuracy he was able to hold the aircraft straight and level within the required limits. We were even worse off, for we had absolutely no experience at all.

What is involved can best be appreciated by considering briefly the limit figures set down by the rules. First of all, once having chosen the

altitude at which we wanted to fly, we were not allowed to go outside
that height by more than 2,460 ft. This was not too difficult. However,
having started the actual run, within that height band, we were not
allowed to lose more than 328 ft. during the whole run, including the
regulation 7½ kilometres which preceded the measured course. It was as
if you had to fly through two invisible circus hoops many miles apart,
7¼ miles up in space, accelerating violently up to twenty miles a minute
under re-heat. Once you had entered the course, you were committed to
going through both hoops. They were actually a little smaller in
diameter than the overall height of St. Paul's. Put another way, flying at
the speeds we had in mind it takes only about 1/120th of a second to
cover 328 ft. – rather less time than it takes you to blink an eyelid.

The object of this rule is perfectly understandable. It is to prevent the
pilot getting any additional increase of speed by diving. However, no
matter how understandable it might be, it was still cold comfort to know
that we had to put it into practice, and that, if we were only a single foot
outside this speck of a bull's eye in the vast open sky, it would be
immaterial how fast we flew because the run would be disallowed. We
spent days analysing the problem in theory to the last possible detail, but
of course we would not know what other unknown factors might come
in to disturb our plans in the actual flights because we would have no
time to put our plans to the test before the actual bid itself. The three
essential aims of the pilot were: to establish the height of the first entry
gate at the beginning of the approach run; to maintain an almost
imperceptible climb from a few seconds after this point until the end of
the run, in order to be certain of keeping within the height limitation; and
to keep within the overall height tolerance during the turn at the end of
the run when we were coming round to make the return journey. It should
be emphasised that what was in fact quite a tight turn to us was really a
considerable pear-shaped sweep by normal standards. It would take me
out to within sight of the French coast before I turned to come round
Beachy Head for the second approach. We were not bound by the rules
to keep within the height limits during this turn, but we decided to do so
in order to avoid any possible inaccuracy due to having to make any
appreciable height adjustment at the last second, in order to be straight
and level and in the middle of the hoop as we came into the course.

All these conditions were aimed at ensuring that we went along the
course in the right position. It did little to solve the most difficult
problem of all – how to pass through the second hoop within 328 ft. of
the first one. To whoever made the actual flights, whether it was to be
Gordon Slade or myself or both, this was the paramount problem and
one which called for every bit of skill and experience we had amassed

in years of test flying, together with not a little plain good luck. The problem was accentuated by the fact that one's altimeter readings do strange and sometimes unpredictable things at these hitherto unexplored speeds. As you go through the sound barrier, there is a flick on the needle, and the needle then stabilises itself at a slightly different value, even though you may still be flying at the same height. This phenomenon was well understood and we could make the necessary adjustments for it. It did not worry us because, of course, we were well the other side of the sound barrier during the run. But it did lay one trap for the unwary which had to be watched. This transonic flick could very well alter the altimeter reading by as much as 600 to 800 ft., and this made it very easy to misread the meter.

There are, as most people know, two needles on an altimeter, one moving round comparatively rapidly and showing hundreds of feet, while the other one shows the total number of thousands which have already been clocked up. Thus the actual height is the sum of the two. With the hundreds needle flicking almost over its complete range, it was very easy to take, instead of the correct thousands reading, one that was in fact a thousand feet above or below. I found it confusing when selecting the correct thousand reading at which to fly, and had to watch it carefully because such an error would put us well outside the permissible height envelope. However, the main trouble was on the actual course itself, where we needed absolute accuracy from the altimeter as never before, but where, as we were to find out, the reading tended to vary slightly as we accelerated. There were no rules in the text-books to overcome this. It became very much a matter of flying one's instruments as well as the aeroplane, building up experience from one run to another, and compensating by judgment rather than any accurate application of science.

On some of the early runs we were also handicapped by the fact that the pilot's altimeter was reluctant to move until far too much error had accumulated. One was lulled into a sense of false security, congratulating one's self on the fact that exactly level flight was being maintained much more easily than one had anticipated, until suddenly the altimeter would jump to the extremities of the permissible limits. We went outside the 328 ft. limit several times before we realised that the needle was sticking, and then we changed it.

One of our most important jobs during this final preparatory phase was therefore to calibrate the altitude and air speed systems, as it were, to the last decimal place. As the error varied with the speed, it was obviously necessary to do a complete range of calibration tests covering the entire speed range in which we were working, so that we could produce in effect a calibration curve to prevent our being misled by our own instruments. With an ordinary subsonic aircraft this is a fairly simple thing to do. The normal practice is to take the top of a building, or any landmark of accurately known height, and fly the aeroplane past it at varying speeds. Each time you pass the landmark you photograph your own aircraft relative to the top of the building. At the same instant, a recording camera in the aircraft also photographs the height shown on the aircraft instrument. That way, a direct comparison is easily obtained which shows the variation between the apparent height recorded by the instruments and the true height as shown by the actual physical height of the building.

Needless to say, if you want to use this method with a supersonic aeroplane flying at the altitudes we were flying at, you would have to jack your building up to 40,000 ft., so we had to find other methods. We enlisted the help of a specially calibrated Venom aeroplane from A. & A.E.E., the Aircraft and Armament Experimental Establishment, which was equipped not only with two special sensitive aneroid altimeters but also a camera operator. This aircraft was to be, in effect, our standard, and in fact its own calibration had been no mean achievement. They had worked for several months to ensure the degree of accuracy necessary. The plan was for the Venom to go up to 40,000 ft. and let the Delta fly past it. At a signal, which I gave from the cockpit, the photographer in the Venom photographed his own true height and, at the same time, observed and photographed the relative height of the Delta to the Venom. Also at the same instant, the pilot of the Delta recorded the reading on his own sensitive aneroid altimeter, and the forward speed. It was, of course, quite impossible for me to guarantee to fly exactly level with the Venom every time, but this did not matter. The photograph showed how much higher or lower I was, and we then made a simple correction in our figures to bring us into line. My actual air speed and height errors were then shown simply by the difference between the results given by the Venom's instruments and the indicated reading on my own.

In order to give the visual signal to the Venom, we simply installed a taxi-ing lamp on the port side of the Delta fuselage and wired it to operate when the auto observer operated.

Our main difficulties were due to the enormous difference in speeds between the two aircraft. I could climb so quickly that we had to send the Venom off at least five to seven minutes before we started the Delta up. Had we not done so, we would have used up all our fuel waiting for the Venom to get there.

At this stage, we hadn't yet discovered how to make condensation trails to order, and we only produced them if we were lucky. Thus, it was no easy matter for the two of us to make contact. We enlisted radar aid, but, even so, making a successful rendezvous at the higher supersonic speeds was anybody's guess. Remember that the Venom had some minutes' start; in addition, I had to start my run anything from up to twenty-five miles behind him in order to accelerate up to the speed that was to be checked and, at that speed, not only had to find him but pass him as closely as possible and at the same height. There is only very limited visibility from the Delta and this, combined with the "vastness of the space" around 40,000 ft., made visual contact very difficult. Fortunately the Venom was fitted with smoke-laying equipment, and this proved invaluable, particularly in establishing initial contact and getting on the right track for the long run-in necessary for runs at the higher speeds.

Even at the lower speeds, the exercise was not without its difficulties. In fact, we were already quite well resigned at this stage to the fact that nothing in connection with this record bid happened without apparent difficulties rearing their heads at the most unexpected moments. When I talk about lower speeds, it should be understood that the term is relative. The lowest point for calibration was Mach 0.75 (approx. 500 m.p.h.). We had thought it would be possible, at these subsonic speeds, to fly together, keeping a sort of Fred Karno's flight formation comprising the much-instrumented Venom and the little Delta with a flash lamp hooked on to its port side. It turned out to be extremely difficult, for a number of technical reasons which we had not anticipated. Also, as we approached the sound barrier, a sort of oscillating pitching action started to take place which, I found, I only succeeded in aggravating when I tried to make the necessary corrections. In the end I found it more satisfactory to leave them to damp themselves.

The highest speed at which we made calibrations was at Mach 1.69 (approx. 1,100 m.p.h.), for which I switched in reheat some twenty miles astern. At these speeds, judging exactly the right moment to start the warning count of "three, two, one – Now", so that the "Now" would synchronise with the actual instant I passed the Venom, and we could all take photographs of each other, was no easy matter. It needed only a split second's error of judgment to be miles away. I have much reason to be grateful to Mr. Inglesby of A. & A.E.E., who was the observer in the Venom, and to Group-Captain Bruin Purvis and "Doc" Stewart, who were pilots, for it was very much due to their skill that we carried through this rather tedious but highly important series of calibration tests with success and without undue delay.

One interesting point came out of this, which had nothing to do with the actual tests themselves. Anyone who has ever heard a supersonic bang on the ground must be wondering what it felt like in the Venom when the Delta passed it at speeds considerably in excess of the speed of sound. So did the Venom crew. Curiously enough, even though we passed at close range, all they noticed was a slight bump. Just as curiously, this bump did not increase as we increased our speed.

The next job on the agenda was to make sure that I would leave behind me a good fat condensation trail. Now, the forecasting of the height at which a good con-trail will form, and the conditions required to form it, are by no means an exact science. It was decided that by far the safest way was to forget science and find our con-trail empirically. This was very readily and efficiently laid on for us by Meteor aircraft of 29 Squadron, stationed at Tangmere. They set up for us what was effectually a "Con-trail Height Reconnaissance Flight", which went up half an hour or so before I did each morning and flew around the sky within the limits of the height in which we could operate, until they found the best trail-making altitude.

As it happened, during the whole period of the bid, this turned out to be at 38,000 ft., which was exactly where we wanted to make the run. But this was pure luck. It could quite well not have been so, which would have meant that we were doing the run at an altitude that wasn't necessarily the most efficient ideal height for the Delta's own characteristics. Had that happened, we would have accepted the situation and flown at that height, because without a good trail there wasn't a chance of the timing-camera operators getting us in their sights. It is a curious thought that the ability to see the aeroplane was more important than flying at the ideal height, but this was just another of those odd little quirks which characterised the whole project. At least we were never in danger of being bored by routine.

As I drove home that evening, I suddenly realised that I had unintentionally set up another quite unofficial record. During the final calibration tests with the Venom, when I was flying faster than we had ever flown the Delta before, the closing speed between the two aeroplanes, even taking into account that the Venom was moving in the same direction as I was, was over the speed of sound. It was probably the first truly supersonic interception to be achieved. Certainly it was the fastest successful interception ever made at that date. How well the Venom crew carried out their calibration is proved by the fact that the "height separation" was never more than ninety-eight feet.

The sense of urgency was now beginning to be felt through the whole team. We all began to feel that we were nearly there, and there was a steadily increasing atmosphere of excitement during this weekend as, piece by piece, this tremendous organisational jigsaw, that up till then none of us had ever been able to visualise as a whole, now started falling neatly into place.

If I had been kept fairly busy in the air, there was even more activity going on on the ground. The two camera crews, who in many ways had more responsibility than I had in making a successful bid, were in position and were now desperately engaged in carrying out calibrations of their own which, as we shall see, made the job that I had had to do calibrating the instruments in the aircraft, accurate though they had to be, appear crude by comparison.

It is necessary here to describe briefly how these cameras worked, so that the immense difficulties involved can be appreciated. In the subsonic era of speed records, measuring the speed over the actual stipulated course was a comparatively simple matter. Firstly, by comparison with ourselves, all such records had been carried out at low level, so that the aeroplane was a reasonably sized object to viewers from the ground, whereas we were asking them to pick up and pinpoint an aircraft which was quite invisible to the naked eye. Secondly, a split-second error, which would not have made very much difference to the final figures on record attempts previous to ours, now became of such vital importance that they could very well make the difference between the record or just missing it.

Imagine, therefore, two invisible pinpoints in the mass of space, $7\frac{1}{4}$ miles up. The instruments had to be able to record the aircraft at the precise instant it flew through these invisible pinpoints hung high in the sky. The general principle, much simplified, was to site a camera, as it were, firmly on the ground and immediately underneath each pinpoint. Then, as long as the camera was aiming absolutely vertically up into the sky, the middle of the lens would be pointing directly at the pinpoint. Now, if the first pinpoint corresponded to the starting point of a course and the second pinpoint corresponded to the finishing point, all you had to do was to take a photograph on each camera as it got the aircraft exactly into the middle of its picture; and, at the same time, to trigger off a timing mechanism which would start the timing at the moment the first camera took the first picture and which would finish it as the camera on the second site took the second one.

In theory, this may sound a comparatively simple thing to do. Probably the most obvious suggestion from most people as to how it could be done would be to stick two cine cameras on end, pointing to the sky at the two appropriate places, and set them running, with some sort of timing device connected to the camera mechanism in order to trigger off the timer at the right instant. However, for this kind of record bid cine cameras are simply not good enough. They had been used quite successfully in the early days but, in fact, had been abandoned after 1945, when the first Jet record was made.

For a number of technical reasons which we need not discuss here, the cine camera method has, ever since then, been replaced by the use of special types of single-exposure plate cameras, which take their photograph at the exact moment which it is needed to record. The technical difficulties involved in achieving this are of a very high order indeed. First of all you have to be absolutely certain that, when you think the camera is aiming straight up into the sky, it is in fact doing so. The first job was to contrive and build special bases and mountings for the camera equipment on the two camera sites. If there was any movement in these at all, it would be quite sufficient to put the whole calibration right out of count. Then, having put the cameras on their mountings, the fact that they were looking upwards at right angles to the ground had to be calibrated very carefully by checking the horizontal alignment of the base, or the horizontal lie of the ground, and then checking the vertical position in relation to it. If the two were at right angles to each other, and the camera was correctly sighted on the invisible pinpoint, then all was well. If either of the cameras was even only a fraction of one degree out, the error, negligible at ground level, naturally becomes greater and greater as the object it sights on becomes further away. Thus, at our height of around 40,000 ft., the smallest angular error of the cameras from the vertical would have been magnified into one which would appreciably and drastically have altered the length of the course that was being measured. (Anyone with a knowledge of elementary trigonometry can very quickly work out the actual error for his own amusement.)

The camera teams solved this tricky problem of initial positioning by setting up the camera points at night and taking photographs of known stars, which then became their absolute reference point for correct positioning in the vertical plane. The horizontal positioning was checked by sighting on markers which the specially prepared local Ordnance Survey Map showed to be exactly on the same horizontal level as the camera points themselves. As a result of this extremely careful work, which was carried out over several days and nights immediately prior to the actual runs, they achieved such an astonishing accuracy that they measured the beginning and the end of the course to a precision which was within a quarter of an inch. Thanks to the scientific wizards on this team, we had thus been able to achieve the seemingly impossible feat of, in effect, laying out an invisible course 15 kilometres long and 7¼ miles high in the sky considerably more accurately than, for instance, the running tracks laid out for the last Olympics.

It was purely by chance that we had these facilities at our disposal. If they had not been available, I have not the least idea what we should have done instead. No one in this country had ever had to face this particular problem before and we ourselves certainly had no experience of it whatever. Neither would we have had either the funds or the time to set about developing some special measuring technique. It had simply so happened, purely coincidentally and certainly without our knowledge, that the Instrumentation Department of the R.A.E., Farnborough, under Mr. N. E. G. Hill, B.Sc., M.I.E.E., had, for the whole of the previous year, been studying this problem of producing special timing equipment of very high precision, including the measurement of high-speed flight. This particular equipment had only then just been completed. Had we wanted to do the run any earlier, we would not have been able to because there would not have been measuring equipment ready.

Accurate setting up of the cameras was only the first half of the problem. The camera teams now had to find a way of ensuring that they would succeed in photographing the Delta exactly at that spot when the camera was precisely in its vertical position. No human operator could possibly judge when, for instance, to release a shutter and take the photograph at anything like the accuracy required. In fact the chances are that he would not get the aircraft in the picture at all. It was thus arranged that the camera operator should pick up the aircraft some distance away, and long before it came overhead, in a very special type of viewfinder. This viewfinder was made from a telescopic theodolite, the type used for following the tracks of meteorological balloons. The telescope viewfinder of this device could be swung along the line of the course. The camera operator thus "shot" his camera at the Delta in very much the same way as a sportsman would try and shoot a bird coming to him from some distance away. He would pick the Delta up in the telescope at a fairly low angle and then keep it in the sights as the Delta approached and the angle increased until it reached the vertical point. This elaborate viewfinding device was so arranged that, when it came up to the calibrated vertical position at which the camera was set, several very ingenious electronic arrangements came into action and automatically released the camera shutter, simultaneously starting off the timing circuit. This signal was passed along the G.P.O. line which linked the two camera sites and triggered off the timing circuit of the second camera, at the end of the course, so that they were synchronised.

The camera operator at the second camera followed exactly the same procedure, the only difference being that, when his camera took the picture, the timing circuit was stopped.

On the return run, the relative positions of the two cameras were, of course, changed over. The one that had been at the end on the first run now initiated the timing mechanism while the other camera marked the end of the run.

There was no time to change the plates in the interval between the out-going and the return run. Each plate therefore carried two exposures, one corresponding to each run. There was an arrangement whereby the plate could be moved across slightly at the end of the first run, so that, although still on the same plate, the two images were not superimposed. Two separate images were thus obtained which could not possibly be confused.

For the more technically minded camera enthusiasts, the lenses were of eighty-inch focal length, using the Dutch mirror lens which gives higher accuracy for this kind of work and allows the focal length to be achieved without having to build a camera nearly seven feet long to do it. It may come as a surprise, though, to know that the shutter speed employed was only 1/300th of a second. It was actually perfectly adequate and resulted in a perfectly clear unblurred image of the Delta, because the altitude of the flight had exactly the same effect as if you were photographing an object over seven miles away from you. There was one unexpected and interesting factor associated with this. The photographic image of the aeroplane was so small that, for measurement to obtain the final speed figure, it had to be examined through a microscope; this had to be done because, obviously, it was necessary in the final reckoning to find exactly where the photographic image was in relation to the centre of the lens. If it was slightly off-centre, due allowance had to be made. As will be seen later, when we describe the record-breaking run itself, this became a matter of vital and heart-aching importance. The line made by the trailing edge of the Delta wing was selected as the actual point of the aircraft to be used for reference, in preference to the nose, because the nose of the Delta comes to such a fine needle-point that it was difficult, even under the microscope, to tell with sufficient accuracy exactly where it finished.

Like all backroom boys, without whom nothing could be achieved at all, these camera teams received far too little credit for their immeasurably valuable work. I would like to redress the balance as far as I can here, by putting on record my own admiration for the way they carried out this most difficult task, and by placing on record the names of those in the teams.

That weekend was a fairly restless one for all of us. Everything now, we felt, was as ready as it ever would be. We had done everything we could think of doing. The aircraft instruments were calibrated. The cameras were set up. Radar, R/T., and the G.P.O.'s telephone network were all tested and re-tested, almost to exhaustion. The camera teams were doing dummy runs over the course, using the No. 29 Squadron Meteors from Tangmere, and seemed quite satisfied with the results. But even I, who had been involved in the project since its very inception, could never have conceived the tremendously complex inter-connected mass of specialist units and personnel necessary to contain a record bid of this sort. In practice, usually, even if everything else worked satisfactorily, there would be a minor snag in one department. I would find myself going out of the 328 ft. margin on a trial run. The camera team would find that, if an aircraft flew only fractionally to either side of the actual course on which they had their cameras laid, it was almost impossible for them to pick it up. As far as the regulations were concerned, this deviation did not matter in the least because, of course, exactly the same distance was still being traversed at exactly the same height. But it was a matter of life and death to the camera operators, whose problem it was to keep me in their sights. How could I be certain of coming in on the line as accurately as they wanted me to, when all my attention would be concentrated on achieving accuracy on the two things that really mattered – the line of the course itself and, above all, the height?

Hanging over all these manifold worries and anxieties, and making them look quite insignificant by comparison, were the dark grey skies of early March. I do not recall that, from the moment we first started with our initial preparations for the record several months previously, there had been a single day in which the weather would have been suitable for an actual record flight. Now, in these last few days, in spite of all our statistical charts and meteorological probabilities, there seemed no immediate prospect in the days ahead. Then, on the Monday, March 5th, the weather began to clear. We warned everybody and put the whole team on immediate readiness. For forty-eight hours we hung around, waiting for the moment. Various units kept reporting a fault here or a fault there, or someone else would come through to say that he had a new test or a repeat calibration of some sort to make. The weather started to clear and then began to look as if it was going to close down again. For a time, tired and keyed up as we were, we could see the whole of our work in the past few months and, come to that, all of our dreams pass into nothing. As so often before a big event, I think we were all suddenly feeling deflated.

Then, almost by magic, on the Wednesday, the first day when everything was ready and the whole organisation was tied in and purring quietly and smoothly, the weather cleared up and stayed bright for days. It was quite fortuitous and quite phenomenal, bearing very little relation to all our carefully analysed meteorological statistics which showed that this sort of thing never happened in March. It was a fantastic piece of luck. A chance in a million. And, if it had not happened, the Delta never would have got the record, because we needed every single moment of every one of those days; and it was on the last possible moment of the last of them that we made the one and only successful record run. We made eight runs in the days before. On every single one of them we had beaten 1,000 miles an hour. But, in turn, on each one of them, human frailty in one form or another had made it unacceptable for official recognition. The weather, notable for its unpredictability, suddenly gave us the miracle of five consecutive days of perfect flying weather to compensate the shortcomings of our own only too predictable human fallibility.

12

READY TO GO

So many times I've been asked, What did you feel during that period of waiting, with the ordeal of the flight still in front of you? And just as many times I failed to give a satisfactory answer. Here yet again I must disabuse anyone who, having read thus far, has any vestiges of romanticism left. The simple truth is that most of the time I didn't feel anything out of the ordinary at all.

If this seems impossible to believe, as apparently it has to many people in the past, let me emphasise that when, after the record, I told the Press that it had just been another routine flight, I wasn't being coy. I meant every word of it. That is exactly what it was. Had it gone on much longer, it would have become a chore instead of a record bid.

And it was the same throughout this period immediately before the flights, when there was nothing to do but wait for the moment. I do not deny that there were times of heightened stress. But there was only one period of real tension, and that was after it was all over and we had to sweat it out through the week-end, not knowing whether the timing records were going to be allowed. And even then, after an irritating hour or so, I went home and pottered about the garden.

Certainly I didn't spend this waiting period chewing my nails, or thinking dark catastrophic thoughts. I simply left the event in its pigeon-hole until it was needed for action, and this is just what I've done all through my life.

To put yourself truly in my shoes for the record bid you would have had to have been in them since the time the Delta 2 had been a few lines on the drawing board. We grew up together stage by stage. So that flying her now, record bid or not, was every bit as familiar a part of my routine working life as anyone else's ordinary working day. The actual record flights called for a bit more accuracy. But that was on account of getting maximum speed recorded by the cameras, not on account of safety or any inherent danger.

I assure you there was far less tension than I experienced the first time I waited for the Boxing Party in the Day Room at Sherborne.

The actual waiting period was tedious and therefore probably irritating in a different kind of way, but I do not recall that it worried me anything like as much as one might imagine. I've always been able to shut myself away quite happily into the present. I am one of those people who can withdraw quite easily from the things around him. I can live alone quite happily for long periods. I like people, and I like to know that they are there, but I don't have any of the obsession for company that plagues the lives of people who can't bear to be alone. There are those around me who have told me that, at times, I seem to be alone even when they are there. I hope it isn't true, but I suspect that sometimes it may be.

My war experiences, also, taught me to wait with a large measure of equanimity. After all, most of one's war service was taken up waiting. There was day after day on the merchant vessels waiting for a shoot-off that never came. Later, it happened night after night on Intruder operations, where you simply hung about over enemy airfields waiting for something to pounce on, so like the falcons I'd trained in the years before.

What I did find exciting about the record bid was that it broke up a long series of routine tests that could become very dull after a while. In fact one of the first things I'd learnt at the Empire Test Pilot's school, where I graduated as a qualified test pilot, was that, most of the time, a test pilot's life could be as repetitious and boring as any other job.

But probably the most exciting thing of all was to see all these terribly complicated arrangements, sometimes apparently quite unworkably complex, suddenly all fall into place. That was an organisational excitement, an intellectual one if you like, but it was very real nevertheless.

And there was an aesthetic excitement of quite another kind, too, feeling the Delta respond when the re-heat was lit or looking at her as she stood on the tarmac. And realising the fantastic gulf in development that man's ingenuity had bridged in a mere decade and a half, a period which to me, just then, seemed to be only yesterday. The gap between the Delta standing there, and the Fairey Battles I had first gone operational on. It no longer means much, I suppose, because developments since have pushed it back into limbo. But it seemed a pretty tremendous thing to me then. And it does now.

In those hours of waiting to prove just how good the Delta was, I wasn't looking for courage. I was looking for weather.

13

WE BEAT THE RECORD – AND FAIL

On the Monday the whole team went on to immediate readiness and we installed ourselves in the County Hotel, Salisbury, so as to be within easy access of Boscombe Down. As we watched the skies, hoping that the fickle March weather would give us our opportunity, we knew that this was the point of no return. Before the week was out, we knew, it would either be blazoned in banner headlines across the world's press, or else we would have crept wearily and hopelessly away into some dark corner to eat humble pie and admit that the critics who had dissuaded us from the start had been right all along.

It was Wednesday afternoon before we began to see the kind of skies we wanted. Already, with half the week gone, we began to feel that the record bid was already on borrowed time. That afternoon we managed to make two final proving flights to give the camera-timing system a final check. The weather now, quite miraculously, looked as if it was set fair; but no sooner was our anxiety allayed on that account than we were faced with another. On neither of these final proving runs were we recorded by the camera. For the moment it blew the bottom right out of all our hopes. These runs were not done at record speed, but they were pretty fast for all that, and I had found that, given reasonable luck, I could hit the two invisible hoops on the course where I wanted to and keep the height limit within the required 328 ft. I had not worried unduly whether I was a few miles or so one side or the other of the actual course line, because this did not affect the conditions set down under the rules. For that, all I had to be certain about was that I went over a course of the proper length and at the required height. The cameras had been arranged so that they could actually be swung to take in up to 30° either side of the course, and I naturally relied on this to compensate for any small lateral amount I might be off the nominal course. No deviation I was likely to make would be anything like as much as the cameras could cover with this amount of angular swing.

However, when we tried it on that afternoon, the camera operators found that, although this should have worked perfectly easily in theory, it would not work in practice. The method used for angling the cameras over in this way was somewhat unwieldy. The operator already had much more to worry about than he could handle in much too short a time; getting the Delta into the middle of his theodolite sights and keeping it there was a full-time job on its own. It was almost impossible to swing the camera at the same time and still keep the Delta in the picture.

I, too, had my hands pretty full maintaining the height regulations, and I was horrified, on discussing this last-minute snag, to find that, in order to make quite certain that the Delta was in the picture, I would have to keep my position to within less than a mile of either side of the nominal course line. This was a fantastic accuracy to be asked to keep at that speed and height and, for a moment, it seemed as if we would have to rely simply on luck, hoping that on at least one of the runs we would be close enough.

In our own hearts we knew that trusting to luck was simply not good enough. The camera sites were also having trouble getting the initial sighting or pick-up at all. Our plan all along had been to use the radar stations to tell the camera operator what angle he could expect to see the aircraft to pick it up. Now, however, we found that the time-lag was altogether too great.

Neither of these situations need have arisen at all had we been able to mount the record bid in a reasonably backed and supported way, instead of doing it as a part-time operation. The difficulty in picking up the aircraft in the camera sights was due, more than anything else, to lack of practice; for, remember, we were asking these Farnborough crews to use hitherto untried equipment and to bring it off first time without ever having had a dress rehearsal at all. The question of lateral displacement could also have been solved easily by quite simple modification to the equipment, but this equipment had never been developed for air-speed record bids and we had had to accept it – and indeed did so very gladly – as it stood.

None of us got much comfort out of appreciating the situation. There was only one thing to be done. I would have to fly within the limits they needed. But how? It was here that my chief, Gordon Slade, made a tremendous personal sacrifice.

Up till then it had been arranged that Gordon and I would take turns flying the Delta on the bid, until one or the other of us got an accepted run at over the four-figure mark. By sharing the flights, also, the pilots would be spared the considerable continual strain and fatigue involved in making one flight after another without a break. Gordon Slade and I had been the only two pilots who had flown the Delta and, consequently, we were the only two who knew intimately and instinctively what kind of instruction for correction could reasonably be passed to a pilot in flight and with what speed and accuracy he could carry it out. It thus became apparent that one or other of us should stay on the ground beside the camera operator. During the initial phase of tracking, the operator would know if the aircraft was laterally more than the allowed one mile out of position, and could tell this ground observer who would then pass on final very fine corrections to the pilot by talking him into position on the R/T., in much the same way as a bomb-aimer passes last-minute instructions to his pilot. This, in fact, became the key operation in the whole complex set-up.

Because a chief test pilot's duties and responsibilities leave him less time for actual flying on any given aircraft, I had had more practice and experience with the Delta than had my chief, Gordon Slade. He, therefore, immediately proposed that he should relinquish any attempt to make one of the runs himself, and should stay on the ground during the whole of the project, talking me into position. It was a magnificently unselfish gesture. I have often wondered, looking back, whether, had the positions been reversed and I had been Chief Test Pilot at the time, I could as willingly have thrown up my chance to fly. I want to place it on record here that, had it not been for Gordon's magnificent gesture, we would never have got officially recognised record figures; because, without his directions from the ground, I was quite incapable of flying within the limits that were needed. This incident serves to illustrate one characteristic, which cannot be over-emphasised, and which was very much part of the whole record project. Throughout, the team spirit was simply magnificent. I think it is true to say that at no stage were individual ambitions allowed to come between the record bid and whatever had to be done to achieve it. There was only one individual. The Fairey Delta itself.

We worked late into that Wednesday evening and when eventually we got back to the County Hotel we were much too tired to worry about what might happen tomorrow. We left a call for 6 a.m., and went straight to bed.

The next day, Thursday, 8th March, we made our first run, taking off at 8.35 a.m. The Delta flew beautifully, and I knew that we had beaten a thousand miles an hour on the run. But I knew it was a failure, even before I landed, because of difficulties with height-keeping and with camera tracking. No further flying was possible that day, but, once again, it was very late in the evening by the time we got back to the hotel. So many things had had to be done to ensure that, given the gift of another fine flying day tomorrow, we should have ironed out the snags in the system. Going back to the hotel that Thursday evening, we could think of little else other than the weather prospects for the morrow.

Miraculously, as Friday dawned, all the signs of a perfect flying day were there. This would be the day, we were sure. But it wasn't. By now there was a sense of desperation in the knowledge that time was running out. We made our first flight at 8 a.m. And then I went up again at 10.15; at just after 12.30; and at 5.15. I was dog tired, as indeed was everyone else in the team. As the light began to go, we looked up at the sky and wondered if we had lost our chance for ever. Four times that day I had gone twice over the course at speeds which I knew were well over our target of 1,000 m.p.h. Each run failed to qualify for one reason or another. Either I had been unable to hold her to the 328 ft. height variation limit, or the cameras had failed to see us. Four times in a single day, with only time in between for refuelling and resetting the instruments, and with no maintenance on the aircraft at all, the little Delta had gone up in the sky and done everything we expected of her. It was we who were failing her. And now the light was going and we wondered whether we would ever have a chance again. We did not dare hope that, against all predictions, we would get another fine day on the Saturday.

But we did. Once again, up at 6 a.m., and out of the hotel before the day staff had come on duty. I looked up at the sky towards Boscombe Down and, to my immeasurable relief, saw the contrails already laid there in the sky by the Meteor squadron, and knew that Providence had given us another chance.

And yet, we failed again. I took off at 8.10 a.m. and was back on the airfield at Boscombe Down by 8.25, only to be told that once again the tracking system had not been able to keep pace with us. By now, as the flights had dragged on through the Thursday, Friday, and finally this Saturday morning, we began to get progressively more worried also about a security break. By this time, of course, we had had to take a large proportion of the people at Boscombe Down into the secret. Had we succeeded in making the record on the first day we tried, this would not have created any danger. But now it seemed to us that the whole project must have become almost common knowledge. We got every issue of the newspapers and, each time, we expected to see the headlines that would show that one paper at least had guessed at what we were doing. There was one thing we could not put under security – our supersonic bangs. Throughout the week we had been getting a swelling number of complaints from all over the place. There was for instance a nurseryman, Mr. Leslie Green, of Bishops Waltham in Hampshire. He was already claiming that supersonic bangs had caused about £16,000 worth of damage to his nursery in the past few months, and there seemed little doubt that a great deal of this was due to ourselves. In fact, when the record bid was finally announced, Mr. Green threatened me with legal action personally and gave an interview to the press in which he said that he had consulted a Queen's Counsel with a view to starting proceedings as "this is the first time the pilot of an aircraft has been named after supersonic damage. I am seeking to restrain him from flying over the district, and to bring him to account for damage already done". He said that during the week we had shattered something like three hundred of his windows, which may quite well have been true.

Much though we regretted Mr. Green's windows, we were much more concerned about the security aspect. You can get away with one bang without giving any secrets to the public. One bang is O.K. So are several bangs at different places. But we were making bangs day after day in the same place. Vapour trails appeared regularly along what was quite obviously a consistent straight line that could have only one obvious reason.

In point of fact, the story was facing the press and they never saw it. During that week a local reporter on a Portsmouth paper made some intelligent deductions and published a story with the headline, as far as I can now remember it, "Is this a speed record bid?". When it appeared, we were absolutely horrified, and we were quite certain it was only a matter of hours before the whole of the national press had the story. But they didn't follow it up, thinking probably that this was a piece of local exaggeration. So, in fact, the whole lot of them were scooped by the initiative of a local paper. To this day, I cannot imagine how the national press missed getting on to this story before we announced it ourselves. Everything was there to guide them to it. There was the fact that the Delta was known to be undergoing flight tests. There were the con-trails, there were the supersonic bangs. When the official story did eventually break, there were some nationally famous air correspondents who were to be seen kicking themselves as hard as they could in their own pants.

Now, after that Saturday morning run, it became even more important that no story should break. I waited for the aircraft to be refuelled and, for the first time, I wondered whether, with all these terrible technical difficulties that had to be overcome and co-ordinated all at the same instant, we were ever going to succeed. We looked up at the weather, and we knew that we had time to make only one more run. The system had failed on seven. How, on this final chance, were we to make sure that it would not fail us again?

14

PRIVATE LIVES AND PUBLIC IMAGES

By the end of the next chapter, I'll have become public property, with the press taking me over lock, stock and barrel. Before this happens, there are some aspects of my personal life that have to be clarified. Of course the press had to have a human interest story. There were photographs taken at home with my wife, Vera, and my baby daughter Sarah, looking quite a poppet at eighteen months, which indeed she was. It was all terribly homely. Idyllic. The whole romantic picture in a nutshell. There was the smiling record-breaking hero, and the brave little woman who sat at home and waited, and the happy united family at home like any other family on a Sunday afternoon.

The truth was that, even at that time, my home life was practically non-existent. It was already breaking up. And it was largely the things that made me a good test pilot that also made me a bad marriage partner.

There'd been a wartime marriage that had broken up as well.

These are very difficult things to write about oneself. I'm certainly no paragon of virtue. Neither do I wish to give the impression that I was simply a wolf in pilot's clothing who jumped in and out of bed and marriage with complete irresponsibility, nor that I allowed the so-called "glamour" aspect of my work to go to my head and considered myself above normal moral and human values. I very much hope this isn't so. Looking back at it all, I don't think I've been any more fly and loose than anyone else of my generation who grew up on operational sorties in the war.

Certainly my first marriage was immature. We met while I was in the States on the Naval mission in 1944 . . . I was only 23. She was quite a bit older. It was simply one of those flash-point wartime marriages that should never have been anything but an affaire on either side. She lived for the theatre. It just wasn't my world, and I found it very difficult to make head or tail of her friends, her interests. I was completely absorbed in flying. Once the mutual enchantment of it all had worn off, I don't see that she could have had any interest in my friends or what I was doing either. Had it been any period other than the war, one would have foreseen this complete vacuum of common interests. Our two careers also meant that we were apart a great deal, she on her theatrical work, me on mine. It was bound to fail – like so many wartime marriages failed. And I don't honestly think it was a thing of lasting importance to either of us.

This marriage was still nominally in existence when I joined Fairey's in 1946, but we'd already been separated for some time, and finally were divorced.

My second marriage was altogether different. Vera and I had been close friends since my days in the Intruder squadron during the war. I flew in her husband's squadron, and he was one of my friends. He was killed on active service, leaving her widowed with two children. Once again, she was older than I. None of this seemed to matter at the time, but I can see now it did, although it wasn't the main reason that the marriage failed. There was nothing acrimonious. It just drifted into pieces and then finally broke up.

I'm certain that the real trouble was that for the whole of our marriage I was test-flying. Now, even to Vera, who had been close to the flying world the whole of her adult life, this life of test flying was something quite different. There are many things in test flying which put marriage through unfair stresses. The job has something to do with it, but the prime factor is the kind of personality which you have to have, whether you like it or not, if you're going to be a good test pilot . In a very real sense much too much of you goes into the job, and before you know what's happened your family life is playing second fiddle to it. This in itself endangers any but the most solidly stable marriage. Test flying is only part of it. There is also everything that goes with it – parties, many of which you go to without your wife – travelling all over the world, with no certain settled period at home. You might be home for a month or so at a time; or you mightn't be seen for weeks on end; or you might be in hospital with a bent back. Meeting dozens of people, attractive women.

One would have to have been a saint not to have fallen occasionally. There were affaires. They weren't important. They wouldn't have wrecked the marriage by themselves.

It is the complete self-absorption of the job that makes one impossible to live with. The job was more important than my marriage. I knew it. I admitted it. I couldn't question whether it was right or wrong, because right or wrong didn't come into it. My home life became practically non-existent. For months on end sometimes. One's working environment absorbed so much of oneself, emotionally, intellectually, physically, occupied so much of one's capacity for interest that, even pottering around, ostensibly doing all the normal things one does at home, one was still detached from it. Withdrawn. No longer an integral part of the unit you're supposed to be in.

You can't expect any wife to put up for ever with whatever residual fraction of you that your job doesn't want.

Perhaps I was selfish. Perhaps I was self-centred. Perhaps I expected everybody else to adapt to me and didn't try to adapt myself to them. Quite possibly. I don't know. I am not trying to absolve myself from blame. I am simply putting the thing down as honestly as I can so that you can see it as I believe it was.

And then I met Cherry. And, for the third time, I married. Doubtless the psychiatrists would put the failure of my previous marriages down to my early upbringing. The moralists can just as smugly tell themselves that you can never trust these pilot types. The cynics can sit back and wait for this one to fail too.

But now there is one vast difference. I'm not test-flying any more. Cherry never knew me during my test-flying days. To her, I'm the husband who works just across the other side of the river you can see from the bedroom window. Developing high-speed sea-going boats. I'm still capable of being completely absorbed in the work I'm doing. And I know that there is still this solitary part of myself. Just as there is a part of herself, too, that is withdrawn and probably perpetually inaccessible to me. But there is a stability behind it all that never existed, never could have existed, during those years of test-flying.

Thank goodness, for both our sakes, that this time we are free of the test-flying environment, the aura that hung around that March Saturday in 1956 waiting for the final speed record run, the atmosphere that had wrecked my previous marriage. The test-flying phase is now something in the past for me, and has always been in the past for Cherry – a phase to which this book is, in a sense, an epitaph. It was not I who wanted to write it – it was Cherry. She kept on at me until it was done. In that former phase, I don't think any marriage could have survived. Because, if I am to be completely honest with myself, I have to admit that, never at any stage during my test-flying career, was I ever in a position to see marriage as anything other than incidental to test-flying aeroplanes.

It was on that Saturday morning, with only one run left, that this phase reached its climax. Looking back at it from my present life, it seems as if I am looking at someone I only half recognise.

15

OUR LAST CHANCE

I stood on the tarmac waiting for them to finish refuelling for the final run. For the first time in the whole series I was feeling taut and strung up, with an over-burdening sense of tension. This had nothing to do with the physical situation of having to make yet another flight, which was a comparatively simple exercise, but was a function of our acute awareness that our time had run out. Until this moment there had always been a next run. Now, there was no future. It was now or never. All of us were feeling a great deal of tension that morning, and it was probably accentuated inasmuch as we were getting the cumulative effect of being continuously keyed up without a break for four days. For myself, there was certainly much more tension then than there had been at any stage in the Delta's life before, except perhaps in that time way back when we had had the fuel starvation. But that had not been a record bid. That had simply been a bid to keep the aircraft in one piece, and there had not really been time in that critical situation to feel tension at all. This time there was. I had to wait while the refuelling proceeded at, what seemed to me, a snail's pace – taking an infinity of time to complete. We had to sweat it out. I found it very much more uncomfortable than the situation when you have a clear-cut emergency needing immediate attention and absolute concentration, because these things themselves absorb all your nervous tension and leave you only the job on hand.

As I looked at the Delta on the tarmac, I realised how very much better she had stood up to these gruelling four days than we had. During this period it had been quite impossible to give her more than the absolute minimum necessary servicing. Each day the fitters and maintenance team were starting at four in the morning to get her ready. They, even more than myself, had been living on their nerves and with practically no sleep. With conditions like this day after day, even the best team of men begin to flag. This is the danger point, when some small but unimportant detail gets overlooked. In fact, I knew that there were some what we call "acceptable defects" which we had accepted and were prepared to tolerate on this run, simply because there was not the time to do anything about them. They were nothing really to worry about. But one was conscious that no machine or man can be absolutely certain after that kind of flogging. Before these runs we had never had her up to speeds of this kind. We were in unknown country, and the unknown has a habit of reacting suddenly. In retrospect, I realise that I was pretty tired myself. And that this was certainly not the moment for thoughts of this kind.

Nevertheless, those three hours of waiting, between the first abortive run on that Saturday morning and the one that I was about to make now, were amongst the most difficult of the lot. We were tired and very frustrated, in fact, we were all getting a bit teased out. There was no question of making another run if this one failed. We knew that, whatever happened, it was the last run of the day. We wondered if we would ever get everybody doing the right thing all at one time.

The fact that on all the abortive runs we had actually beaten the record only helped to frustrate us further. I found myself quite unjustifiably blaming it on the camera teams. We had to rely on them and they'd muffed it again. Of course this was quite unreasonable and terribly unjust to them, but in the circumstances I hope it was to some extent forgivable. I think my attitude was probably accentuated by the fact that in these final moments I was becoming more and more acutely aware that the boot was in fact on the other foot. The onus was very much more on me in these latter stages, to keep the height absolutely accurate; and, of the two of us, it was I who was much more likely to be the fallible one. They were getting better and better on the cameras as time went on and they were beginning to get some of the actual practice that they had never been allowed before the bid started, and I was – well, it had been a long four days. I began to half-doubt my own ability to keep up my own standard in spite of frustration and fatigue. I could not help thinking: this is our last try. Supposing, this time, the cameras, whom I have been criticising so unfairly in my mind, bring it off and I fail by going out of height. It would be myself in the last analysis who had failed the bid, not them.

Right back in the early days of the bid, on the Wednesday, which now seemed an age away, we had agreed amongst ourselves, once it had become apparent that we were in for a prolonged series of runs, that all abortive runs were to be regarded simply as trials. There would be no acrimonious postmortems nor criticisms. This situation was normal. Cameras could be expected to fail on trial runs. And many pilots only get one chance at the record, because record aeroplanes are usually not built for shuttling indefinitely across fifteen kilometres of sky day after day. I kept on telling myself that this was exactly the position I was in

Top left: Leading Airman Peter Twiss, Wilton 1940.

Top centre: The author's mother, Wendy, and brother Paul, Wilton 1940.

Top right: The author by his Seafire, 807 Squadron, on board HMS *Furious*, 1942.

Bottom: 807 Squadron, August 1942. Standing left to right, S/Lt. Madley, Mid. Ford, S/Lt. Rowland, S/Lt. Terry, S/Lt. Lloyd, S/Lt. Powell, S/Lt. Harvey, S/Lt. Brooker, S/Lt. Hargreaves. Sitting left to right, S/Lt. Twiss, S/Lt. Baldwin D.S.C., C.O. Lt. Fraser-Harris D.S.C., S/Lt. Rankin, (unknown).

Top: *Left to right*, Gordon Slade, Flood, Twiss, Humble and John Cunningham at Lympne, 1947, for the High Speed Handicap race.

Bottom: Fairey Primer flying over Hamble River, piloted by the author, 1949.

HM Queen inspects prototype Fairey Gannet at Lee-on-Solent, early 1950s.

Top: Fairey Firefly on production test, piloted by the author, late 1940s.

Middle: The author deck-landing a Meteor, early 1950s.

Bottom: Test flight of a Fairey FD1 from Boscombe Down, 1954.

Top: The author lands the Fairey FD2 at the Farnborough Air Show; note the braking parachutes.

Bottom: The author with Chief Engineer Robert Lickley, centre, and Maurice Child, Boscombe Down, 1954.

Top: The team mainly responsible for keeping the FD2 in the air, Boscombe Down, 1955.

Bottom: Author with Gordon Slade, Chief Test Pilot and Maurice Child, centre.

Top: Engine failure results in 'wheels-up' landing at Boscombe Down.

Middle and bottom: Plan-view of FD2 (*above*) and with wheels down and nose lowered.

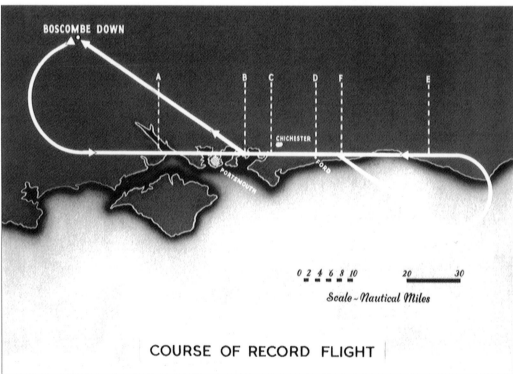

BOSCOMBE DOWN

A   B   C   D   F   E

CHICHESTER

PORTSMOUTH   FORD

0 2 4 6 8 10   20   30

Scale~Nautical Miles

COURSE OF RECORD FLIGHT

Top: The specially calibrated Venom flashes past the control tower at Boscombe Down at zero feet.

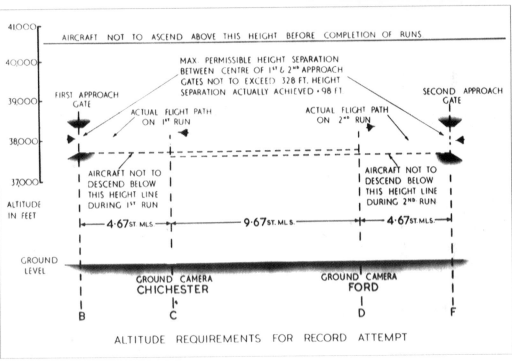

41000 — AIRCRAFT NOT TO ASCEND ABOVE THIS HEIGHT BEFORE COMPLETION OF RUNS

40,000 — MAX. PERMISSIBLE HEIGHT SEPARATION
BETWEEN CENTRE OF 1ST & 2ND APPROACH
GATES NOT TO EXCEED 328 FT. HEIGHT
SEPARATION ACTUALLY ACHIEVED ·98 FT.

39,000 — FIRST APPROACH GATE · SECOND APPROACH GATE

ACTUAL FLIGHT PATH ON 1ST RUN · ACTUAL FLIGHT PATH ON 2ND RUN

38,000 —

37,000 — AIRCRAFT NOT TO DESCEND BELOW THIS HEIGHT LINE DURING 1ST RUN · AIRCRAFT NOT TO DESCEND BELOW THIS HEIGHT LINE DURING 2ND RUN

ALTITUDE IN FEET

← 4·67 ST. MLS → · ← 9·67 ST. ML S. → · ← 4·67 ST. MLS. →

GROUND LEVEL

GROUND CAMERA CHICHESTER · GROUND CAMERA FORD

B · C · D · F

ALTITUDE REQUIREMENTS FOR RECORD ATTEMPT

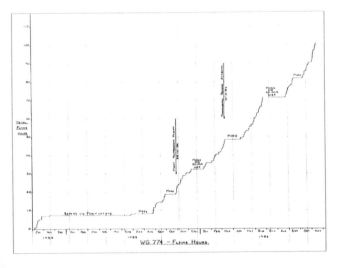

WG 774 – FLYING HOURS.

Top left: A timing camera crew in action 10 March, with Aero Club officials in attendance.

Top right: View of timing camera. Contrail of FD2 is just about visible (*centre*).

Above: Altitude requirements for the record attempt.

Left: Flying hours October 54 – October 56, showing time on ground after engine failure. The upward movement of the graph illustrates the number of flights possible during 1955/1956, because of the FD's excellent serviceability.

Top left: How one of the newspapers reported the record.

Top right: The official certificate of the record.

Bottom: FD2 flying at Farnborough with full post-record paint scheme.

Top left: The author at Boscombe Down after the record.

Top right: Executives of the Fairey Company pose with Peter Twiss under the portrait of Sir Richard Fairey.

Bottom: The author and Maurice Child with the group from Dassault, at Cazaux 1956.

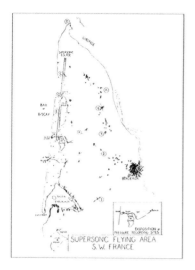

With congratulations and best wishes from the Daily Mail — and CHRYS.

" It's this infernal air of coy modesty that gets me ! "

Top left: Map of the supersonic flying area in SW France.

Top right: Chrys' view of the FD2 at Farnborough 1957.

Bottom: The author in a Tipsy Junior landing on *Ark Royal*, October 1957.

Top: The smallest plane ever tested, the Fairey Nipper.

Bottom: The Duke of Edinburgh examines the Tipsy Nipper with Peter Twiss and Bernard Meefs, an Avions Fairey test pilot, at White Waltham in 1960. The Duke arrived in the Mini visible behind him.

Top: The author with Billy Butlin at Hamble before the *Daily Express* Power Boat Race in 1961.

Bottom: The *Fairey Huntress* which won the first prize for a production boat under £4,000 in the 1962 *Daily Express* race.

Top: *Fairey Huntsman*, with the author at the controls, during the Poole Power Boat Race, 1963.

Bottom: Action shot from the film From Russia with Love (1963). Sean Connery is in the first boat with Peter Twiss firing at him from the second.

The author at Lasham, 1994, with a replica of a 1926 Slingsby Falcon glider.

now. All the other flights had been trials. Now this was the real thing. It was a normal situation for a world speed-record bid. But, although I knew it was true, this kind of self-philosophising made me feel no better, and only succeeded in making me laugh at myself.

Then the Delta was ready. I settled into the tiny cockpit and began the forty-item check that had become routine in nearly a hundred high-speed flights since I had first taken her off the ground. She had been wheeled out and lined up on the great concrete runway before I climbed aboard, because the fuel margin was so small that we could not afford even the small loss of fuel used for taxi-ing. Now, with most of the cockpit checks completed, I signalled for the ground crew to start the Rolls-Royce Avon turbo-jet. From this moment, not a second could be wasted, or the fuel might run so low during the second speed run that I would have to break off in the middle and dive for home. I felt an even greater urgency to get away quickly than I had in the previous run, for the awful thought of failing just because I had run out of fuel crossed my mind.

The last few checks were made quicker than I have ever made them before. I heard the coding signal come over the R/T., "three . . . two . . . one", and switched on the recorders. The control tower had already given the green light for take-off and, within seconds of the engine starting, we were streaking down the runway and into the air. Operation Metrical's last attempt was under way.

Far over to the left, at 38,000 ft., I could see the contrails produced over the measured course by the Meteors, and mentally I ticked off another vital check-point. There was not a cloud between the contrails and the camera sites. Still in the climb, I heard Gordon Slade come through from the camera site, telling me that they were ready and that the radar operators, who played the major part in getting me centred in those invisible hoops at the end of each course, were tied in.

From now, the whole thing was a confusion of voices on the R/T., the sounds and vibrations of the aircraft, my instruments in front of me and the need to concentrate wholly on one thing singly and yet everything together without letting slip for an instant on any single item. Normally I welcomed plenty of R/T. conversation, because it stopped you feeling lonely. But now I could willingly have pulled the radio out of the aircraft. Coupled with the tenseness of this final run I found the stream of instructions terribly irritating, and I had an illogical desire to tell them all to shut up and let me get on with the job; yet, at the same time, I knew that I was wholly dependent on them and that, without them, the operation would be quite impossible.

I was listening to the R/T. and correcting course as necessary, and was still concentrating on climbing at precisely the right speed to reach the 38,000 ft. altitude at geographically exactly the right spot and without wasting any fuel by climbing in any but the most economical manner. Even a slight inaccuracy in the angle of climb could have cost us a precious ten to fifteen gals. of kerosene, and have wrecked our chances.

I was watching the altimeter continuously, correcting and correcting again to compensate in accordance with our calibration tests made with the Venom, determined that this time there should be no variation from the regulated height limitations. At the same time I had to keep constant watch on the fuel gauge, the temperature of the jet pipe, the Mach-meter, and a dozen other dials and gauges, while all the time this continuous stream of instructions came through my headphones.

I made a wide sweep to the west of the course, to come in for the first run. Over the radio I heard Tommy Thompson: "You are twenty-five miles from Point Able. Vector good," and braced myself for the first reference point on the ground to come up.

"Timing check, Timing check. Three . . . two . . . one."

This was the timing signal from the ground. I pushed a switch to mark the recording tape and knew that, at exactly the same instant, the official Royal Aero Club observer $7\frac{1}{4}$ miles beneath me on the timing site had synchronised with the same signal. Already I was supersonic and accelerating rapidly. All the concentration I had ever possessed was now focused on lining the Delta up for the centre of the first of those invisible hoops that represented the gates to the speed course. I had been airborne $4\frac{1}{2}$ minutes and now the crucial moment was here.

"You are over Point Able." Tommy Thompson's voice again, calm, unhurried, reassuring, as if we could not possibly fail. From the cockpit I could see only the coast of France, but knew that I was over the New Forest. "Afterburner – Now." The re-heat exploded into life, and I was pushed hard back against my seat with the sudden shock of acceleration, as if I and the aircraft had suddenly been released by some enormous invisible catapult. I was able to report "Lit up O.K." on the R/T., and knew that they should now see my contrail lengthening in their direction, coming towards them at fantastic speed. Gordon Slade's "Contact, Contact," confirmed this. I could imagine the camera operator, weary after four days' trial and error, now clinging to the front of the trail, holding it in his sights and following it as if he was physically tied to it through all the miles and altitude, swinging up through a great arc until I passed overhead.

And then there was nothing in the world but watching the height, steady a little, steady, steady, watching the altimeter as if its needle was the forked tongue of some deadly snake that would attack me if I didn't do exactly what it said: flying by the altimeter and making the apparent, almost imperceptible, climb to compensate for the needle's variation as the acceleration increased, knowing from past flights that the result of this would be a straight and level course.

We had not enough fuel to build up top speed before entering the measured course. For the whole run, I was pressed hard back as the Delta 2 continued to accelerate, through the first hoop above Thorney Island at one and a half times the speed of sound, over the timing-camera at Chichester, along the course and over the second camera at Ford Naval Air Station.

"Cancel, Cancel," from Gordon Slade, told me the first leg of the run was over and it was safe to cut the afterburner. I cut it instantly with a reflex action, already conditioned to the knowledge that any additional split second with the afterburner on might run us out of fuel for the second leg. There was a sudden deceleration, throwing me forward in my straps, like the shock of catching the arrestor wires when you come in to land on an aircraft carrier and the hook engages and you are pulled up dead. The first part of the job was over. Fifteen kilometres – nearly $9\frac{1}{2}$ miles – about half a minute.

Then I felt the "g" as I made the wide sweep out to sea to turn round on to the return leg, with the Thames estuary away to one side and the French coast on the other. I noticed fields being burned off in the Pas de Calais and how the smoke was blowing right across the Channel to the white cliffs of England.

"38,000 . . . 38,000" – a reminder over the R/T. of the height I had gone through the first hoop on the run, a reminder, as if I needed it, that I had to do it again now and that the whole success or failure depended on my ability to hold the aircraft straight and level on that invisible thread in the massive volume of space. This was the most critical moment of the whole flight. There was no sensation of speed, yet every second brought me 1,000 ft. nearer to the gate of the speed course. I was sweating, partly from tense excitement, but partly also because air friction even on the super-smooth skin of the Delta had already caused a temperature rise of over a hundred degrees in the few seconds we had streaked along at "eleven hundred plus" and the cockpit was beginning to warm up even though, outside, the air temperature was minus sixty or very near a hundred degrees of frost.

Gordon's voice again: "Contact, contact, left, left, steady, a touch more, steady, steady, hold her there, you are lined up beautifully," talking me gently and efficiently, as if there was all the time in the world, into the infinitesimal corrections of course that would bring me into the middle of the camera operator's sights. "Point Edward." Once again the Delta ramming me in the back as I switched the re-heat on $7\frac{1}{4}$ miles over the little port of Peacehaven.

Through the hoop, accelerating, accelerating. Hold her, hold her steady, watch the altimeter needle. Follow the needle, ease, gently, gently, steady. My eyes watching nothing except the altimeter and the fuel gauge. Knowing that, this time, we had done the straightest run of all, and holding my breath as the fuel level gauge dropped lower and lower, in case it dropped too low and the automatic cut-off came into play to close the afterburner before the course was run. Thirty seconds of the utmost tension. And the Mach meter needle at its highest ever.

Then, after what seemed to me the longest half-minute in history, the R/T. was speaking again with the most welcome sound I have ever heard in my ears: "Cancel, Cancel."

It was over. I felt a great surge of relief as I switched off the re-heat and banked round for the smooth, quiet, peaceful descent towards Boscombe Down, forty-five miles away.

I was happy, and excited, and now relaxed. I was convinced that we had kept well within the height limits and that we had flown faster than we had ever flown before. Approaching the runway, I lowered the "droop-snoot" and, as the wheels touched the runway, noted that we had been airborne for just twenty-four minutes. It seemed impossible to believe. At that instant the whole of time seemed to have been consumed in those few minutes in the air, as if it had been going on for ever and nothing had existed before.

It had, as I thought, been the fastest run of all. And we had kept the height variation to the fantastically close limit of a mere ninety-eight feet. We had clocked 1,117 miles an hour on the first leg of the run and 1,147 miles an hour on the second, giving us an average of 1,132 miles an hour.

It is impossible to describe my feelings at that moment. It was a wonderful moment for the whole team, everyone of whom had played a vital rôle.

In those first moments of elation we forgot that all the instruments still had to go to Farnborough for official checking, and that the camera plates still had to be developed.

I had landed at 11.45 a.m. For a brief space in time, the world was ours. Then, shortly after mid-day, the bombshell dropped – knocked the bottom out of everything. The plates had been developed. But the camera site at Chichester showed only the Delta's contrail. It ended a few millimetres from the right-hand edge. Those few millimetres were enough. The start of the contrail was there, but the Delta wasn't. By an immeasurably small error, the photograph we looked at now was one which must have had odds of something like a million-to-one against it. We could see the point immediately behind the aircraft where the contrail formed, fully defined and clear cut, and to the right of it, the few millimetres that, we knew, separated it from the tail of the Delta. And then there was nothing.

16

SWEATING IT OUT

Of course this was a moment not easily to be forgotten. A moment of quite shattering dramatic climax. The last run of the day. The final chance ever. Whatever had happened now was there for good and all. Immutable. Success. The fastest run of the lot. And then the anti-climax. The timing cameras had missed us.

"You're not on the cameras again." I don't remember now who it was who said it. It was echoing round and round my mind, and wouldn't stay still long enough for me to grasp it. My feet wouldn't move from the spot which pinned them to the airfield. There was absolute silence. In the vastness of space, $7\frac{1}{4}$ miles up, the last remnants of the tell-tale trails had drifted away. There were a few perfectly ordinary March clouds where the invisible line had been. It was almost as if the whole thing had never happened. I started to say something but the words wouldn't come. Then, as if I was listening to someone else from an immeasurable distance, I heard my own voice say simply, "What a bloody waste of time the whole thing has been."

I was being unreasonable and I knew it, but in that sentence was all the weariness and all the anti-climax, all the frustrations, the countless limiting conditions imposed from outside, the endless handicaps of unnecessarily constricting circumstances, which we had had to combat throughout the long tiring months of preparation. Everyone had dispersed by then, because the bid was over and there was nothing more that could be done, and it was the weekend anyway. It was like being left alone to clear up a party the morning after. The only one I knew who was still on the airfield was Maurice Child, the flight-development engineer, whom I knew must be feeling just as badly as myself.

We turned our backs on the little Delta which, I felt at the moment, we had failed, and walked slowly away from the airfield. I don't know what it was I had in mind to do; probably my intention was to get in the car, drive back and pick my things up from the County Hotel, and then go home. It was exactly as if I had been dazed by a blow, and my mind was still muzzy. But then, suddenly, my head cleared and I knew this wouldn't do. A curiously aggressive, truculent mood set in quite uncharacteristic of my normal personality. I couldn't leave it at that. I couldn't just sit down and let this happen to us. We had beaten the record, and I knew it, and everyone else knew it, and I was not going to let us be beaten at this final stage. I would fight it – with what, I did not know.

Together, purposelessly, as if to do anything no matter how useless was better than doing nothing at all, we wandered across the airfield to the photographic laboratory to watch them develop the other film, the one from my recording equipment in the aircraft which would have my height trace on it. At least, we thought, we might as well make sure that we had done something right. This was normal routine and maybe we did it just out of habit, because, if the camera had really missed the Delta, it didn't matter now how good or bad my height-keeping had been. The film was developed and ready by the time we got there. It showed that, throughout this last flight, the height had been spot-on with a total overall variation of only ninety-eight feet. It was unbelievably good.

This should have given me a tremendous personal boost. Flying the Delta within the height tolerance had been the most difficult piece of flying I had ever been called upon to do, and it needed a very great deal of skill. I had never flown as accurately as this in any of the previous flights, and in assessing my own capabilities, I had certainly never expected to be able to keep inside one hundred feet. But this was simply a matter of personal pride and, at that moment, I had none. It was the Delta I was proud for, not myself, and this could do her no good now. Curiously enough, instead of making me feel better, this evidence that my own part in the flight had been successful beyond any possible expectations simply made the whole thing more galling. We could have done it a thousand times and it still would have been simply a waste of time if the report about the timing-photograph was right; and we knew that it was.

From here on, I drifted around for a while in a world of empty loneliness, abjectly depressed. Maurice Child had filtered off; when I looked for him he was no longer there. I don't remember him going, nor do I remember where he went. I assumed vaguely that he had given up the ghost and gone home. After all these months of living in the close secret-shrouded world of the record bid, I suddenly found myself deposited again alone in the ordinary world of everyday life where what had won the 3.30 was more important than whether the Delta had beaten the record; an empty world of Saturday afternoon where everybody had gone home to their own routine pleasures; a world where no one even knew that the record bid had taken place.

This should have been one of those moments of elation which you experience only once in a lifetime, when for once you can let your hair down and forget false modesty and know that you have achieved something, it should have been a moment of deep happiness and, above all, camaraderie, with the team celebrating together and champagne flowing to toast the wonderful little Delta; it should have been a gregarious, spontaneous moment with the bottles cluttering up the mess bar and the place full of smoke and everybody talking at the same time, and what would it matter if we opened a bottle or so too many. Instead, in a mood of complete frustration, I left the laboratories by myself to try and get a drink and some lunch before I packed it all in and went home. At least, I thought, I'd find some people in the mess that I could talk to. Of course, I had forgotten that it was the weekend. There was hardly anyone in the mess at all. None of them knew of the record bid anyway, so we could not have talked about it and let off steam. There were two R.A.F. officers on late lunch whom I knew vaguely by sight, and no one else. The untidy emptiness, a few empty glasses and the day's papers sprawling on empty chairs, of a place deserted. The mess steward found me a bit of cold and dusty veal and ham pie. I ate it alone.

The important personal moments of crisis in life are so often just such periods of inaction rather than action. Periods of awful anti-climax, as this was. Periods when you haven't got the spoken word to rely on to stimulate your memory, because they were moments when you were absolutely alone. Either because there was no one else to talk to or, even worse, because even if there had been you couldn't possibly have communicated what was going on in your own mind. These are the moments when you could burst and no one would know. And this was one of them for me. But you can't really remember such things. You can only remember something of what you felt like. And I'm no nearer to being able to communicate that now than I was then.

But I have asked myself since whether it really was all that important to get official recognition of the record. Sometimes when you look on something that seemed terribly important to you at the time, and ask yourself why it seemed so important, it isn't easy to find an answer. Just how important was this moment really? Would it have made any difference to the Delta if, as we all certainly thought then, the record had been disallowed? None at all. Official recognition couldn't alter the fact that the Delta had done what we believed she could do; and that, furthermore, she had gone on doing it longer than we'd ever had any right to expect. We'd got the information we wanted, and now we could go ahead with routine testing on the basis of that knowledge, which was what we wanted fundamentally. Would it have made any difference to the future of Fairey Aviation Ltd.? Not one iota. We got no contracts as a result of the bid. So we would have lost nothing. The firm had to sell itself to Westland anyway. Did it make any difference to my future? None. It was the sale to Westland that determined my future, not the record bid in the Delta. Did it make any difference to the British aircraft industry? I can't see how. The scaled-up version we hoped to be allowed to build never materialised anyway. The other things we wanted to know were all found out as part of the routine testing along the lines for which the Delta was originally commissioned.

But if you'd tried to make any of the team – including myself – see it like that, at that moment, they probably would have shot you.

This was the anti-climax supreme. To those who like the usual happy endings to their world-speed-record stories, I must report that the facts were very different from the happy hero's homecoming that popular imagination loves so dearly. Believe me, this time there was no stepping out of the cockpit to be garlanded with laurel wreaths and champagne corks popping all over the place. Instead, it was a lonely solitary beer and pie while I waited for the dusty answer from Farnborough to confirm what we had already been told unofficially, and to which I was now already resigned. Tired, unhappy, everyone else's life went on around me. I felt completely detached from it, as if I could not make contact with the life around me again. All around me, but dissociated so that I could not touch it, the continuity of their lives went on unbroken and meaningful for them, but leaving me even more in miserable isolation. I was held outside them by a secret much more potent than the secret of the record bid itself; it was the secret that we had failed.

It was not so much self-pity I was feeling in those moments, but a complete deflation of everything that we had lived for up to this day. And the fact that it didn't make the least difference to the world outside one way or the other simply served to accentuate my sense of isolation. To bear success alone is possible. To bear failure alone is soul-destroying.

A dreary lunch in a weekend mess was the end to all our high-flown hopes, and it was I who had started the hare in the first place. Not I alone, of course, but all the time I'd been pushing the thing forward as far as, in my somewhat limited position, I could. And certainly I had been the first, on that October morning six months ago when we had gone supersonic for the first time, to believe with complete conviction that we could beat the world. I who had had the temerity as a comparatively humble member of the flying staff to tell Sir Richard

Fairey at a shooting party that I knew we could, and believed we should, go out and do it.

And the end was a negative without a picture on it. Or, rather, a photograph with everything on the picture but the one thing we wanted to see. The aircraft was missing.

I am not by nature morbid, and I knew this mood could not last for long. I was gradually becoming resigned to the whole thing, returning slowly to face the hard facts of life. I had not the least doubt that the report we had received was true. And yet I could not leave the thing alone. I simply could not make that final decision to tear myself away completely from the whole thing, forget it all, and drive home. Something kept me still helplessly gnawing at the bone.

Simply because there was not anything else I could do, and at least there would be someone at the other end I could talk to who knew what we had been doing, I phoned Farnborough again from the mess. This time there was a ray of hope. True enough, the Delta was not on the plate. But the end of the contrail was, as we had been told, and the people at Farnborough thought that this might at least make it worth while to take the plate to the official judges to be examined more closely.

A breath of optimism came over me, and then immediately left me again. I kept asking myself what they could possibly expect to find even if they examined the plates through a microscope. I knew, and so did the people at Farnborough, that the Delta simply wasn't on the plate. There was the end of the condensation trail and then blue sky and then – by a 10,000th of an inch or so – the Delta beyond the edge. Nothing. Perhaps the Delta had never been there, had never been through that part of the sky at all. Perhaps we hadn't done it at all after all. Anyhow, whoever heard of a speed record being confirmed on the strength of a photograph of a vapour trail? It might have been anybody's trail. It might even be cooked if one was ruthless enough. It might have been one laid by the R.A.F. Of course it wasn't, but in this mood one had anything except hope. I didn't believe for a minute that this new development was going to make any difference. We had beaten a thousand miles an hour, and no one was ever going to know it. The whole thing was going to die with a whimper into obscurity; with no flowers at the funeral, no mourners, with a few pages of officialese in triplicate for a funeral oration, and a dusty piece of veal pie for the silent wakes.

I knew, of course, that the fact that the camera had got the end of the contrail on the picture did in fact prove that we had beaten the record. But whether the officials would, or indeed could, accept it was another question. The faulty photograph was at the exit end of the run.

Obviously, therefore, the end of the contrail must, as it were, have passed the winning post a fraction of a second later than the Delta itself; for the Delta must have passed that way to leave the contrail, even if it had passed out of the picture in the process. I began to see an argument, even if I did not yet see hope. We could quite easily prove that, if they measured the record from the tip of the contrail that was in the picture, instead of using the trailing edge of the Delta wing as the point of reference, they could not possibly be in any danger of accrediting us with a speed we had not obtained. This was obvious, because the appearance of the contrail was an event which could only take place after the Delta had passed. Thus, any measurement on this basis must unavoidably accredit us with a speed slightly slower than the speed we had actually attained on that run. The judges would therefore be running no risk at all. There was never any doubt in anybody's mind that we were quite willing to make this very minor sacrifice. I knew that there had been plenty of speed to spare. We could afford to give them a few miles an hour in barter for official recognition. All it added up to was that, at the instant the cameras photographed the vapour trail, they were already behind the event. Let them judge the run on that, and to hell with whether the aeroplane was in the picture or not. We would give them those few miles an hour with the utmost pleasure. It might mean that the record would turn out to be 1,130 m.p.h. instead of 1,132. But what odds did it make. It was still far and away a new world speed record.

This kind of mental exercise was all very well. But I strongly suspected that I was rationalising the situation, trying to swing the balance by the sheer weight of wishful thinking. I knew the official mind so well, or thought I did. I was quite certain that they would not see it our way. After all it was I, before, who had complained because the American record had been allowed under a security barrier which kept their measuring arrangements a secret. Now that the boot was on the other foot, had I any right to expect that an exception should be made in our case? Had it been the Americans instead of ourselves who were waiting now for the answer, would I have been so much in favour of pushing it through? I honestly did not know. I could appreciate that the rules were stringent, and I was the first to agree that they should be so because I knew the reason for them. I had no reason to complain now if they operated against me. My whole mind was in a state of ambivalence. No sooner had I convinced myself of the need for setting up the rules and sticking to them whatever, than I remembered what it had been like streaking across the speed course in the Delta that morning. And I remembered too, that, no matter what might go down in the history books, the Delta had been the first aircraft to take off from the ground and fly faster than a thousand miles an hour. Immediately, the other side of me told me that just to know this was not enough, that the Delta deserved more recognition than the unofficial knowledge that she had done it; but that now, if we were disallowed, without every condition laid down, fulfilled, witnessed, confirmed, the record had never happened. The Delta might just as well never have flown. You could prove the reliability or otherwise of what was on the plates till you were black in the face. It would make no difference.

It was late afternoon. and the day was already closing in when I decided to chuck in my hand; it seemed now impossible to perceive it as the same early March day in which, only that morning, I had felt the thrust of the Delta pushing me hard against my seat as we climbed to altitude, and, over the Pas de Calais, the fields still burned and left their own smoke trails oozing slowly, miles below, across the Channel to the English coast, and there had been the triumphant moment when I heard "Cancel, Cancel" through the R/T. at the end of the run and the whole of space was full of future and the sun. Now it was getting cold and the sky was empty, and there was no use hanging about any longer. I went out to the car and drove back into Salisbury where I picked up my bag at the hotel – and then pointed it home. I remember the dreary trip along the A30 with the weekend traffic all around me. All part of quite a different world, a different weekend to the one that held me in its isolation. Traffic, misery, saturated weariness, driving the Zephyr into anti-climax.

And then the gates were in front of me and there was a sentry on duty. I had not driven home after all. I had driven to Farnborough. Even still, it seemed, I couldn't leave the thing alone, or it would not leave me; although what good I could expect to do at Farnborough I had no idea.

I found it difficult to appreciate exactly why I was there at all, and I could not remember having made any positive conscious decision to drive there. I found it difficult to find anyone there either. Quite reasonably. I was not known by the people at the gate. I was not wanted by the people inside. I was in the way.

But there was no sense in coming all this distance and then doing nothing about it. I dug them out eventually. I had no idea in my mind what it was I thought I was going to say to them, but I found one of the judges and tried to give him what I thought was a simple layman's sensible point of view, explaining my reasons for accepting the record from measurement of the contrail instead of the photographic image of the aircraft. He was a Farnborough man, on the staff of the R.A.E., who had been appointed by the Royal Aero Club to act on their behalf. He was getting pretty fed up with the whole thing by then himself, anyway,

I think. It was not his fault; he had his rules and his job to do. He explained to me with the utmost reasonableness, but ice-cold and detached and completely unemotionally, as if he were reading the minutes of the last meeting, that it was their job to make the decision. I felt that I was the last person who was wanted there at that particular time.

On looking back, I realise that it was most unfair of me to approach him at all, let alone to root him out at this hour of the day, for it might well have put him in a compromising position. As an R.A.E. man, he must have had the interests of the British aircraft industry just as much at heart as I, and it must have been an agonisingly conflicting decision he had to make within himself. Hour after hour, ever since the photographic plates had been flown up to him as soon as we had landed from the run, he had been wrestling with the predicament we had so unwillingly forced upon him. He must have been under greater tension than any of us, for he knew that the whole of this very costly project's success depended on a single decision which only he could make. He could put British prestige right up in the sky – or kill the whole thing. And yet he never showed it, nor did he show any resentment when I opened his door and walked in uninvited as the unwanted ghost at a feast that was already macabre enough. Perhaps his was the worst decision of all to have to make.

That was my last shot. I went back out through the gates, and drove home. It was not as late as I thought it was. It was only about teatime. I was tired and disconsolate, and all the fight had gone out of me. It has never been part of my personality to brood over what might have happened. If it had, I never would have become a test pilot in the first place. I had a wash, and put on some clean clothes, and had a drink, and then I felt better. There was nothing to do but to accept the situation. We still had the evening, and tomorrow was Sunday and there were things I wanted to do in the garden. On Monday morning we would continue routine flight testing on the Gannet programme.

We went out to dinner that night, simply because it was a thing we often did at weekends. It was certainly no celebration, and we were back home early. On the Sunday morning I had been pottering about in the garden; for weeds won't wait even for a world's speed record. As I came indoors I heard the 'phone ringing. It must have been about 10.30. I lifted the receiver. Gordon Slade was at the other end. He said: "The record has been accepted." For a moment I couldn't understand. Already I had shrugged off the day and had made an armed truce with defeat. In a sense, I believe I was afraid to accept it, afraid of another big build-up only to see it topple like a pack of cards. It was a rumour, or some other snag would crop up and the position would be reversed again. I had to see it in black and white. Was it in any of the papers yet, or anywhere where it could no longer be revoked? Gordon told me that it had been too late by the time the judges had made their final decision to make the Sunday papers. Even the later editions would already have gone to bed. They had released the story just that minute. It would not break till Monday. I pondered about this for a minute, and then a ridiculous thought struck me and I started laughing. The record judge must already have known about this decision when I forced my way into Farnborough to talk to him. It must have been a great temptation for him to tell me then that it was O.K. But of course he couldn't. It had to be announced through the official channels.

I went out to the back of the house and started to collect together some of the things I had been using in the garden. I was deliberately putting myself back into my everyday routine, and already finding that it fitted familiarly and comfortably like a well-worn glove. It was still, in a sense, as if nothing had really happened. Gordon Slade's 'phone call had had no apocalyptic effect. Certainly there was no upsurge of emotion, no great elation. There was nothing left emotionally to do it with.

Half an hour later, Gordon rang again. All he said was: "Stand by for the deluge." They had decided after all to release the story immediately. I thought his remark was simply an offbeat joke. That afternoon some friends of ours whom we hadn't seen for about five years came in. They must have thought that they had walked straight into a South American revolution. For, directly behind them, came the deluge. They had no sooner sat down, when the 'phone started – and never stopped. It rang and rang and rang until in the end I had to leave the receiver off. At the same time the door bell started; first they came in ones and twos, and then more, till finally we got tired of opening the door and just left it there. An irrepressible tide of reporters, newspapermen, photographers, totally engulfed our unfortunate friends before they could utter a single word, and then engulfed ourselves, and finally more or less took over the whole house. The last we saw of our friends that evening, they were being pushed relentlessly away into a corner in the mêlée.

Goodness knows what time we got rid of them all, but it was as if a swarm of locusts had been through the place. It had been quite a day. As I went a little uncertainly upstairs to bed, perhaps not entirely sober, I reflected on the fact that, if I never achieved anything else in my life, I had at least achieved one ambition. I had been the first man to take an aircraft off the ground and fly faster than the sun. For that, incredible though it may seem, is how it was. You have to twist the fundamental laws of the solar system a bit to do it. The sun does not, in fact, move around the earth, as everybody knows. It is the earth that moves around the sun. And it is not earth's orbit that makes the sun rise and set each day, but its rotation on its own axis. But the earth does have a circumference of 24,000 miles, and, as it rotates once every twenty-four hours, the sun has an apparent speed of a thousand miles an hour. For a few seconds in the longest 10th of March history has ever known, I had flown at 1,132 miles per hour. The comparison may be a trifle shaky scientifically. But it sounded fine to me.

About the last thing I can remember that night was thinking that, if you flew at that speed at the Equator, taking off at dawn, you would leave the rising sun behind and fly into night; or, if you preferred it the other way, you could catch up the setting sun, pick it up out of the horizon, and put it back in the sky where it belonged. Even today, even in this new era where men measure speeds in terms of escape velocities, it is still a pretty exciting thought.

17

ONE SWALLOW. . .

Oh yes, that was quite a moment. And yet, five years later, sitting in the living-room of our present home where the garden runs down to the river's edge and, as I watch, the sun sets behind the moored yachts and the power-boats, I know without any doubt at all where the lasting reality lies. It is here. Those hectic days of the record bid already seem something in the long-distant past. How much of it is so nearly forgotten already. Sitting here, trying to re-imagine it all so that I could recapture it as fully as possible, I realised how very seldom I now thought of those days except in the most general terms. A great deal of the detail has gone for good. A lot of the rest, when I started to write it down, I found had to be dug up laboriously from a reluctant memory now occupied with other things.

You won't find any reminder of it in this room either. There aren't any photographs on the wall or anything like that. I don't keep a trophy room like the big-game sportsmen of previous generations used to do. There is a small model of the Delta, but it isn't there because I flew the world speed record in it, so much as because I think it is decorative. There's also a similar model of the Rotodyne. The only unusual features in this room are a hi-fi amplifier stacked rather untidily on its chassis on the floor – I built it some time ago and haven't anything to put it in – and a wonderful old spinet which we picked up one day in the country for a few pounds. I've half a mind to put the hi-fi amplifier in the spinet, but I suppose that would be something of a sacrilege.

There were trophies as a result of the record, of course. Dozens of them. All sorts and shapes and sizes. Medals, medallions, plaques, others that defy description. Some in bronze, some in silver, some in gold. I've no intention of listing them here, because they're of no interest. They've all been put away in a drawer together and I hadn't had them out for goodness knows how long until the other evening when a friend, who happened to be here while we were discussing this book, asked to see them. We got the drawer out, and there they were, all jumbled together, and we didn't try to sort them out. I came across my wartime D.S.C. as well.

You know, I've been extraordinarily fortunate. What luck it was that all this happened right at the end of my test-flying career. Supposing it had happened in mid-career, as it could so easily have done if the company hadn't changed its structure, I might quite well have lived to find test-flying a burden, perhaps even bored by the day-in day-out routine after having had a taste of the heights in this way – although I find it difficult to imagine. As it was, when the time came to quit, I was ready for it. What grouse could I possibly have? I'd had about twelve years test-flying altogther. And when I left it there wasn't a single unfulfilled ambition. That phase of my life had rounded itself off in as satisfactory a way as any mortal could ever wish.

I suppose many people think that during those years I must have amassed some phenomenal total of flying hours in my logbook. This isn't so either. It is something like 4,000 hours, which is absolutely nothing if you compare it with the logbook of, say, an international airline pilot. But it does represent a tremendous number of flights. About 12,000. Test-flights are usually only a matter of minutes. About 12,000 take-offs and landings. There, I probably have the edge on the air-line pilots by quite a way. Of my 4,000 hours, only a few hundred of them were on the Delta, all told, and, of those, the record flights accounted for less than three hours. The press made it look as if we flew records all the time.

Equally vividly in my memory are the enormous contrasts in types I had to fly during those years. For instance, no sooner was the Delta schedule finished than I was taking a refresher course and learning to fly helicopters. I flew a helicopter at the S.B.A.C. show at Farnborough on one occasion. And, as Chief Test Pilot, I was responsible for the test schedule on the Fairey Rotodyne, although I left the test-flying to others better equipped to do it than I.

I remember one incident which illustrates the absurdly contrasting type of situation that was always likely to crop up. I'd completely forgotten about it until when, developing and demonstrating power-boats, I got a letter from Richard Dimbleby. It was an enquiry in connection with my present work but, in the course of the letter, he reminded me we'd met before. It had been at the Shuttleworth Trust, that remarkable institution which keeps historic aircraft in flying condition. I suppose he'd been doing a programme on the Shuttleworth Trust – and I'd taken him up in one of their Bristol Fighters, that redoubtable First World War aircraft. This must have been three or four years ago, and I'm sure he won't mind if I now put it on record that the most memorable thing about the incident, to me, was the problem of equating the limited control of the Bristol Fighter against the not insignificant weight of Richard Dimbleby. In fact, I had the greatest difficulty in keeping the stick far enough forward to hold level trim.

Every now and then the Shuttleworth Trust used to call in one or two experienced pilots to fly their historic collection, and this gave me a wonderful opportunity. I remember also flying the Sopwith Pup there. Of the present generation of Sopwiths, I raced against Tommy Sopwith on the 19th August, 1961, only this time it was boats. The first British International Offshore Power-boat Race. He won. I didn't finish.

There was a fascination in flying these old aircraft, and I much regret that I never had the opportunity to fly the Trust's Blériot plane. These old aircraft fly without trouble providing the wind is right. And, even with all our present-day technique and know-how, I'm certain that Blériot had something over us. How the old French fox managed to coax the horse-power out of his original aircraft that he must have done to get her across the Channel, 1 just don't know. He flew the twenty-two miles, or whatever the exact distance was; yet it is quite an achievement to fly a mile in the Blériot plane at Shuttleworth. I reckon he must have been packing a lot of willpower into his engine as well as petrol.

Crude though they were, these early aircraft were extraordinarily well thought out, although, by today's standards, they were quite absurdly simple. But then, in those days, it was quite something to achieve a flight at all. You got up and landed again with nothing going wrong in between, and it was really something to talk about. On any cross-country flight the pilot naturally expected a forced landing or two on the way, as a matter of course. I flew one of the Bristol Fighters from Shuttleworth Aerodrome down to Kenley on one occasion, and ended up with a very strong fellow-feeling for the chaps who flew them in those days. I got there without having to put down on the way, but I must admit I plotted out a course on the map which gave me bits of open country or water to follow all the way, just in case.

The biggest contrast of all was during the time the Delta was based at Bedford. I did a test flight on the Delta, and stepped out of it right into the Bristol Fighter. Two aircraft that just about span the whole of practical flying history up until then. Fascinating.

So, also, was the helicopter I flew at Farnborough, although on that occasion I'm not quite sure who was in charge of who.

Oh, there was much more to my years of test-flying than the bit that made the headlines. I did make a desultory attempt to collect some of the headlines together at the time, and got as far as buying a child's shilling scrapbook. But I never got around to sticking them in. It put me in a spot when I wanted to find a few quotes for the next chapter, because they are of some interest to this story and some of them are important. Luckily Fairey's publicity chief, Derek Thurgood, had done a better job than I had. He had the lot.

18

AND THE PRESS SAID . . .

If I had thought about press reaction to the flight at all before that Sunday, when the deluge from what we came to call the "sporting press" descended upon us unannounced and, in full flood, carried my private life with it, bobbing and weaving and buffeted and half drowned in a sea of half-truths as the flood gates burst, it had been only in the most general terms. The difference between the true picture of a test pilot, any test pilot, and the image of a test pilot which the sporting press habitually gave the general public was, of course, something to which I was already in a general way conditioned. I had been the unwilling victim of it in a minor way on previous occasions, and, in the past, could remember having derived quiet amusement at the discomfiture of personal friends and colleagues like Mike Lithgow and Neville Duke who, having made record bids in 1953, suddenly found themselves given the full glamour-boy treatment. But I was quite unprepared for it to happen to myself. Like every test pilot I have ever known I am, if anything, rather more reserved than even the average individual, and I was horrified now at the prospect of becoming a sort of supersonic male Marilyn Monroe having the most intimate details of my private life strip-teased in public on the front pages of the popular press.

On that Sunday everything had happened too quickly for me to realise fully what it was all about. At one moment I had been pottering around the garden resigned to the fact that the whole record bid had died an unnatural death the day before under the scrutiny of the judges. The next moment Gordon Slade had been on the 'phone and I was the official world's air speed record holder. There had not been time to take a deep breath, or even to appreciate fully this wonderfully unexpected news, when the press arrived. Through these last forty-eight hours I had been alternating so rapidly between tremendous elation and utter dejection, climax into anticlimax, active hope into dull, passive resignation, that I don't think I knew any longer where I stood emotionally amongst all this. This process of being swung repeatedly from one end of the emotional scale to the other over a sustained period has a most curious effect. It is, in fact, exactly the same process that forms the basis of brainwashing techniques. In the end you accept almost anything, and nothing seems to be able to touch you directly any more. It is a sort of emotional exhaustion. I knew that all these things were happening to me, and I was excited about it, but now it was as if my own personality was separated from the things going on around me, so that I could watch myself being excited and elated in a curiously detached way where I seemed really to be feeling nothing at all.

The press invasion of my Sunday afternoon stopped as abruptly as it had started. I suppose that, being good newspapermen, they either had to be there immediately or not at all. For an hour or so it was absolute chaos, with myself in the middle of a seething, humming mass of questions following me like a tropical atmosphere before the monsoon wherever I moved. It was certainly not an atmosphere in which a considered answer could be given to a considered question. The whole thing in fact was quite light-hearted, even gay, a party to celebrate the news I had had on the 'phone; a party to make up for the one we hadn't had the day before. Apart from a certain amount of jostling, it was all good clean fun.

It was after they had all gone that I began to have some awkward moments. I suddenly realised that all these superficial questions and equally superficial answers were going to be splashed across the front pages of Monday morning's papers. I found the whole idea terribly embarrassing, and I was very apprehensive about the whole prospect. I realised now that I was the focal point of a full-scale hue and cry, with the whole of Fleet Street, noses pressed firmly to the scent, in hot pursuit of my personal life. I had become the victim of the public's insatiable demand for a human angle. Every banality I had uttered during the afternoon would be transformed into a cosy little quote several inches high across four columns. I was not worried so much about the general reader as about the people I knew. Because I had talked to the press, because the press had descended upon me unawares and had presented me with a situation which I neither wanted nor could avoid, it was going to look as if I had courted personal publicity, as if I was trying to get personal kudos from the record. This was the very last thing I intended to do. In a sense, I suppose I had been gratified and even flattered to think that the press considered me of sufficient interest to give me this quite phenomenal attention; but I was also terribly embarrassed, and very much concerned lest they angled the story around me instead of round the team. The very idea of someone running the "There-was-I-38,000-ft.-up-alone-at-a-thousand-miles-an-hour" kind of story was enough to send shudders of awful anticipation down my spine. I racked my brains to try to remember what I had said, but I could remember nothing except that someone had wanted to know about my flannel trousers and someone else had asked if I liked hard-boiled eggs for breakfast. The whole situation had been one for which I had been completely unprepared. Until only just before the press had arrived, I had never expected any press at all because, until Gordon had phoned, I was convinced that the whole thing had been a washout. Then, when I heard that we had succeeded after all, I had expected that the thing would be done at a press conference where the whole of the team would face the press together, as indeed did happen the following day. Later, Derek Thurgood, who was responsible for all the press relations on the record, told me that he had in fact tried to keep the press away from me on that Sunday; but of course he was quite impotent to prevent them coming down to my home on their own initiative.

In a way, I had a great deal of sympathy with the press, because the story had broken for many of them in the most awkward possible way. The Sunday papers had missed it altogether. And the evening papers were in something of a spot too, because the Monday morning papers would have had plenty of time to go to town on the story, and the evening papers would have to take what was left. From our point of view, it could not have been better. We were not courting the casual Sunday reader. Above all, it could not have fallen more happily into the laps of the aeronautical correspondents, who usually put their stories together over the weekend anyway. I was particularly sorry for the reporter on the Portsmouth *Evening News* who had the story sitting in his lap on the Saturday, the day we had flown the record, and apparently just did not realise what the facts he was reporting added up to.

The story appeared on one of the inside pages under the headline: "Air Ministry asked to investigate the City bangs." The story went on to report that the C.in-C. Portsmouth (Admiral of the Fleet Sir George Creasy) had requested the Lords Commissioners of the Admiralty to invite the Air Ministry and the Ministry of Supply to investigate the "unexplained" explosions in the Portsmouth area recently. More bangs, the writer continued, had been heard over Portsmouth that morning and three residents had telephoned to the Lord Mayor's office complaining about them. A member of the Observer Corps at Chichester had claimed to have identified a Fairey F.D. 2 flying over Chichester that morning. Its appearance coincided with a very loud bang which was also heard in Portsmouth. The plane, continued the report, was flying from west to east and a few minutes later was seen flying in the opposite direction.

These clues alone should have been plenty to give the game away. However, the reporter had obviously been doing some additional following up and, by the time he finished, had found out a great deal more. For instance, he had interviewed Mr. R. Clegg, a mains engineer on the Southern Electricity Board, who told him that a plane appeared at the same times each day and flew in the same direction. At 8.10 the previous morning, Mr. Clegg said, a plane had crossed Portsmouth travelling from west to east. The plane had left a vapour trail which started as a thick line. As the trail thinned out there was a bang. At 8.25 a.m. a plane appeared travelling from south to north and disappeared over Portsdown Hill. More bangs followed. A similar pattern had been followed at lunch time, when he had heard more bangs. There had been a heavy one at 5.30 p.m.

Mr. Clegg had certainly been persistent if nothing else. Continuing his interview, he told the Portsmouth *Evening News* reporter that he had kept watch again on the Saturday and, at 8.10 a.m., a plane appeared travelling from west to east and leaving the same vapour trail across the sky, producing a heavy bang. Then, fifteen minutes later, a plane appeared flying from south to north, again disappearing with a bang over Portsdown Hill. Mr. Clegg stated that the sound barrier appeared to be broken in level flight.

This story was reinforced by a letter sent to the *Evening News* by Master David M. Paul, of Petersfield, who wrote: "One of my friends, who is a keen spotter, said today he thought he had seen the F.D.2 leaving a vapour trail. To support this another of my friends, also a keen spotter, said he saw the same plane. Less than half an hour later I saw a delta-winged plane again leaving a trail. From this trail I deduced that it was single-engined, and a jet from its speed. I heard bangs myself at 10.30 a.m. on Friday in Portsmouth – I attend school there – and my father in Petersfield also heard them. My mother in East Meon heard another bang at about 12.45 p.m., and finally I heard a very dull one at about 5.30 p.m. at home in Petersfield. I looked for a plane and was rewarded with the sight of a single-engined jet leaving a vapour trail and heading west-north-west."

Not a bad report for a schoolboy!

The story finished with a little tailpiece to the effect that, for a change, there had been no one at the Halland Cross Nurseries of Mr. Leslie Green of Bishops Waltham but, on the Friday, having only recently refitted new glass in his greenhouses, it had been shattered yet again. This was, of course, the Mr. Green who subsequently threatened to sue me personally.

It seemed a little unjust that the Portsmouth *Evening News*, so close to the truth on the day the record was actually flown, had to sit helplessly by and watch themselves scooped by the official release twenty-four hours after they had dug it out for themselves.

Monday morning, came the dawn – lurid with newsprint. This was something I could not have anticipated even in my wildest dreams. Every single paper seemed to have it splashed across the front page. The cumulative effect was unbelievable. Derek Thurgood, whose job was to get as much publicity as he possibly could for Fairey's, had been champing at the bit all the previous week because we had not been able to tie the record down until the last moment. Then, when there was the final doubt over the photographs and the whole thing was held over till the Sunday, he thought he had lost his story altogether. Normally, many people would maintain that the middle of a Sunday is not the best possible time to put a story release out to Fleet Street, because the news editors have the whole of the weekend's news to choose from, with the result that something gets squeezed out altogether and everything else tends to get somewhat less than it would otherwise have been given. Derek, however, had always maintained that a Sunday release would pay handsome dividends, and on this occasion luck played straight into his hands. It so happened that, as far as the news desks were concerned, this had been one of the deadest weekends for hard news in Fleet Street's memory. They were digging the bottom of the pile for a front story lead when, as if by a benevolent providence, the Delta story fell into their laps at exactly the psychological moment.

The *Daily Sketch*, I remember, gave us the whole of the front page with the exception of a panel which announced the most exciting contest ever run by a newspaper – "You can own the Derby winner." Beside this was about the most lurid three-line head across five columns I have ever seen. It announced to the world: "Twiss or Burst." The second story on the front page was date-lined Ibstone, where I lived. I read with horror: "How I did it – by sky's fastest man." The story spread over on to the middle pages and must have been the handiwork of one of the deluge that had descended upon me on the Sunday morning. From it I learnt that I was thickset, and that I waved a self-deprecating hand as I told everyone in front of my cottage log fire how dull the whole thing had been.

You might have thought that the *Daily Sketch* at any rate was fairly happy with what it had got out of it all. But not on your life. At that time, they also ran a feature inside called "Inside Information". On this occasion they used it to give our publicity boys a rather tetchy rap over the knuckles. It is worth quoting here because, much though one may dislike personal publicity, I still had to admit that they had a point:

Tut, tut, Sir Richard. What a frightfully English way your Fairey Company chose yesterday to announce that the world air speed record had been smashed.

Into this office came three uninspiring sheets of paper headed "Press Release". I read: "Fairey Delta 2 smashes world speed record. First to exceed 1,000 m.p.h."

Followed a lengthy technical explanation – and appended was the 'phone number of your Public Relations Officer in case anyone should want to know more.

It was, of course, in the glorious tradition that is England.

"You might be interested, old man – don't want to boast – but I flipped along at 1,132 m.p.h. yesterday. . . ."

It set me dreaming how Americans might have tackled a similar situation. Programmes interrupted, pilot's voice heard over nation-wide radio hook-up, TV close-ups arranged. Planes standing by to fly newsmen to the spot. Designer on "How I did it". Special facilities for foreign correspondents. Examination of machine.

It was just a dream. For this is England. A nation of understatement. Where such things are not cricket . . . specially on Sunday.

I kept a stiff upper lip when the Fairey Company, while being as helpful as they could, decided the pilot and designer could not be interviewed until today.

"I mean, after all, old chap, they're awfully tired . . ." It was all – so frightfully British.

I think the *Daily Sketch* must have been shorter of news than anyone else that Monday; for, not only did they spread the story all over the front and middle pages, but they also had an editorial leader on page 2. This they called "Glorious Monday"! At this time the Cyprus situation was much in the news, and I remember that, immediately adjacent to the leader, was a wonderful cartoon showing a typical British Colonial Administrator pouring out his chota peg with his native servant standing at a respectful distance behind him, holding replacements on a tray, while underneath the table was his faithful bulldog, and his solar topee. Addressing him, on the steps to the verandah, was the spokesman for the native African population, backed by a crowd carrying banners and, incongruously enough, including the smiling figure of Archbishop Makarios. The caption was: "Bwana, we come to demand union with Greece." One could not help reflecting how anyone who reads newspapers could ever be expected to get a balanced view of what was happening when a speed record bid could take up most of a paper while some of the most crucial questions and problems and crises of that time were relegated to one off-beat cartoon.

It had been a dreary period for both British foreign and domestic policy and, I suppose, they jumped at anything that could show a note of optimism. This was the period of Suez; of the crisis following the banishment of Makarios from Cyprus, the beginning of the credit squeeze with threats of more to come; and so on. In this period of difficulty, disappointment and frustration, so the editorial leader noted, the Delta brought news of a brilliant triumph for a change, from a quarter where it was least expected. Our aircraft industry had been denounced, left, right and centre for sluggish inefficiency and failure to deliver the goods. We had been told that we were badly behind the top performance both of the Russians and the Americans. And now, it continued, literally out of the blue, a British plane had shattered the world speed record. It had even done more than that. Its margin of superiority of speed over any existing plane had been equal to the speed of an ordinary passenger aircraft; this, the leader writer exhorted us, was an achievement that should brighten the day for all of us and remind us that there are no difficulties we cannot overcome if we have the will, the confidence and the initiative to take the lead from the whole world and show them all the way.

Brave words, fine words, but, alas, only words.

The Daily Telegraph gave a sober account by their Air Correspondent, Air Commodore L. G. S. Payne, and there was a big splash also in the *Guardian*. The *Guardian* also gave us a piece on the leader page. On reading this, I was interested to discover that, at the speed the Delta had flown, I could have covered half a kilometre in a second or that I could have gone from Manchester to London in ten minutes perhaps smoking the same cigarette the while. I was also rather taken aback to read that, "Speeds of this magnitude are speeds of a kind which could, on paper, let people escape from the earth altogether." This, as everyone knows by now, is of course quite wrong. The escape velocity, to be able to fly clear of earth's gravitational force, is some 23,000 m.p.h., which made our record look pretty small by comparison. However, in those days, space satellites were still a fiction-writer's dream. Another interesting point they made was that during my flight I might have had time to notice that nearly a tenth of the normal force of gravity had ceased to act on me. That one, I must confess, made me laugh; I had noticed almost everything else acting on me, primarily the Rules of the F.A.I., but this gravitational point had passed me by. This editorial piece went on to consider what would happen if designers started producing commercial aircraft that could travel at supersonic speeds. I had some sympathy with the writer of the final paragraph:

"Some airline operator will be able to promise his customers lunch in London at noon, followed by morning coffee in New York at 11 a.m. Those who set off in the evening see the sun set in the east on the way. What advantages – apart from the sensation – this will have it is hard to foresee. There can be very little point in so shortening a journey that you spend most of it in the Customs Shed. Indeed already there is strong support for the proposition that we go too fast as things are."

The *Daily Mail* had another "How I did it" piece, from which I gathered the flight was little more than routine, and that, on the day of the record, I got up at 6 a.m. and had a boiled egg and toast. In their main story, by T. F. Thompson, I was glad to see that the team aspect of the project was given fuller credit than it was elsewhere. "One man and one aircraft get the glory for the new record – but to make it possible a team of several hundred worked at high pressure for nearly a week". In its third article in the same issue, someone had worked out that a plane flying at the Delta's speed would make the journey between London and New York in a little over three hours and would "gain" two hours on the flight. Thus, if it left London at 10 a.m. Greenwich time it would only be about 8.10 a.m. when it touched down at New York, where the time is five hours behind that in London. A flight from London to Moscow would take about $1\frac{1}{2}$ hrs. One of the evening papers had picked up the fact that, as a joke, someone had put a plaque up in the County Hotel where we had stayed saying "The fastest man on earth slept here". I believe the plaque is still there to this day. I have always thought that the slogan had something of a double meaning which, perhaps, was not altogether unintentional.

Other papers had got a cabled message from Horace "Dude" Haynes, the previous record holder, from Edwards Air Force Base in California sending us congratulations on the bid.

And so it was right through the press from the serious headlines of *The Times* and others, to the "Peter Flew in Flannels" type of headline in the *Mirror*.

I was glad to see that one paper at least gave credit to Geoffrey Hall, then assistant managing director, who had had so much to do with the whole project. At the time of the record, Geoffrey Hall had already had twenty-seven years with Fairey's, starting as a 27s. per week apprentice. He was one of those executives who, also being a pilot, could appreciate the problems to be met in the air as well as those on the ground. Really, the story of the record, I suppose, started after the war when Geoffrey Hall headed a research team of six to study future trends in flying. At that time all they had was a derelict building which they had to get decorated themselves. It was this building that grew into the Weapons

Division of Fairey's. And it had been from this division that the Delta had come.

Looking back on the press cuttings of the time, it is ironical to note that the speed record lifted the shares of the Fairey Aviation Company by 1s. 3d. to 22s. 6d. Ironical, because once the White Paper came out, even the speed record could not save the firm.

The way in which the record caught the imagination of the public amazed me. I found it completely overwhelming. However, of course, there were also our critics and we should not forget them in this present story. For instance, only four days after the record, Viscount Hinchingbrooke, then Tory M.P. for Dorset South, acted as spokesman for the diehard fraternity, expressing the opinion of a great majority of those who held the political reins. We throw our caps in the air and congratulate ourselves that we have defeated the United States, the Viscount told the House. But, he supposed, it was about the most inflationary thing this country could do to spend that money on this aircraft. One wondered whether we could afford these extravagances. This type of plane, he said, was too fast for the cold war and out of date when it came to long-range ballistic projectiles with atomic heads. What use to mankind, and at what a frightful cost, were these experiments that were going forward on fighter aircraft, radar and all the defensive equipment, he asked. It was not fair to the taxpayers to have the Ministry of Supply grossly overstaffed with people working on what he called projects of a Wellsian conception when, in an H-bomb war, they were no earthly use and, in the sort of Colonial war we would have to fight in the future, they were of no use either.

Reading through that, the only possible comment that came into my mind in reply was: "Was your journey really necessary?"

In somewhat lighter vein, as a result of all this personal publicity that I had received, I found myself about a week later on the B.B.C. television programme "What's My Line" on the night when poor Gilbert Harding achieved a certain amount of notoriety by being in one of his tetchiest of moods and taking his coat off in the middle of the programme. I had to appear as the "Celebrity" and my identity was very soon guessed. First, he refused to put on the mask which the panel were meant to wear for this part of the programme, so that they could not see who the celebrity was, complaining that it was covered with lipstick and greasepaint. Having found that his handkerchief, which he proposed to use instead, was not big enough to be used as a blindfold, Barbara Kelly offered him her scarf. In the end, however, he did put the mask on. Then, while I was being interviewed, there was a sudden roar of laughter from the studio audience which doubtless bewildered those looking in. What had happened was that, out of camera, Gilbert Harding had done what hundreds have been tempted to do under the blazing heat of the TV camera lights. He stripped off his dinner jacket and was sitting there in his braces. Unfortunately for him, the cameras switched rather too suddenly on to Mr. Harding just in time to see Barbara Kelly nursing him back into his coat again.

Personally, I found Gilbert Harding kind, courteous, and very human. In fact the thing I remember about that particular incident was Gilbert's efforts to apologise to myself and to the other guests on the programme for the lack of hospitality offered officially by the B.B.C., consisting of the unconsumed portion of the day's ration of a single bottle of whisky. And we only had the opportunity to make the most even of this somewhat modest offering because, immediately the programme was over, Gilbert Harding had disappeared. He had collected together some dirty glasses from somewhere on the set and we found him in a near-by lavatory washing up in the handbasin. We had a couple of stiff ones there and then, dispensing water from the cold tap.

For myself, I was vastly relieved when, almost as suddenly as it had started, all this hullabaloo died down. We were no longer news. And we could now carry on with our normal test-flying routine. The Delta did not fly again for some time, as of course she was due for a major overhaul. But the Delta had always only been a part of our job, even at the peak period when we were building up to the record. There had always been the day-to-day work on other aircraft, notably the Gannet. There were also many things we still wanted to do with the Delta, as soon as its much overdue maintenance schedule had been carried out and it was ready to fly again. In particular, there were further supersonic tests which we wanted to carry out and which, as we shall see, were in many respects just as difficult and just as important as the record bid itself.

19

THE YEARS AFTER

I was very tempted to finish my story here. Anything that follows now must be anticlimax, except to myself who, in the final period that followed the record attempt, had to face up to the prospect that my test-flying career was coming to an end and that, at an age when most people are already solidly established, I would have to start an entirely new career.

There were still a couple of years to go before I went on the shelf as a test pilot. And very interesting they were, too, in a different kind of way. Some of that time I was supervising the test schedule on the Rotodyne. And there are still two incidents worth telling about the Delta, when we took her first to France and then Norway. They had their humorous moments, those two incidents, although they were both achieved only after a struggle with the Ministry of Supply, or the Misery as we called it.

Before we wrap that up, however, there is still one facet of the popular test pilot image left to shatter. And this one, I'm very much afraid, is going to shake any would-be test pilots who may have strange dreams and visions of the wealth that is going to drop into their laps.

When I joined Fairey's in 1946 I exchanged the uniform and pay of a Lieut.-Commander in the Fleet Air Arm for a flat salary of £1,000 a year. If I'd stayed on in the Service, my gross income, what with allowances and so on, would probably have been higher than it now was as a civilian test pilot, and certainly my future would have been more secure.

Nevertheless, it was what I wanted to do and, at the time, a flat salary of £1,000 a year seemed a tremendous amount of money to me. For some reason it seemed very much more than the same amount made up of pay and allowances as is the way in the Navy. I suppose it had something to do with the fact that I could now think of myself as a "thousand-a-year man", whatever he is. In point of fact, it was well below the rate for the job. True, it had been a tremendous salary in 1939. But what you could buy with a pound in post-war Britain was very different from what you could buy in 1939. And, in fact, test pilots' salaries were pegged to the 1939 level, because they had been frozen right through the war in order to keep them more or less in line with the equivalent Service pay.

Salary increase was based on a somewhat peculiar arrangement that I'm quite certain no industrial trade union would have tolerated for a moment. Such increases that came along as one took on increasing responsibility were rated so that your income would just keep pace with the rise in income of the average Service officer of the same age group you were in, assuming you would have got promotion at the same rate. All this, of course, was highly arbitrary. What is the average serving officer anyway? And didn't one have to be a little bit above the average to become a senior test pilot, perhaps?

After test-flying for ten years for Fairey, and after the successful record attempt, I reached my all-time peak. I was then Chief Test Pilot at £3,000 a year. Perhaps this is enough. How can you judge the commercial value of one skilled job against another? However, people who had spent their lives in the commercial field, and who had reached what I would have judged to be about the same level of executive responsibility, certainly didn't seem to think it was very much. It certainly wasn't the kind of salary that would let you drive an E-type Jaguar around.

There is no financial recognition for obtaining the world speed record. It is all part of the day's work. The only "prize" is a certificate from the F.A.I. One of the signatories on my certificate, incidentally, was Lord Brabazon, President of the Royal Aero Club. Fairey's gave me a car to drive around which was virtually my own, and this was given as some sort of recognition. I did, in fact, pay for its running expenses, as required by the tax authorities. Not that I'm complaining. Far from it. I owe Fairey's far more than they owe me. But you ought to know the hard facts of life before you become a test pilot instead of a tycoon.

A certain engine manufacturer was the kindest of all, and I think I probably made rather a fool of myself there. Naturally, they didn't owe me a thing. The boot was very much on the other foot. But they thought they owed me something, and I was very grateful. After the record, someone got in touch with me and explained that they'd like to do something to show their appreciation because piloting the Delta through the thousand-an-hour mark had indirectly given them some considerable prestige. They said, we're not going to insult you by giving you money, we couldn't anyway, because it'd be against the rules, but we'd like to give you something. What would you like?

I've often wondered about that since. Do you think if I'd asked them for a Jaguar I would have got one? There have been moments when I have thought that that was perhaps just what was intended, because it might have had some publicity value. I said I'd like an electric cooker!

And that was about the only thing I could think of at the time that I really wanted, so you can see that I personally had no grouse about the salaries paid to test pilots. It certainly came in handy because we were moving into a new house at the time. It had a large country-style kitchen you could live in. And no cooker. Thereafter we cooked our meals by courtesy of one of the world's best-known engineering firms, which still seems a curiously offbeat way of going about things.

I also earned a bit through advertising and so on, but nothing really worth mentioning. Unfortunately the tax authorities didn't agree with me on that point.

I do sincerely think it is important to bring this out, even at the risk of being misunderstood for my motives, because so many people have said to me at one time or another: "Oh, yes, of course, you're the chap who did that speed record, aren't you? You must have done pretty well out of it." And then they go and tell the next chap; and so on.

The bare facts are that, in the end, I lost financially on the outcome of the world speed record because the income-tax man – or so it appeared to me – turned smartly round, having read the news along with everyone else, and really went for me. In the meantime, the social side of being a celebrity, which was a side I never really cared for although I knew I couldn't very well avoid it, pushed up my cost of living willynilly in various diverse ways which could never be represented as legitimate tax claims.

Really, though, it is the lack of security that hits hardest of all in the end. Test pilots' salaries have now improved. We tried all along through our own organisation to keep abreast of the commercial fliers and the services, but we kept slipping behind all the same. We were never an organised negotiating body in the same way that a trade union is and, indeed, test pilots are such a small and specialised group compared with the industry as a whole, that it shouldn't be necessary. We were covered for insurance by the firm, of course, and this would have looked after my dependants if I'd flown into the next world. I think Fairey's covered me for £20,000 for flights made on the company's behalf. I was in fact worth a great deal more dead than alive.

So, you would-be test pilots, enjoy your flying days as I am sure you will, and when you reach your forties do not expect to find yourself rich, but brace yourself for a change in salary! Money is not everything but it is mighty useful sometimes!

Had I decided not to return to Fairey's and gone to another firm, perhaps I could have done better financially. On the other hand, from their point of view they were by no means getting a bargain. Not many firms these days will take on a new man on salaried staff at forty, and with no previous experience. They gave me the chance to re-establish myself in a completely new field. The fact is I wasn't worth any more to them than they paid me. If anyone reads this and thinks I'm complaining about it, they've misconstrued my motives completely. I am simply putting down the hard facts. The only gold you're likely to see as a test pilot is on the clouds when the sun starts to go down below the horizon.

Anyway, who could have regrets over a career that has given one so much? It's been a career with many wonderful moments. And many amusing ones. My experience at Cazaux was one of them.

20

WAS IT FOR NOTHING?

This chapter might well be called: "After the Lord Mayor's Show". For this was the period of aftermath, of let-down, in which there were to be many moments in which we wondered whether in fact we had achieved anything worth while at all. There were, of course, two distinct facets to the Delta project at this stage. The first of these, to design, build, and test a supersonic research aircraft under contract to the Ministry of Supply, was almost completed; and in this respect the speed record bid had been an extraneous, unnecessary, and indeed a somewhat unpopular additional exercise. But now, although probably only the Board knew it at that time, there could be seen a secondary aspect which had arisen out of the first one and which was now assuming greater and greater importance. The end product of this aspect was to turn out to be no less than the survival or otherwise, as an independent entity, of the Fairey Aviation Company who had been responsible for bringing the Delta from the drawing-board up to the world speed record.

No aircraft firm, particularly in this day and age, can hope to exist on experimental and development contracts alone. These contracts are quite nice while they last, and they can be reasonably profitable, but they are not available with sufficient regularity nor do they provide the manufacturing quantities which could keep a firm continuously in work with the knowledge that there were at any rate sufficient contracts in hand to cover the tremendous overheads involved in any aircraft firm.

True, the Gannet programme had gone very well, but orders for Gannets could not be expected continually and that aircraft, in common with any other, was likely to be superseded at any moment in this decade of continual flux. There was also the Rotodyne, but it was impossible to rely on this as security for the future, because its design was unorthodox and there were considerable difficulties, both political and otherwise, in obtaining production contracts.

To some extent, the future of the Company depended on whether the additional prestige we had been able to obtain by beating the world speed record could now persuade the Ministry to give us a development

contract for a fighter version. Questions in the House, including those
made immediately after the world record had been obtained, indicated
that the Ministry was far from convinced that this was an advisable
policy. In fact, as we have already noted, there were those who were in
no two minds that the whole world speed record bid had been a
complete waste of time and money, believing that the supersonic fighter
aircraft was now completely out-moded by the guided missile. It is very
easy to be wise after the event, and one appreciates the immense
difficulties of assessing future military requirements in the air at that
particularly fluid time in aeronautical development. However, it is a
strange coincidence that, when I first wrote this chapter, I opened the
morning papers (Monday, July 10th, 1961) on the day that the Russians
put on their big fly-past for the Russian public, and obviously the world
outside as well, at Tushino Airport, near Moscow. A lot of new aircraft
types appeared in public for the first time at this show and, indeed, a
great number of them had been unknown to the West. The show
undoubtedly took the West very much by surprise, and there was a
feeling of shock throughout the whole of the British press. The most
significant thing to me is that, as far as general policy and at least two
of the aircraft are concerned, the Russians have obviously carried out a
development programme resulting in military types along almost
precisely the lines that we had in mind at Fairey's. In the helicopter
field, they had what some of the press actually called a Russian answer
to the Rotodyne, although in fact it doesn't use the unique principles of
the Rotodyne, now fully developed and apparently in use as a huge
troop and cargo-carrying vertical take-off plane. It was, in fact,
demonstrated, and a photograph was shown of it carrying a complete
prefabricated house. Even now, the Rotodyne principle is not fully
accepted in this country.

Even more significant than this was the first appearance of their
Sukhoi-Delta interceptor fighters, which had been known to the West
for some time but had not been photographed before. The aircraft is not
strictly comparable with the Fairey Delta, of course. However it does
carry forward the complete principle of using a supersonic delta-winged
fighter aircraft as part of national air armament in this day and age. The
Russian aircraft is said to be able to fly at about twice the speed of
sound, which is not all that much faster than we were doing in the record
bid, and to be capable of carrying air-to-air rockets under its wing.
Discussing this unexpected display of new and very advanced Russian
aircraft, one experienced air correspondent in the British press summed
up the conclusion of most of them: "What was shown more clearly than
anything was that the Russians are not putting all their faith in missiles.

Since the last air show in 1958 they have clearly developed an air-striking power which is second to none in the world." In other words, Russia, who was the one power who might justifiably have been expected to believe there was no future in supersonic fighter aircraft and to concentrate on guided missiles, in view of their admitted lead in technology in the rocket field, have now shown quite conclusively what we had believed all along – that the day of the fighter was by no means over and that there was a great and urgent need to develop a supersonic fighter arm.

Six years back when we gained the record, in 1956, opinion was very much against us.

James Hay Stevens, the well-known aeronautical writer, summed up the views of all of us at Fairey in an article he wrote at the time ("The Case for the Triangle"). At this stage of aircraft development, as he noted, the swept wing had more or less been ruled out and the design battle was between the thin straight type of wing, such as the Lockheed F-104 Starfighter, or the Delta type of wing which we had adopted. Stevens was one of the few experts who was not surprised that we had broken the speed record by such a large margin. He had always admired the F.D.2 as a design, and gave it very full credit as "a fine technical achievement by a Company in which high-speed experience had hitherto been restricted to missile work". He also pointed out that the Delta was only the second British supersonic man-carrying vehicle.

It must be remembered that the Delta design was then still comparatively new. It was not until as late as 1950 that the British and American manufacturers had in fact flown a pure, tailless, Delta aeroplane. These were the first Avro 707 and the Convair XF-92A; although by 1952, when the design work on the Delta 2 had been finished, quite a considerable practical experience had been built up with designs of this type. The very special Fairey F.D.1 had flown, although it had a special tailplane; two variants of the Avro 707 had been going through tests; and so had the Boulton-Paul P-111 and the Douglas Skyray. One Avro 707 and the Convair XF-92 had both crashed due to difficulties of handling at low speeds. But the essential difference with the Delta 2 was that it was the first of the thin-wing designs, on which there was absolutely no background of experience.

Ours, then, was about the sum total of general experience available on this type of aircraft at the time we made the record flights. It was, therefore, perhaps too much to hope for that those at ministerial level would be as enthusiastic about the design as we were. In point of fact, to themselves, to give a development contract for a scaled-up military version would have involved a considerable gamble not only on the design itself but also from the point of view of future military requirement, at a time when their policies were already being heavily criticised. It is worth here quoting the conclusion from Stevens' article:

> Inevitably, invidious comparisons are drawn between the F.D.2, the X-1, the F-104 and so on. It largely depends upon the nationality of the writer or reader, which view is taken upon their relative merits. What really matters is that each one adds to the West's knowledge of supersonic flight and to potential supremacy over the East. The ultimate aim is still to produce the fastest and most usable weapon. Speed alone is not the answer, the ultimate fighter must have a practical endurance, the strength and controllability to manoeuvre accurately at great heights and the ability to discharge its weapons with a sure aim.
>
> Which brings us to that vexed-question: When will the missile supersede the man? The piloted aircraft is bulky, it has to be able to take off and land controllably (instead of being boosted to Mach 2 in a couple of seconds) and much of its guidance system is applicable to manned aircraft, but for all that none of its complicated electronic gadgetry can think. It is true that computers can calculate precise interception courses at lightning speed, but they cannot reason and decide like the human brain. Furthermore, the missile is expendable and therefore very expensive when produced in worthwhile numbers. Peter Twiss's precise flying at almost 20 miles per minute is an indication of how infinitely adaptable the human brain can be. The range, endurance and manoeuvrability plus "pilotability" of the F.D.2 suggests that the formula is a practical one for a supersonic fighter. It should, one would think, be possible to add military load, with more power, of course, and still make a fighter less than twice the present size. Moreover, such an aeroplane should have a practical endurance and the undoubted power to manoeuvre at great heights.

At least, although we were still in a minority, we were no longer crying completely alone in the wilderness. The record flight had in fact gained us quite a number of supporters although, as it subsequently transpired, not in sufficient quantity nor in the appropriate quarter to alter existing policy. Besides farseeing objective observers such as Hay Stevens there were others, such as a certain Wing-Commander who was one of the few people outside ourselves to fly the Delta and, having flown it a couple of times, put in a report to the effect that: "If the Air Council doesn't order some of these, I'll eat my hat in public." Being a man of his word he must have had a very indigestible lunch, for of course they never did. Maybe he was a bit before his time. Maybe if all those who had been responsible for planning Britain's future aircraft at that time had been, like the Wing-Commander, practical flying men, we could have let each one of them have a flight and let the aircraft speak for itself. The Wing-Commander was fully behind the project and was absolutely sold on the Delta as a practicable aircraft. However, of course, he could do no more than we could to push the thing through at high policy levels. He could later, when he was high up in the Air Ministry. What a pity he didn't get there just a few years sooner.

By and large the appreciation we received at this period did encourage us to believe that it was worth continuing with the possibility in mind that a scalable fighter version might still be approved. This immediately meant that we had to do considerably more flight-testing than we had done already. Up till now, the Delta had really only undergone extensive testing at the higher altitudes. It was imperative now that we should also carry out tests throughout the whole of what is known as the flight envelope, that is covering the complete specified speed range within all the altitudes at which flying would be carried out under operational conditions. In particular, it was essential that we should carry out some low-level tests, since very little was known at that time about low-level supersonic flying and the effect on aircraft control and performance.

One might think that, with the possibility of proving a valuable new future aircraft type, every conceivable facility would be laid on from the highest possible level and the utmost encouragement would be given, so that the only question was whether the aircraft was ready and adequate to carry out the tests required. But it was here that, for the second time, we came up against a solid brick wall of "obstructivism" which, at one time, made it look as if it was virtually impossible ever to test-through a supersonic aircraft to meet military requirements in the British Isles. This in fact turned out to be the case and eventually we had to go abroad.

First of all, there seemed absolutely no way of circumnavigating the regulation, only then recently introduced, whereby aircraft were not allowed to fly supersonically over populated areas in the British Isles, at altitudes lower than 30,000 ft. What areas might have been found sparsely enough populated were quite useless for our purposes because, being a small island, wherever we flew, it would be absolutely unavoidable to make supersonic bangs over adjacent prohibited areas.

The considerable amount of press which our own supersonic bangs had achieved for us during the record bid had done nothing to help the situation, and if anything the position had now somewhat hardened. Several questions were asked in the House to ensure that no one was going to have his greenhouse panes shattered in future. Although we could understand this perfectly well, it was also difficult to see how we could possibly test our aircraft. The only possible areas were over the sea, but the regulations had in fact already either endangered the lives or actually cost the lives of pilots flying near supersonic speeds by the fact that their aircraft had got into trouble and, being over the sea, there had been no hope of rescue. It would have been sheer madness to have attempted low-flying supersonic tests under such conditions.

In the end, we turned the situation to our own advantage. There were several reasons, both personal and technical, to commend the idea of doing such tests abroad, provided we could find suitable sites. Not the least of these reasons was that, ever since we had started flying tests on the Delta, we had worked very largely as an independent and closely integrated team detached from Headquarters. This had many advantages. I was discussing this aspect recently with Maurice Child, and he unhesitatingly gave this as the major factor in having brought the Delta forward so very quickly up to the time of the record bid. To quote his own words: "I have always considered that quite the most important factor in the rapid development programme of the Delta was that we were not at our own base." Thus, all along, the main effort had fallen on a small integrated team of people, some stationed more or less permanently at Boscombe Down to look after the aircraft, and the remainder of us commuting every day between White Waltham and Boscombe Down by the Rapide communications aircraft. This commuting could be very tiring. At the end of a day's flying at Boscombe Down, it would often have been nice just to be able to climb into our motor-cars and go home. Instead we were always faced with the commuting trip in the Rapide involving another half-hour journey, often in bad weather, to get us back to home base at White Waltham.

However, this was a very small discomfort to accept in return for being detached and away from home base so that we were left very much on our own. Apart from reporting to the various directors, engineers, and so on to let them know how things were going, we were thus left very much alone to get on with the job. This situation also kept us very closely knit together as a team even during the most trying periods, because this separation from the main organisation was something which we all held in common and, further, we were relieved almost entirely of all the multitude of red herrings inevitable when you are physically within the organisation itself, and which can so easily pull pieces of a team apart and disrupt its integrity. In our little team everyone was doing something vital, something significant and, even more important, they knew that they all had a vital wanted part to play. They knew that they were wanted just there, doing just what they were doing. They were no longer just part of the impersonal organisation of Headquarters. Maurice Child summed it up by saying: "If we had had to do the record on the firm's doorstep, it would certainly have been done some months later if we had ever managed to get it done at all." By this, he was not meaning to criticise the organisation of the firm. It is simply that, on a project such as this, a small team left to themselves can very often achieve things which the entire potential of a large organisation cannot.

Maurice Child, who had a very great deal of organisational responsibility as flight-development engineer, made a habit of taking this philosophy of detachment to its very limits. As a consequence, we also kept the boffins out of our plans as much as possible during all preliminary phases. This didn't mean that we simply disregarded all the safety factors and developed the aircraft faster than it should have been developed; we still had to jog along methodically step by step. But Maurice's philosophy – and I must say that it was borne out by practice – was that by keeping detached we could progress to each next step safely faster; because, if you ask an organisation for permission to go to the next step or if you ask a boffin, there is always a perfectly good technical reason why you shouldn't. Similarly, he believed very strongly that with a little diligent handling it was nearly always possible to steer the research boys almost anywhere you wanted to steer them. He used this gambit to great effect when we now started lobbying to go abroad to do low-flying tests. Although we might criticise the rules and regulations that wouldn't let us do low flying supersonically here, we were in this instance quite definitely making most of the running to go out of the country. We therefore "managed" the research boys quite gently and harmlessly, but nevertheless efficiently, to let them think up the idea of a series of low tests abroad for themselves. The tests were in fact of some very great importance, since they concerned the whole control aspect of the aircraft.

There is always a compromise in design between how an aircraft behaves at the high altitudes and how it behaves at the low. In some ways, the two requirements are in conflict. The low-level flights show the effect of high air speed much more critically than flights at high altitudes – where the air is much less dense – and you are apt to get a lot more distortion, and more departure from the predicted behaviour than theory leads you to expect. Absolutely nothing had been done in this range by anyone in Europe at that time, and we could find no records of any serious measurements on such flights ever having been done previously. Thus it was that the team put up its case to be allowed to study low-altitude aspects – knowing full well that we would have to go outside the country to do it.

R.A.E. at Farnborough were willing to go along with us, at least as far as giving us moderate support. We felt that they were perhaps a little lukewarm. So we brought up reinforcements to lobby our cause for us just in case they were needed; we put forward the suggestion that, at the same time, we could make some hitherto uninvestigated researches into supersonic bangs. This ploy was so successful that we finally dragooned them into sending a complete research team with us to France specially to carry out these tests. They did in fact produce some very interesting results, but for us the noise test was only a sprat to catch a mackerel. While they played with their bangs, we were carrying on quite happily with our aircraft behaviour and characteristic tests.

So far, so good. If we could not do low-level tests in the British Isles, we would do them outside. And now we had fairly powerful support behind us. Next, we had to find somewhere to go. In this we were very lucky, for we had very good relations with the French Air Ministry, and the French firm of Marcel Dassault, and we were offered an excellent testing site in south-west France, at Cazaux.

On 11th October, exactly seven months after we had made the record, I flew the Delta across from Bedford to the French Air Force Station at Cazaux, near Bordeaux. By that time I was Chief Test Pilot of Fairey's, Gordon Slade having gone upwards to bigger and better things. Forty-seven supersonic research flights were made before we returned on 15th November.

But there were still some formidable obstructions to be overcome, and which we had not foreseen, before we got there.

21

ENGLAND IS BARRED TO US

Cazaux seemed an ideal base for our low-level tests, from all points of view. Situated S.W. of Bordeaux, it belonged to the French Air Force but was being used primarily at that time as an Armament Training Centre for NATO and American squadrons. The French Experimental Establishment, the Centre d'Essais en Vol at Bretigny, and Marcel Dassault also had a detachment there for carrying out armament trials. Air traffic tended to be somewhat too dense for our liking during the summer, with up to five hundred movements a day; but, at the time of year we proposed to be there, traffic would be comparatively light and was not likely to cause us any concern at all. Fifty miles to the north of Cazaux was a desolate area of pine forest and swamp which gave us the sparsely populated forty-mile run we wanted for supersonic testing. The course ran parallel to the coastline, some five miles to the east, and along the coastline were coastal resorts such as Lacanau-Océan, and Le Porge-Océan which, filled with holiday-makers through the summer, were now fortunately empty except for local inhabitants. To our north was the mouth of the Gironde. The site made the best of two worlds because, not only was it desolate enough to allow us to make all the supersonic bangs we wanted to without fear of repercussions but, to prevent us becoming too desolate ourselves, French civilisation was an easy motoring distance at Bordeaux, only about forty miles from Cazaux itself.

All in all, the set-up seemed pretty nearly ideal. The French Air Force were obviously going to go out of their way to give us the best possible French hospitality. The site was technically ideal. And we could be pretty certain of the gentle climate that characterises the south of France at this time of year. The snags, we felt, were bound to come. They did!

First, we came up against M.O.S. again. When we approached the appropriate quarters, through the Ministry of Supply, and told them what we wanted to do, they were horrified. They pointed out to us in no uncertain fashion that, even if we had forgotten that we were flying a Ministry of Supply research aircraft that was on the security list, they certainly hadn't. In their view, it would be a most unorthodox exercise to take such an aircraft out of the country to carry out tests of this nature. It would in fact be tantamount to a breach of security. Of course we were all perfectly well aware of this, but it is difficult to think what else they expected us to do. Sooner or later, if a truly supersonic aircraft was ever going to be developed and brought to a production stage in British industry, low-level tests would have to be done; and the regulations left no possible loophole for doing them in the British Isles. It was Hobson's choice.

Eventually we got the green light and, even though we felt there was perhaps a lack of full-hearted enthusiasm behind it and the light was still a bit pallid, we did at least receive formal permission to go ahead. Then the great insurance joke started.

The problem was one of third-party insurance to cover any possible claims for damage due to supersonic bangs. After the usual negotiations the appropriate French Government department had eventually agreed to provide the flying facilities and to confirm officially the generous offer of the French Air Force to lend us Cazaux as a base. Naturally enough the French Air Force could not give us permission on their own initiative, and we had been waiting for this confirmation to come from whichever appropriate part of the French Air Ministry might be concerned. In giving us official permission, they made one condition. They insisted, very reasonably I think, that the British Government should reimburse them for any claims that might result from damage caused by the supersonic bangs which we were deliberately setting out to produce. Doubtless they had already had some troubles of this nature, and the very considerable press which we had been given before the actual record story broke, with many of the headlines telling scarifying stories of thousands of pounds' worth of damage done to property, and glass being shattered wholesale, obviously did nothing to reassure them. If this sort of thing could happen at 38,000 ft., what was going to happen when we did the same sort of thing, only more so and more often, more or less on the deck.

It was true that the area we had selected was just about as desolate as you could find in Western Europe and, at that time of the year, was only sparsely populated. Nevertheless, the towns and villages along this part of the south-west French coast are all popular summer holiday resorts, and consequently, though there was only a negligible amount of people around to be irritated by bangs, there was considerable capital investment and acres of glass windows in various hotels, pensions, estaminets, and so on, simply waiting to be shattered by the first bang that happened to point in its direction.

To all of us the French authorities' request seemed quite reasonable. We approached the British Government. And the British Government said: "Not on your life."

This rather surprised us at the time, because it seemed little enough for them to do after all the French had offered us. We were a little sad at their attitude but not unduly worried. If we couldn't get official Government cover, we would have to get it through the normal commercial channels. British insurance companies are famous for their willingness and their spirit of adventure in undertaking to satisfy even the most eccentric customer.

Naturally enough, we first approached the insurance company with which the firm normally placed all their business. We imagined that getting this particular cover would only be a formality and could be settled in no time at all. The man listened to us and nodded his wise well-insured head as we explained to him what it was we wanted. Certainly, he said, his firm could cover us against damage to French civilians or property by supersonic bangs. They had indeed had many stranger requests than this in their time. However, he continued, he was quite sure that we would appreciate that a new kind of risk like this naturally involved charging a somewhat higher premium than was usual. There were no statistics on such accidents or what the amount of claims were likely to be. They were very largely taking a gamble and he was quite certain that we would see their point. We quite understood. We expected to be charged a few shillings in the pound extra per flight. He went away and worked out a quotation. We looked at it. We did not believe it. The premium worked out at something of the order of £1,000 per flight. We were envisaging doing forty flights or more. The whole thing was quite absurd.

We approached another British company, still not believing that this could be a representative figure. However the wise well-insured head of the man at the second company nodded in just the same way as the first one. News spreads very quickly, we discovered, around the insurance fraternity. Naturally enough he was not going to undercut his friends in the game. He quoted us almost exactly the same premium.

When we had first heard from the French officials that they wanted this insurance cover, we had treated the whole thing very lightly and with some amusement. There was something refreshingly off-beat in being asked to insure against supersonically banging somebody's windows out. But now the whole truth dawned on us. It was a matter of the utmost seriousness, because the French were quite adamant that permission could not be given until we produced the insurance cover they asked for. And, on their part, the British insurance companies were equally adamant that we would have to pay through the nose to obtain it. From the firm's point of view, we could obviously neither afford to carry the risk ourselves nor pay these enormous premiums which the companies were asking.

For the first time we realised that a ridiculous situation like this, if we were not very careful, was going to be perfectly adequate to stop all further tests being carried out on the Delta. We could see no possible way round it. A few days later we did in fact write to our French hosts explaining the position to them, thanking them for their co-operation, but most regretfully declining the facilities they had offered us. The whole exercise was called off.

In this we had seriously under-estimated the traditional resourcefulness of the French official mind. Feeling pretty sad about the whole thing, we rang up Paul De Plant, chief engineer to Marcel Dassault, to tell him we wouldn't be coming over after all. All he said was: "Well, why don't you take out the insurance in France?" It was a good suggestion. We had not seriously considered it ourselves because we had no reason to believe that it would be any easier there than in England; after all, insurance is a pretty international business, and what one country does the other is just as likely to do as well.

Anyway, without any real hope of success, we flew over to Paris to see what we could do. Our own experience of Paris being limited to things other than insurance agencies, we first went along to see our French representatives and ask them if they could suggest a French insurance company that might give us the cover we required. At their suggestion, we went straight to Marcel Dassault, who had the answer without a moment's hesitation. "But of course," he said immediately, "but of course," in the way only a Frenchman can, "when do you want to see him?" He gave us the same name that other contacts in the French aircraft industry had already suggested. They too seemed to assume that there would be absolutely no trouble at all. We 'phoned the insurance company concerned and arranged to meet their representative.

I shall remember the rest of this incident for the rest of my days.

If I had ever stopped to think what a French insurance agent might be expected to be like, doubtless I visualised him as being exactly like a British insurance agent – only French. One imagined taking a chancy ride on the crest of a Paris taxi-driver's horn to one of the lesser-known side streets in the Parisian commercial quarter where the buildings would be dark and dingy, with a heavy front door and a brass plate and a concierge at his desk inside, like the indigenous and traditional bourgeois respectability of the old business houses you see in the Maigret series. One might imagine that we would find our insurance agent probably on the first floor, in an overfurnished office with a mahogany desk framing a clinical specimen of the French upper middle classes. He would listen to our proposition, look at us coldly and clinically through rimless glasses; and then doubtless quote us whatever the equivalent premium of £1,000 a flight might be in French francs.

We were not a little surprised when, 'phoning him from our hotel, a cheerful and authoritative voice answered us from the other end and suggested that, if it was of course convenient to ourselves, it would perhaps be most appropriate if it met us at our hotel where the matter could be discussed in civilised surroundings and, it had no doubt, a suitable arrangement could very soon be found.

We entirely agreed. There was a very pleasantly equipped little bar in the hotel which, at that time of the season, was not over-populated and which had more than adequate supplies to soften up even the most adamant insurance agent. We got well dug in, as it were, expecting a fairly lengthy and drawn-out discussion. We had not expected him so soon, so that now, sitting in the bar where we had agreed to meet, we were hurriedly marshalling all our facts and arguments in order to press our case home. Everything was laid on to give him the V.I.P. treatment. We put the bartender on immediate readiness, and mentally prepared our tactical approach by deploying the various gleaming bottles behind the bar. We would put our case gradually, discussing the weather and the French Air Force and whatever, plying him the meanwhile adequately with drinks until, in a happy haze of cognac and well-being, he could not refuse to give us cover.

While we were plotting all this, he arrived. Efficiently, he introduced himself to us and came immediately to the point. What was it exactly that he could do for us? He looked quite unlike what one might have imagined a French insurance agent to look like. In fact he wasn't the agent at all. He was the head man.

Well, of course, we said, in a moment we would explain the whole problem to him. But first, of course, we should have a drink? He smiled agreement. Yes, yes that would be very nice indeed. Could he please have a Perrier? I can remember that bottle of Perrier mineral water to this day. The bartender gave us our cognacs, and then poured his Perrier into a wine-glass. It looked cold and depressing, and quite the wrong beverage to soften him up. It had a bit of lemon stuck in it. He sat down and asked what our problem was. He didn't bat an eyelid when we told him what we wanted to do. As we were talking, he found a piece of scrap paper somewhere and jotted some figures down. We told him the bare facts, as succinctly and as quickly as possible. There was no point in gilding the lily on a glass of Perrier. When we had finished, he glared for a moment at the figures he had put down. Then, without any hesitation, he made a few quick calculations which, he said, of course he would confirm formally later, took a few more sips of his Perrier, and said: "Very good. We shall cover you. It will be round about forty pounds."

He finished his Perrier, stood up and thanked us for giving him the opportunity to do business with us, and left just as quietly as he had arrived. We could not believe our ears, and were quite certain that we must have misunderstood. Forty pounds as compared with the British insurance company's £1,000 a flight. It just didn't make sense. We waited to receive his formal cover note when, we were quite sure, we would find that somewhere or other a " nought" had been left out of the conversation. But when the cover did arrive the next day, we were even more surprised. The figure was perfectly correct. And it was not, as we had supposed, forty pounds per flight. It was only around forty pounds to give us complete cover against any claims for damage for the entire time we were operating from Cazaux. We retired to the bar, considering that this certainly was an occasion which deserved to be marked in the appropriate manner. We marked it all right, but not on Perrier.

Between the 11th October, 1956, and the 15th November, we carried out no fewer than fifty-one flights over the Cazaux test site, of which forty-seven were supersonic. Our helpful French insurance man could still continue to drink his Perrier with complete equanimity and with a slice of lemon in it, for we did not get a single claim against us.

The flight across to Cazaux was uneventful but nevertheless interesting, because it was the first point-to-point flight that we had ever made in the Delta. All previous flights, of course, had been limited either to testing from Boscombe Down or, on occasions, showing our paces over Farnborough. I flew from Bedford via Bretigny, climbing immediately after take-off to the Tropopause at Mach 0.9, then levelling out and cruising at Mach 0.93 till the airfield was in sight, then using the air brakes to reduce speed during the descent to land. The trip took only thirty minutes, but it had its tiring moments because of a feature of the "feel" of the hydraulic controls and other technical reasons, which made it necessary to apply continual lateral corrections to prevent the aircraft rolling. Visibility on the outward trip was excellent. The Atlantic coast, near the south of the Gironde, could be seen as soon as I reached the top of the climb en route from Bretigny, at a distance of hundreds of miles. Gordon Slade was not so lucky on the return journey, where cloud often obscured the land, and the final descent at Bedford was made with a considerable amount of cloud cover. One snag which I encountered during these transit flights was that my own visibility was seriously impaired by misting of the windscreen. The reason for this was that hot air from the engine was used for de-misting. This was now shown to have its disadvantages because, if you ensured that enough air would be made available to the windscreen during cruising speeds when the aircraft engine revolutions were low, the delivery at higher engine speeds and Mach numbers became dangerously hot for the glass. This set the designers a problem, because, of course, the most important time to be absolutely certain that your windscreen is clear of mist is during the descent when it is very necessary to see where you are going, and at this stage the engine speed is low. These two runs showed the limitations of the existing system and, as a result, it was recommended that the system should be modified so that the hot air for de-misting was completely independent of the engine and would operate at a constant level at any stage of a flight. As it was, during the final part of the descent, not only the windscreen but three-quarters of the inside of the sandwich in the cockpit misted over, and the inside of some portions of the hooding not only misted until it was impossible to see through but also froze. On one occasion I had to go round again before I could land, in an attempt to clear the windscreen and get some sort of visibility.

Technically, we obtained a tremendous amount of useful information during this series of tests at Cazaux. Much of it was completely new and of very great benefit for future research into supersonic flight. In particular, we learnt that we would have to make a fundamental change in the power to the control jacks. The control system of the Delta, as I think we have described earlier, was operated entirely hydraulically and by remote control. This sets the pilot a special and rather individual problem. When he flies a conventional aircraft, the pilot knows that the movements he gives to the various flying controls and the effort required to move them bear a direct physical relationship to what is happening on the controls themselves. For example, the force needed to operate the controls varies according to the speed with which you are travelling and the violence of the movement which you are initiating. Now, with hydraulic remote control, all that happens when the pilot moves any of the cockpit controls is that he opens or closes the orifices in various small hydraulic valves. The effort required to do this is constant. The hydraulic valves simply pass a message on to the hydraulic motors which do the actual work. If the force required to move the flying controls varies, the hydraulic motor automatically provides more power to move them. Thus, the pilot has none of the "feel" of the controls that he has with direct mechanical control systems. This can be disconcerting. Very broadly speaking, it is as if you were steering a car by twiddling a knob instead of using the steering wheel; the steering would respond to everything you asked it to do, but you would not have the least idea what strain you were putting on it and you would be into a skid before you knew where you were. Quite apart from this aspect, there is also the danger that, with sudden manoeuvres, the pilot could actually strain a control beyond its structural limit. As I have probably mentioned, this was overcome to a certain extent in the Delta by building in artificial loads to the various controls so that they did give an impression something like the "feel" the pilot would obtain if he were using direct mechanical controls. However, this obviously cannot go all the way unless a very complicated differential system is evolved which would take into account all the other variables such as speed, effect of "g", and so on. Prior to the Cazaux series, this sort of artificial gear ratio between the controls and the elevator and aileron actuators themselves had been so arranged that it was possible for the pilot to vary either individually throughout its entire range. It was therefore possible during these low-level tests to assess the optimum gear ratio required for low-level flying. As a result of these tests we made the very important discovery that something like twice the power that we had been using up to now was needed at these low levels. As it was, so much control had to be used to trim the aircraft under some of the flying conditions that there was too little control left for safe manoeuvring.

Apart from the ordinary range of flutter tests of control displacements, at transonic and supersonic speeds, which we had been carrying out throughout the testing routine of the Delta at Boscombe Down, we also carried out a number of manoeuvres to test both the quality and the response of the aircraft's handling characteristics throughout the true speed and Mach number range. I put the Delta through a number of rolls both at subsonic and supersonic speeds. On some, the aircraft was rolling at a rate of about 250 degrees per second, which I was relieved to find that I could tolerate without any embarrassment. This was a manoeuvre which I approached with a certain amount of caution, because I had had an unfortunate experience doing the same thing previously on the F.D.1 experimental aircraft after one of the Farnborough Air Shows.

The series of tests on supersonic bangs also brought to light a great deal of hitherto completely unsuspected information, which largely debunked the general belief that the lower the aircraft the greater would be the damage from any supersonic bang. The course we used for these tests was in a southerly direction and was some forty miles in length. Recording sites were positioned on the ground at the southern end of this area and along a line crossing it from east to west, thus telling us what spread of sound we produced from various heights. The central recording tower was on top of a line of sand dunes about 250 ft. high and some $2\frac{1}{2}$ miles from the coast. The recording was made by sensitive microphone type pressure pick-ups. The flying technique was to climb the aircraft northwards from Cazaux towards the mouth of the Gironde. I was given my position as accurately as possible so that we came down along the same position on the course each time, using radar and instructions from the ground passed over the R/T. I stabilized the speed as soon as possible at the pre-arranged Mach number. At the lower speeds this involved short bursts of re-heat followed by a period of coasting. Supersonic runs were made from 30,000 ft. down to 2,500 ft.

Due to the concentration of "bangs" on the village of Lacanau-Océan, we moved the measuring sites to a more isolated position when it came to the lower altitude runs since we thought that this village had already had its fair share of the noise. The new sites were at Le Porge, on the beach some miles south of Lacanau-Océan. The results were finally put together in a very full report by the R.A.E. Farnborough team who carried out the experiments. A few points are worth mentioning here, however. At 25,000 ft., flying at a speed of Mach 1.5, the bang had a very considerable spread. Ground observers at three positions to the south-east of the course and some forty to fifty miles apart all heard the bang distinctly even if not loudly enough to disturb them unduly.

As the height was reduced, the spread became less until, at 5,000 ft., flying at a speed of Mach 1.125, it was actually possible to fly between two of the observation points only a few miles apart, with each of them hearing only a comparatively harmless rumble while another ground observation point nearby heard nothing at all. In fact, to obtain the required results, we found it necessary to change the flight path to seawards and actually to overfly one of the positions. This particular ground observation point was situated on the outskirts of a small coastal summer resort with a winter population of about four hundred. In summer this rose to over ten thousand, but at the time we did the tests most summer residences had then shut up with the season at an end.

So we annoyed no one, caused no damage, and learnt a great deal – but why the hell did we have to go out of our own country to do it?

22

ON THE SHELF

So much for Cazaux. And if it seems to you a pretty irresponsible way for one of the world's leading aeronautical nations to carry out the kind of development tests so vitally necessary if it is to continue being one of the world's aeronautical nations, I can only agree with you. But this was nothing compared with the Norway excursion. We went to Norway quite by accident.

After the Cazaux tests we had a period of some months embodying the results and making improvements. Then, these achieved, it was quite essential to carry out a further series to try out these modifications in flight, and to complete the development programme on the Avon engine itself. Once again the requirement was for low-level supersonic flying. And once again Security regulations said No.

The French had given us such wonderful co-operation that we didn't give it a second thought this time. We went straight back to them and asked if we could use Cazaux again. Unfortunately, one of those political situations that seem to be with us so much of the time had resulted in the situation between the French and ourselves having hardened quite considerably since we'd last been out there. They wouldn't give us permission to use Cazaux again.

Instead, they offered us a base in North Africa, in the Sahara – Colomb-Bechar. We had to turn it down because the climate there was quite unsuitable. Quite apart from the difficulties of sand, servicing facilities, and so on, the high temperatures of the North African summer would have been enough to squash the idea out of hand. We'd scheduled the tests for round about July 1958.

For the second time we found ourselves sitting around like unwanted orphans. We weren't wanted at home, and there was nowhere else.

Curiously, the Ministry did not seem perturbed by all this. At least, that was the impression that most of us on the Delta development team got. Seeing our situation, they wasted no time rubbing it in, pointing out that they'd been telling us all along we shouldn't embarrass everyone by doing this sort of thing. There were times, and this was one of them, when we began to wonder whether, in fact, they weren't right.

Then chance turned up trumps for the last time, in this story at least.

After we'd got the record a lot of my time was taken up giving lectures to all and sundry. One of these took me to Norway, to give a lecture in Oslo to members of the Staff College.

One of the senior officers present was a personage with the redoubtable name of General Bull. He was in command of the Southern Norway Air Forces and, after the lecture, he invited me to dinner. It was all very pleasant and, in the middle of it, I told him something of our problem, having already had some discussions with our Air Attaché. He listened attentively, although obviously bewildered at the possibility of such a situation arising at all, as I told him we would very likely have to scrap the pay-off series of final tests on the Delta simply because we weren't allowed to do it in our own country. And we couldn't find a piece of desolate country anywhere else in Europe where we were allowed to go.

He gazed into his glass for a moment. Then he said: "I don't understand. Where are you now, but in a desolate piece of country?"

I said that surely there must also be a lot of difficulties about coming to Norway. He simply answered: "I don't see any."

At that very dinner party, there and then, he told me: "You may come and use our facilities whenever you like, and there will be no charge."

The offer and the spirit it was given in remain vividly in my memory to this day. I was subsequently given quite a number of pats on the back from high quarters for arranging the Norway trip. However, as you can see, I didn't arrange anything. It came out of the blue.

All the same, even if the ideal offer had come out of the blue, we were by no means out of the rough. Back home again, of course, the Ministry wouldn't hear of it. Cazaux had been bad enough from their point of view. But Norway! The whole idea was outrageous. Didn't we realise how close Norway was to the Soviet border?

We got there in the end, but only after a great deal of paper had gone to and fro, through all the usual channels and quite a few unusual ones as well. Thus it was that, on the 5th June, 1958, I flew the Delta to Norway. We took off from the R.A.E. airfield at Thurleigh, Bedford, refuelled at Newcastle – and then flew direct over the North Sea, Newcastle-Sola, 363 statute miles, in forty-five minutes.

The site was ideal. The terrain we were to fly our tests over was a plateau of four to five thousand feet in Hardanger Vidda, some forty miles inland from Stavanger, wild and desolate country with a population only in summer, consisting of farmers and hunters.

The trip across the North Sea was quite a stretch over open water for the Delta. I had a Hunter as escort but I don't think I ever saw it, because the Delta was somewhat too fast for it and it very soon got left behind.

That was virtually my swan-song, as far as the association between the Delta and myself was concerned. As soon as we got the series of tests going in Norway, I handed over to Squadron-Leader J. O. (Jimmy) Mathews, and came back home.

Once again I made a report in which I tried to get something done about the impossible restrictions on supersonic test flying in this country. Here is an extract from it:

> The generosity, friendliness and co-operation of the Royal Norwegian Air Force and civil authorities in Norway has to be experienced to be believed. A quite extraordinary willingness to assist was met at all levels. Without this attitude in negotiations the operation could not have been mounted, and without it on the base itself the trials would have stood a good chance of foundering.
>
> Comparison of terrain and population in some of the more remote areas of the British Isles, with that of the Hardanger Vidda, are of interest because, with the present restrictions on supersonic flight in U.K. air-space, the results of this operation would have been impossible to obtain in this country.
>
> Comparisons show the North Western highlands of Scotland to be remarkably similar in terrain and population density. As a sample, if a line be drawn from 5830N/0400W to 5742N/0501W it will be seen that in this distance of almost seventy miles only four roads and one track are crossed. In this mainly sheep-grazing district there are no National Parks and no known bird sanctuaries or game reserves. Throughout the month of supersonic flying in Norway *not a single complaint of aircraft noise was received* and there is no reason why the situation should be different in an area of the U.K. such as the above.

That was my final gesture. I expect it's still sitting in someone's pending tray.

I never flew the Delta again. And it became apparent very soon after that I wasn't going to fly anything any more. And that – without more than an unheard murmur from the people who loved and believed in British aeroplane design – the historic pioneering name of Fairey Aviation was going to lose its independent identity for ever.

The whole situation was so complicated that I'm not going to try and put it down in detail here. The Air Council, I think, would have liked to have seen us with a development contract, but the régime at that time was such that they wouldn't have had the authority to do so on their own initiative. They did put some pressure on, but not enough.

For a while there was a gleam of hope when they brought out an O/R (Operational Requirement) for a supersonic fighter which the Delta could have been developed to satisfy. We were hot favourites. Then it was cancelled. Duncan Sandys and the White Paper put the kybosh on that – and also rang the knell for Fairey Aviation, because the requirements of the White Paper made it impossible for the firm to continue long as an independent entity. It was then, when the Defence Ministry was created and the recommendations came out for the reorganisation of the aircraft industry, that we knew we no longer had any chance of survival at all.

As far as any military development of the Delta 2 was concerned, the writing had been on the wall ever since the Ministry of Defence published its Outline of Future Policy in April 1957. Clause 62 left no room to manoeuvre as far as we were concerned:

> Work will proceed on the development of ground-to-air missile defence system, which will in due course replace the manned aircraft of Fighter Command. In view of the good progress already made, the Government have come to the conclusion that the R.A.F. are unlikely to have a requirement for fighter aircraft of types more advanced than the supersonic Pl. and work on such projects will stop.

Long before the Fairey-Westland reorganisation, in fact, fundamental policy was to drop the Delta, and in the final six or eight months of Fairey Aviation no one flew it at all. I had severed contact completely and, round about March 1959, the Delta was handed over to R.A.E., Farnborough. The key people in the team moved over to other projects.

Then there was one last glimmer of hope for us. The revolutionary "Ogee" wing was beginning to brew up round about that time, and this could have influenced the whole picture if a contract had matured, because we could have applied a modified wing to the Delta. The "Ogee" was the supersonic wing which was then very much in the news for commercial airliner development. Particularly, the French had pinned their faith on it in their plans for the supersonic airliner of tomorrow.

Ironically, the contract was offered – just as Fairey Aviation were sold to Westlands. But then it was too late. Westlands didn't want it, and turned it down. It makes you see red at times. At Fairey's we'd been haggling a long, long time to get Treasury approval for development on the "Ogee" wing. If only it had come nine months earlier! If only we'd actually had the contract and started work when the reorganisation happened! At least, then, Westland would have been forced to take it and continue with it, and it would just about be flying today. But they didn't want it. It was transferred to Hunting. But no sooner had that happened than Hunting were bought up too – by British Aircraft Corporation, in which Bristols were the senior partner. Bristols were already developing the "flying pencil" job, so they thought it was logical for them also to have the Delta for the "Ogee" development.

I could have gone over to Westland in the reorganisation, I suppose. But this I didn't want to do, for a number of reasons. It was a very sad day for me. But somehow it seemed even sadder to think that the name of Fairey Aviation, which had always seemed to me so durable, so much part and parcel of the life-blood of British aviation, could be so vulnerable to the policy-makers. It was no longer enough even to design an aeroplane like the Delta and then fly it on a shoe-string through the thousand-mile-an-hour mark in the teeth of competition from the limitless resources of the United States. It seemed outrageous that Fairey Aviation were apparently no longer fit to survive in the evolutionary rat-race. It was difficult to understand where the true values that one had always hoped existed somewhere actually were.

My test flying days were over. Twelve years previously, I had graduated from the Empire Test Pilots' School and had joined Fairey's. It is amusing to think what might have happened. In those days, very much as a new boy in the test-flying field, I had written round to three or four different firms asking them whether they had any openings for a test pilot. I wrote to Hawker's, and I went to see Jeff Quill at Supermarines, but he couldn't fit me in at that time. Then I got an answer from Hawker's – offering me a job. But, instead of taking it, I wrote another letter – to Fairey's. And I held off accepting the Hawker job until Fairey's answered. Why this predilection for Fairey's? I don't really know, except that I had flown a lot of their aircraft and I knew the people there and knew they were a friendly crowd to work for. At almost the same time they lost two test pilots in rapid succession. They wanted another one in a hurry. They gave me the job and I turned Hawker's down.

It is an interesting conjecture where I'd be today if I'd chosen Hawker's instead of Fairey's. But, of course, such conjectures are idle. Ifs and buts don't really give you any option in your life – not in mine anyway. We could go right back to the beginning again on that basis, and say that, if the airfield at Ford hadn't struck my youthful imagination when I was a farm-hand at Salisbury, I would have been a gamekeeper.

Of course there's another way of looking at it too. If I had joined Hawker's, I might quite well be under the sod instead of writing this. A couple of good friends of mine were killed doing the job that, but for a piece of notepaper and a threepenny stamp, might have been mine instead.

23

SEABORNE NOT AIRBORNE

Many readers may still be bewildered, as I certainly was at the time, over the final outcome of the sale of Fairey Aviation in 1959. Why should such a pioneering firm, whose tradition had become part of the history of the aircraft industry itself, have to be sold at the very moment when it was riding a quite phenomenal peak of success?

I hope that, through this book, I have made clear the general reasons. Regrouping of the industry was inevitable, and was in no sense a reflection on those firms which, even though their names had been household words since the beginning of flying, were now to lose their identity. We who regret their passing are, perhaps, being sentimental rather than realistic, for the past is no longer with us, and the present is a very different kettle of fish.

The present trend in every field of industry is towards the larger group. Outside the aircraft industry one sees it in, for instance, the enormous "consortiums" set up by engineering firms to cope with the tremendous problems of nuclear power station design and construction. Globally, it is evident by the trend in the United States, the regrouping of individual resources in Europe by the formation of the EEC, and, above all perhaps, in the planning of Russia and Eastern Europe, where tremendous production advantages are being gained by rationalising industry on a scale never before envisaged.

Rationalisation of this kind invites bureaucracy; but, if it can be made to work without becoming altogether too unwieldy, it obviously eliminates all the wasteful duplication of effort unavoidable when a lot of small private firms are all engaged quite independently of each other in development work along similar lines.

Industry could well afford this wastefulness of effort in the early days; indeed the system was its life blood, because it was through effectively free enterprise of this kind, with its incentive of competition, that the really great developments have come.

However, I think it must by now be pretty generally agreed, even by the most ardent supporter of free enterprise, that the field of competition has become a global one; it is no longer the cosy domestic thing it used to be. Under such circumstances an industrial nation, or even group of nations, has no alternative but to consolidate in order to survive. This has applied with particular emphasis to the aircraft industry where the increasing complexity of design and technology of manufacture have put any future developments completely beyond the capital resources of any but the largest organisations.

Ted Bowyer, the then director of the Society of British Aircraft Constructors, has stated the situation very concisely in the following figures. A turbo-jet engine may cost £20,000,000 before it is ready for service; and even a medium-sized airliner can cost up to £40,000,000 to evolve, develop, and to tool for initial batch production. One American manufacturer has had to spend £90,000,000 on designing, developing, proving and tooling a large turbo-jet air-liner.

Now, obviously, as an industry the existing structure in Britain was quite inadequate to meet development costs of this order. This is not to suggest that an indiscriminate and apparently endless policy of dog eat dog in industry is the ideal alternative. There must be a limit to the present trend of consolidation into groups beyond which any advantages are more than offset by bureaucracy. At what stage does a group topple over into a condition where it has simply become too large to be adequately managed and controlled? Many of us, too, may still have our doubts as to whether all the firms that were affected by the White Paper were absorbed for the right reasons. Sometimes it seemed more a matter of who could make more out of whom than of what the firm had to offer in terms of consolidated technical know-how. To anyone working inside a firm about to be sold, as I was, it was difficult not to feel as if we were sitting exposed and helpless on some second-hand stall in Petticoat Lane, waiting for the best bid to finish its haggling over the price and take us home.

Immediately before the war, in 1939, there were thirty aircraft manufacturing companies and sixteen aero-engine companies in Britain. By 1959 these figures had been whittled down to twenty-four aircraft and six aero-engine companies; and seventeen of these were already tied up in groups. As Ted Bowyer has noted, in the previous two years no fewer than thirteen companies had been involved in mergers or amalgamations.

The largest group was Hawker Siddeley. In 1958 Hawker Siddeley Aviation was formed as "one single integrated unit combining research, design, development and production". The group involved Avro, Hawker, Gloster, Armstrong-Whitworth and Armstrong-Siddeley.

Then, in the same year, Armstrong-Siddeley merged with Bristol Aero-Engines, to form Bristol-Siddeley. Saunders-Roe merged with Westland in 1959, together with Fairey Aviation.

By 1960 Hawker Siddeley had acquired Folland, the de Havilland group, and three Blackburn companies. Following on the heels of this was the second fixed-wing group comprising British Aircraft Corporation, and combining English Electric, Vickers Armstrong, and the fixed-wing interests of Bristol. Subsequently, Hunting moved yet again, also to be absorbed in this group.

The future of Fairey Aviation was obviously going to be not with either of these groups (as it might well have been had we had any further development contracts in hand on the Delta design), but with vertical take-off interests; our major asset at that period was undoubtedly the controversial Rotodyne.

It was thus that we found ourselves, by early 1960, absorbed into the rotating-wing group comprising Westland, Saunders-Roe, Bristol Aircraft, and ourselves.

No one can doubt that, in one form or another, this streamlining was necessary. However, it is worth quoting Ted Bowyer again before we let the matter rest finally: "We are not convinced that Government decisions are being made with the necessary speed and purpose to ensure that the new-look industry's resources are applied as effectively as they might be. There must be constructive policy-making, quick decisions and firm implementation. This is particularly true of Europe and NATO, where we have lost orders in recent years largely because of the lack of firmness and foresight on the part of the government."

I cannot help wondering, even with the comparatively limited practical experience I had of dealing with governmental and ministerial departments, whether it mightn't have served a more useful purpose if someone had streamlined the Government before they started to streamline the industry.

The Fairey Westland reorganisation period was a very unhappy one for me. I was worried about my future as, indeed, were all the pilots on Fairey's flying staff. We tried without any success to find out what plans, if any, Westland had for us. Months went by with us virtually sitting on the shelf and not knowing whether to hang on or start to look for something else. Amongst the thousand and one things that had to be tied up in this vast reorganisation, we began to get the impression that, as test pilots, we were of no account at all. I suppose it was inevitable but, to this day, I believe that it showed a singular lack of insight into human psychology by Westland, and that something was sadly lacking in the field of human relations. Everyone in my department, myself included, began to get very demoralised and, as a consequence, much bad feeling developed.

Westland were based at Yeovil, and I made many fruitless trips down there from the Fairey plant at White Waltham in an attempt to gain some clue as to the outcome. Eventually, my mind was made up for me by the directors of Westland. When at last I got a hearing, I was told in as many words: "There's no room for you, mate."

Perhaps it wasn't said quite as baldly as that, but the effect was just the same. And they subsequently changed their minds. But it was too late. By then I had an ineradicable impression I wasn't really wanted. Rightly or wrongly, I found that I could no longer believe that a Fairey Aviation division enveloped in the new Westland organisation could ever recapture the friendly family atmosphere that had meant so much to me in the fifteen years I had spent test-flying with the original Fairey Aviation organisation, now passing so ignominiously into limbo.

It was a bitter pill to swallow. Perhaps it was made a little easier when the new policy was made plain; Westland, as the rotary-wing group in the new set-up for the industry, would have no part in the development of any further fixed-wing aircraft. It was to be helicopters, and allied types, all the way.

Although I had been test-flying for years and believed that, by now, I could take anything into the air that could reasonably be expected to get off the ground, I was still a comparative newcomer to the rotary wing field. It is a field which has a technique uniquely its own. Two years of helicopter flying, including a period when I had acted as second test-pilot on the Rotodyne, had been sufficient to show me that I was still learning in this very specialised field. Already rising forty years of age I would be pretty old in the tooth, by test-flying standards, before I could consider myself an expert.

Perhaps, after all, it would be a good time to face the decision I would inevitably have to face in a few years' time anyway, and pack it all in. The decision was not made without a great deal of heart searching. It is always a deflating experience to find that, even though you have been good at your job, you are no longer wanted. It meant, too, leaving many of my closest friends at Fairey's and, quite possibly, never seeing many of them again. I also had to face the depressing fact that the odds against making a new career at forty were pretty discouraging.

Once again, as throughout my life, I let fate decide for me what I should do rather than try to rearrange destiny to suit myself. I handed over my job as Chief Test Pilot to Ron Gellatly who, for some years, had been my senior helicopter test pilot and who was undoubtedly the leading rotary wing pilot in the country, if not in the world. It was so obviously right that the flying future should be in his hands rather than mine; and it would have been very wrong of me if, now the whole organisation was to concentrate on this type of aircraft, I were to continue nominally as Chief Test Pilot simply to maintain a personal position, on the strength of experience that had been gained in quite a different field and which was now no longer applicable.

When the offer came to join Fairey Marine at Hamble, I jumped at it. My long connection with Fairey's did not have to be severed after all, and, remaining with an organisation I knew and in which I had always felt at home and welcome, the transition from test-flying to a life of commerce would at any rate be cushioned to some extent.

Nevertheless, I approached it with some trepidation. There was no difficulty in the transition from aeroplanes to boats; handling a boat in the open sea has much in common with flying. However, the transition to the completely unfamiliar world of commerce was something very different; for myself, with absolutely no commercial background whatever, it would be something akin to trying to land an aircraft you had never flown before on an unknown airfield in the dark.

Geographically, my return to the Hamble was very much in the nature of a sentimental journey. There were so many associations with it right from childhood upwards that I was delighted at the prospect of living there. Even through my test-flying career the Hamble had been a symbol of peaceful relaxation; yachts, and fresh-picked strawberries on hot summer days, and all the things that are conjured up by the sound of water lapping lazily against a hull and sails flapping in a summer breeze.

When I had first joined Fairey Aviation, the Hamble factory had been producing Firefly aircraft, and the prototype of the Primer trainer was also built there. In those days there had been pretty strong competition amongst the pilots at Fairey's Heston headquarters to get the test-flying assignment on one of these aircraft so that we would have an excuse for a few days in the Hamble area. It was more or less standard practice to put ourselves up at the Bugle, a typical local yachtsman's pub.

Now, on my first trip back to Hamble to discuss my future, I looked in at the Bugle again. The setting was still the same, but the quiet yachting backwater atmosphere and the aeroplanes had gone for good. Hamble had become the centre of a thriving new world of power-boating, noisy and full to overflowing during the summer weekends, with the Bugle packed to capacity and bursting at the seams at meal times.

My arrival to take up the new job could not have been arranged at a better time. It coincided with what was to prove to be a new and exciting development in motor-boating. Fairey Marine were in on the ground floor of this new-look in yachting, concentrating a large proportion of their production on the fast day cruiser capable of over forty knots, and able to make open sea passages to the Continent and beyond in all but the worst weather conditions. They were to be the forerunners of a new concept in sports boats. Like miniature MTBs, these craft were being made on newly laid-down production lines replacing the aircraft shops of the previous years, to a hull design by the famous American boat designer Ray Hunt. Fast and stable, they are vastly exhilarating.

To my delight, I was given the responsibility for the development and sales of this new and exciting range.

This was to be the beginning of a new phase in my life, in more ways than one. It was at this period, too, that I remarried and we bought the house at Long Meadow. In fact, the first experience I had with a Fairey power boat was on our honeymoon, when we took one to Italy and back. Then, honeymoons and holidays over, I dived headlong into the commercial world.

I would not pretend for a moment that this was any less difficult than I had expected it to be. After all, test-flying Ministry development contract aeroplanes calls for the absolute minimum of commercial acumen. By comparison, I now found myself in a world where the whole environment was very largely conditioned by a completely commercial outlook, because we were now involved in satisfying a market which was already highly competitive and was becoming more so every minute. But you can get used to anything. I slowly but surely became absorbed into this new atmosphere. And, above all, I wasn't indefinitely chair-borne, because a large proportion of the work was a fine open-air life making test runs and demonstrations.

I found myself completely engrossed in the work. I had not yet once missed my previous life of flying.

Here is one final coincidence. While Richard Fairey was alive, we had often talked of the fast power-boat races held in the States, notably the Miami-Nassau race; and Richard had actually entered his own boat in that most rugged of all races the previous year. The course is 180 miles of open sea and, although Richard's boat did not finish, it is interesting to note that the first two boats home were designed by Ray Hunt who had designed this new Huntsman class for us.

During my first summer at Hamble my previous conversations with Richard came back into mind with great vividness. If we were really to go all out in our plans to develop this kind of seagoing power boating and to publicise it to the yachting world, we must have a similar race in Britain.

I thought about the idea and realised it could only happen with a suitable newspaper to back it. It was inevitable that I should think of Max Aitken. He had been a famous fighter pilot during the war. He was a keen yachtsman. And, as everyone knows, his father was Lord Beaverbrook.

During that weekend he came to Cowes. I put the proposition to him. He looked surprised for a moment, and then started laughing. Then he told me: "It's already arranged. We had a board meeting at the *Express* yesterday evening with exactly the same idea in mind. It's all laid on!" So the *Daily Express* International Offshore Power Boat Race was born.

We built a boat for Billy Butlin, especially for the race from the Solent to Torquay. I was his copilot in the race itself. Unfortunately, we hit an underwater obstruction quite early on and ripped our bottom out, and ended somewhat ingloriously by beaching as quickly as we could on Hayling Island before we sank. Billy Butlin, not in the least deterred, chartered an aircraft to get him to Torquay in time to see the other competitors finish. However our standard diesel-powered Huntsman made up for it all by coming in third place, brilliantly driven by Charles Currey, Fairey Marine Sales Director, and the following year Butlin won first prize for Production Boats under £4,000, and came eighth overall in a 23-foot, single-engined Huntress.

The race has caught hold of the public imagination and there is no doubt that power boating was now very much on the map. It also proved the Fairey design, for we have had prize-winners in several of the various classifications.

One thing which pleased me particularly was that, after the 1961 race, Billy Butlin announced that he would present a Huntsman to the Outward Bound School. So, even if indirectly, I had been able to satisfy another long-held ambition – to do something for the youth movements of today, in return for what they did for me. And so we come full circle. There have been moments of excitement, many, many moments of pleasure and exhilaration, and moments of doubt. Moments of enforced change. One career finishes, another opens. Life always goes on, not perhaps always the way one had expected, but, if one is made the way I am, always with absorbing interest.

EPILOGUE

Developing the Fairey power boats was a wonderful experience. To me, it was a new experience. I knew how to handle a boat and soon became reasonably competent in the finer points of trimming, stability and manoeuvring at high speed. 25-30 knots – fast in those days! I was guided by Charles Currey, a first rate seaman and brought up in MTB's, etc. during the war and our designer, Alan Burnard, who drew the lines and whose speciality was propeller design.

Demonstrations to customers was a pleasant part of the job. Usually the potential customer had some yachting experience and was looking for a fast, seaworthy craft to take him and his family safely offshore. There were always some who thought they knew it all but I found that even they were impressed with the "sea keeping" qualities and performance of the Fairey range of craft.

One always makes mistakes! On one occasion, Peter du Cane, the great power craft designer from Vospers, sent his son-in-law, Nigel Tunnicliffe, down to Fairey's to have a demonstration in the 23 foot *Fairey Huntress*. Lord and Lady Head were going out to West Africa to take up the government post of governor and wanted to take a boat with them. Vospers had a craft, the *Swordfish*, which they thought was very suitable for the Heads, but Peter du Cane thought it would be a good idea to show some other manufacturer's product as a comparison. Nigel T. and the Heads came out in the 23 foot Huntress with me. This diesel-powered cruiser was capable of around 23 knots and had a large open cockpit with a small cabin with sitting headroom.

There was no wind and, therefore, no waves to show off the good riding of the craft at full speed. We often resorted to using the wash of the passing Isle of Wight ferries to demonstrate this feature. So, as soon as I sighted a ferry, I opened up to full power heading for the wash. Unfortunately, as I turned towards the wash and unknown to me, Lady Head decided it was the moment to view the cabin. The Huntress jumped over the waves in good style, but poor Lady Head hit her head on the cabin roof, so hard that she collapsed with minor concussion. I took the craft gently back to The Hamble with profuse apologies and, needless to say, Lord and Lady Head bought the Vosper *Swordfish*!

There were many exciting trips over the next few years in the Fairey boats. Expeditions to overseas, such as to the Paris Boat Show, which had an area on the Seine for demonstrations in amongst the huge barges and other leisure craft. The trip over and back was eventful with fog in the Le Harve estuary, shallow and uncharted parts of the River Seine, locking in and out of the huge lochs with the barges, each one capable of crushing the relatively flimsy Fairey craft.

We had a very enthusiastic French agent who thought that the right place to show the Fairey range would be on the Côte d'Azur. After some discussion with the MD at Hamble, we decided to send a Huntsman 28, on a lorry, down to Cannes and tour the South of France. We had one good prospect, Rex Harrison, who had been to Hamble but had been called away from the demonstration to talk to his director for the key role in the musical My Fair Lady, which was "on the stocks" and the director was after Rex Harrison to take the key role.

Rex Harrison had thought that the Huntsman 28 would be an answer to his boat requirements. This special boat had 2 large V8 petrol engines and had a capability of over 30 knots. He did not reappear after the phone call!

When our demonstration boat arrived in the South of France, I took it along the coast, calling in at all the famous resorts – Cannes, Ville-Franche, Beaulieu, etc. and on to Italy, Genoa and Porto Fino. Sadly, Rex Harrison had bought a boat locally.

One part of the French trip I remembered was the road delivery trip down and back, sitting in the cockpit of the Huntsman, 12 foot up, at 30-50 m.p.h. looking at the French countryside and passing through Paris with a grandstand view!

Shortly after this trip, Fairey's had an enquiry from a film company making From Russia with Love, a well-known Bond story. Part of the film should have been shot in Yugoslavia, with wild country and a rocky coast. The company were unable to find any suitable, fast boats for the scene involving the escape by boat of Bond and his beautiful accomplice, Danielle.

The special effects people approached Fairey's to try and persuade us to take boats out to Yugoslavia. This was an impossible task, or at least totally uneconomical. We suggested using the Western Isles of Scotland which have a very similar coastline. After much discussion this was agreed. All Fairey's had to do was to find 7 boats, drivers, mechanics, etc.!

We had to approach a number of Fairey boat owners to hire some of the boats and were able to supply two or three demonstration boats from our boatyard. The deal was that the film company would pay £1,000 per boat per week, transport, repair damage (if any) and repaint boats all over after the job was completed. The film company also accommodated and fed all the drivers and crew and paid any personnel a daily rate for any scenes they appeared in. Fairey's team consisted of Charles Currey – sales director, myself, my wife Heather, Fairey Marine engineers and boat builder and Ian Anderson, who was understudy to Connery in the driving scenes, etc. etc.

The organisation and set up of a large film company working on a countryside set was quite incredible. The manpower involved was amazing. Catering, miles from any civilisation for 40-50 personnel had to be done sometimes from a substantial vessel with cooking facilities or from mobile kitchens. The film personnel union requirement is for everyone to have a hot, 3-course meal once a day! The chefs produced fresh salmon, steaks, salads and first class sweets, served by waiters in dress suits. Tables with white table cloths, cutlery, glass, and so on. Wherever we were, perhaps on the moors or in a sheltered gravel pit and when on the island scenes, onboard the 60-foot tender, wine was the order of the day, certainly for the actors and directors. We made sure some came our way, of course.

Between scenes, there was always plenty of waiting around, usually in the boats. Out came the cards and the cabin tables were loaded with paper money as the film company and actors played Poker or whatever. Their finances were a bit above our level, so gambling was left to them!

We would set off in the 5/6 boats from Crinan, our base ashore, to the location of the set at 8 a.m. each day. We were very fortunate with the weather – fine for weeks on end. The boats were fuelled and serviced in the evenings. We had made provision for spares, etc. and it is of great credit to the ground staff that we had seven weeks of almost continuous use out of the boats with only one temporary delay of a few hours on one boat to change a propeller.

One of the scenes involved Bond in his boat with Danielle being chased by the "baddies" and in order to make a "get away", Bond was to cut loose three 50 gallon drums of petrol which he was to set on fire on the surface of the water in his boat's wake.

The film company staff had taken two days to set up all the explosives, etc. for the major conflagration to happen between Bond and the "baddies". Communications in those days (1963) were basic and the timing critical. Bond had to fire a Very light which looked as though it set fire to the petrol, etc. This was to be at a precise time. Bond fired the Very pistol $2^1/_2$ minutes early and the boats were all in the wrong position when the "set piece" explosions and fire took place. It took another two days to set up the scene again. The director and Connery exchanged some ripe comments for the mistiming!

In the film, one sees the "baddies" boats burning in the sea of flame, with people throwing themselves into the sea. This part of the scene was done using full sized replicas in the tank at Pinewood Studios and I remember going to witness this and as I drove into the film company's yard, being amazed at the Fairey boats floating on the surface of the tank. Whose boats were these? Surely they were not going to set fire to them? They were a remarkable likeness and even floated naturally, but they *were* fake.

So much for the filming, the result was a really first class movie and a substantial profit for Fairey Marine.

Each year, in August, "*The Daily Express* Offshore Power Boat Race" took place from 1961 onwards. This was *the* power boat race of the calendar, sponsored and organised by Max Aitken and the *Daily Express* newspapers. It was important to take part in this event if one produced a fast offshore craft. To complete this course was an achievement in itself, to take Class prizes was a real bonus. Fairey Marine boats always entered and a works team was usually included. Sheer speed was not always the winning factor – the craft had to be seaworthy and capable of running at a reasonable speed in rough water.

Each year, for about six years, I entered with Fairey craft and usually managed to finish with a Class prize, although never the overall prize.

One year, I was asked by the American owner of a large US boat company, Thunderbird, to race with him in one of their race boats. Merrick Lewis loved race boats and had a 35 foot fibreglass racer capable of 50 knots. He was the President of the Alliance Crane Company which had a number of subsidiary companies, including Thunderbird. He always did things in style and shipped over a massive air-conditioned coach which contained comfortable sleeping quarters, shower rooms, etc., as well as living accommodation. I jumped at the opportunity of crewing with Merrick. We made a good run down to Torquay coming 2nd overall, being three-quarters of a mile behind the winner, *Brave Moppie*.

In those days we had a return race, Torquay to Cowes direct, i.e., not circumnavigating the Isle of Wight. Merrick let me drive this race and we stayed in front of the fleet all the way, winning by several minutes.

On another occasion, I was asked to drive an unusual boat designed by a well-known naval architect and financed by *The News of the World*. Not unnaturally, it was named *News of the World* and was powered by 4 large Foden diesels driving twin propellers, each pair of engines being coupled. A very complex installation and not well tried. We started in great style, but after approximately 50 miles, one gearbox failed. The diesel soot which resulted from running on $2\frac{1}{2}$ engines blackened our faces and took some removing!

The final race I took part in was the "*Daily Telegraph* and BP Round Britain Race" of 1969. Fairey was fortunate to have an order from the Ford Motor Company for 3 boats to join a 4th Huntsman 28 thus forming a team. All the boats were powered by the new Ford diesel the company was introducing at this time – the Ford 2700 Series diesel – and were determined to offer as much power as was reliably possible and provided a good back-up team of engineers and spares. The race was 1400 miles overall and done in ten stages, starting at Southsea, down to Land's End, up to the Isle of Man via Milford Haven and around the Isle of Man up to Oban, through the Caledonian Canal (not racing) to Inverness, down the North Sea and into the Channel, finishing at Portsmouth. A punishing schedule! My crew were Roger Clarke of Ford rally driving fame and Colin Hallet, one of the best of Fairey's boat builders. All four Fairey boats worked as a team. We did not have our eyes set on being overall winners. The boats with large petrol engines of 500 hp or more were likely to be in the first few. However, we won the team prize and one of the Fairey team, Derek Morris, was third boat home, leading the whole team into the next three places.

The Huntsman I drove with Roger was called *Ford Sport* and after the 1969 races it was purchased by Alex Moulton of Moulton Bicycle fame and renamed *Seven O Seven*. The boat is still in pristine condition, 30 years later, with another owner and lying on the Hamble River.

All this racing was done to further the Fairey fast cruiser image and although I had tremendous fun, it did involve many long hours of preparation, and routine sales work at Hamble still had to be done. The expansion of the Dry Land Boat Park was my particular "baby" which helped sales, in as much that we could provide a berth for a customer's boat immediately when most marinas were booked up and a waiting list for a mooring on the River Hamble was 5-7 years. The site at Hamble was ideal for this dry land mooring. Near the mouth of the River Hamble, a substantial slipway was left from the 1920s and 30s when flying boats and seaplanes were made and tested from the site. Launching and recovery could be made using the slipway. The maximum rise and fall of the tide on the Hamble River is 16 feet or 5 metres and launching and recovery could be achieved almost at any tide except the larger spring tides at low water. We developed a unique method of slipping the boats using a Fordson tractor operating, what could be called, a giant hydraulic forklift truck. Each boat had its own cradle made to fit the shape of the hull. Having driven the tractor and forklift trailer, complete with cradle, down the slipway and into the river the boat was manoeuvred either on or off. Up to 100 boats were regularly on the scheme and as it expanded, additional tractors and a second hydraulic trailer were purchased. As I write this, the two original hydraulic trailers are still in use, 30 years later, having been purchased by other boatyards.

From 1961 Fairey Marine started negotiating for planning permission to build a wet marina to accommodate 2-300 craft. We had the land alongside our northern boundary. The whole site was purchased by Sir Richard Fairey in the early 20s and the village was concerned that no encroachment should be made onto Hamble Common. This piece of common land was owned by Winchester College through whom we had to deal while making the marina application. The early responses to our application were, "No, No, No"! However, with the College's support and our undertakings not to upset the local use of the Common, plus the fact that the yachting public were crying out for yacht berths, the application was finally accepted. Much design work was done by Ken Steele, an architect from Taunton, and I was deeply involved with stating Fairey's requirements. We needed to know what size craft were to be accommodated, their draft, beam, and so on. How many of each size, what facilities were to be provided ashore, etc., etc. I started off by asking an associate Fairey company, Fairey Air Surveys, to take aerial pictures of local marinas and rivers. From these we deduced the numbers of yacht/motor vessels, their lengths and beams. We then had a good basis for the layout of berths and could produce a figure of annual income. The parent Fairey company was by no means enthusiastic about the scheme but having seen a positive indication of the levels of income available, became more interested.

Ken Steele did a good job and his plans covered our requirements within the budget allowed. One of the biggest costs was dredging. We had to dig a hole in the mud and remove the spoil some 30 miles to the dumping grounds at sea. Approximately 100,000 cubic yards of mud had to be removed to give us berths with 6 foot draft on the large boat berths and 4' 6" on the smaller ones. An enormous amount of chalk and hard fill had to be trucked into the site from Portsdown Hill to provide a good solid surface for buildings, car parking and boat storage area. Very long Greenhart piles had to be driven to hold the pontoons in position. A steel piling wall had to hold back the excavated land. The Fairey Marine site where the aircraft factory had been and where now the boat building and boat parking were situated, was 2-3 feet below high water and there was a retaining wall, mostly built of mud, around the site.

This was very vulnerable and over the years, flooding had occurred due to the slipway having been "topped" by the tide flooding large areas of the factory. At the top of the slipway there was provision for a flood barrier of substantial boards to be erected. This was around 2' 6" high and only took 20 minutes or so to erect. Even with this barrier, with an exceptional spring tide or tidal surge, the sea would top the barrier. If the team was slow in erecting the barrier, it was almost impossible to do so when the tide started flowing over the slipway. If extra high water occurred during the night, the barrier had to be rigged before the work force left. Sometimes, this did not happen!

Going back to the dredging, as the dredger approached the existing mud wall, removing mud some 30 feet away, cracks began to appear in the sea wall and within a few minutes, the wall was breached and parts of the factory flooded to a depth of 18 inches to 2 foot. The lowest part was the drawing office! The boatshops were usually under a foot and as it happened we were storing approximately 100 new Petter engines for the neighboring company, Petters. These all had to be stripped and treated against salt water corrosion. An expensive mistake, so all dredging stopped in that area. Emergency measures were taken to fill the gap. Hundreds of tons of hard core, etc. were tipped in from landwards and a temporary reinforced plywood wall was erected in the gap and large pumps manned day and night at higher tides until a substantial steel sheet piled wall was erected. This took several months and meanwhile, night crews had to be on watch to start the pumps until the tide subsided.

A dock was built to not only slip marina boats not suitable for the slipway scheme, but also to bring in work on larger boats for Fairey Marine. Also to haul out 63 foot Fairey Trackers being built by Fairey Marine, East Cowes.

During this time, about 1975, I had a call from the Fairey company at Heston. They had received a request from the Libyan government, to whom we had supplied 50 Fairey Marine boats, a few months before. They had ideas of developing leisure boating sites and marinas along the Libyan coast and wanted some advice on the scheme.

The Fairey company decided that I should go to Tripoli accompanied by another member from Fairey engineering. There was the minimum of information and we could only wait until we arrived to see what ideas the Libyans had. We had a Fairey representative in Libya, looking after various projects in which Fairey was involved, among them being the fleet of Fairey Marine boats. The majority of these were from one amazing order received, out of the blue, on telex from Paris for 25 Spearfish and 25 Fantômes. The surprising thing about the order was that no sales staff were involved. The telex just arrived.

I suspected that one of the things the Libyans wanted, was some practical advice on problems they were having on the boats. The police were using the boats, which were stationed in various anchorages along the vast coastline. Most of these anchorages were miles from anywhere. No moorings as such were laid – the boats lay to their own anchors. It appeared that the main problem was loss of power and problems with starting the diesel engines. The first Fantôme I visited had this loss of power. I went out with the Libyan coxwain and it was obvious, straight away, that there was fuel starvation on one engine. All the fuel valves and filters were below decks, so I ventured below to investigate. I was in for a shock. This was August and the heat was intense, the smell inside the cabin was indescribable. I soon realised why. The Libyans had to feed themselves on board; being miles from civilisation, they kept their chickens on board for eggs and any fish caught were also stowed on board (no fridges were fitted). I managed about 2 minutes below, but then had to come up for air!

The boats were clean outside, but sadly neglected otherwise. The fuel problem was due to water in the fuel supply, the filters were half full of water and "gunge". This had worked its way through to the fuel cocks and had partially blocked the supply. All the pipes had to be removed and blown through and the filter elements changed. This was only a temporary cure – the fuel supply from shore was suspect.

There was not much more one could do until this was rectified. Most of the boats away from Tripoli were affected but where shoreside pumps were used, the systems were reasonably clean. I spent two days going round the other boats and was impressed how well the Libyans handled the craft. Wearing their long flowing robes cannot have been easy at 30 knots!

We carried on with our main task. After a short briefing from the Libyans, it appeared that the senior officials (who we never met) wanted to develop the coastline by providing launching and mooring facilities for the "people" to be able to enjoy seaside activities, i.e. swimming, sailing and boating and they hoped they could encourage yachtsmen to cruise the coast as they do in the South of France. Some hope!

The coast is most unsuitable, having a rocky reef lying approximately two miles offshore, totally unmarked. Admittedly, they had lovely sandy beaches, sadly heavily coated with oil, but no harbours to speak of and no provisioning, restaurants, or fuel.

However, we were issued with a long wheel base Landrover with a Libyan Naval driver who had been instructed to take us wherever we wanted to go, along the coast covering 1250-1500 miles. It was a very rough ride. We stayed in villages along the main E-W road, sleeping with the truck drivers in campbeds 6 inches off the ground and with extremely basic washing facilities. Each day we would study the maps and charts and drive down to the shore to survey any likely spots. It was very interesting but I cannot say very productive! We drew plans of likely spots and took a large number of photos. Each day we would cover approximately 150-200 miles. We had a great bonus when we got to Benghazi on the Gulf of Sirte. A hotel for the night and a bath with hot running water.

While in the hotel, we got a taste of Libyan authority! There was an Italian couple who had come in on a ferry from Italy for a holiday in Libya. The husband was very agitated and almost tearful. His wife had brought a bottle of wine in her luggage for their picnics, and had been searched at the docks. All forms of alcohol are taboo and Col. Gaddafi made the police enforce this strictly, so this unfortunate woman was incarcerated in the local jail and was still there when we left.

While we were in Tripoli, our Fairey representative introduced us to some of the other company reps. All of them had stills in their quarters and produced some very lethal "hooch". All were warned not to mention it.

The trip went on for another few days and we then decided we had enough information to produce a report. Back to Tripoli and we hoped a flight back to the UK. Our passports had been taken from us on arrival and the airport was not interested in discussing flights until they were given clearance. We stayed on in a very comfortable, but "dry" hotel until we finally got clearance to leave Libya, but it was a very uncomfortable feeling to be deprived of one's passport. Britannia Airways found room for us and having been searched by Customs, we were glad to be away.

Following a number of rumours, the future of Fairey Marine and Fairey Yacht Harbours looked gloomy. Total profits were not what the parent company wanted. We at the marina had a heavy debt around our necks with the financing of the marina which had cost considerably more than originally expected.

The rumours came to light one day in 1988 when Alan Simmonds, MD of Fairey Marine took me aside and said that, although it was not for general release, "the marine company had been sold to a Dutchman as a going concern". This was a shock, to say the least. I was to be severed from the Fairey group of companies after 39 years.

I had to keep the information about the sale of the company to myself for a while and, indeed, wanted to until I knew more about the situation. First of all I met Robin Pitt, who was a friend of Mijndert Pon, the owner of the Dutch company. He explained the facts as far as they went and reassured me about the Dutch company and who and what they were.

All the negotiations were done through Fairey Marine and the Fairey Company. I was never involved and did not meet the Dutch personnel until much later, but I got a measure of the way they did business very soon. Their senior accountants and Robin Pitt and their lawyers and English chartered accountants sat around a table from 1100 until 1700 and tied up the whole deal with Alan Simmonds, our lawyers and Fairey company directors. Sandwiches were sent down and suitable refreshments, it being determined to do the deal there and then! By this time, I was able to tell the senior staff what was happening, to the best of my knowledge. Fairey Yacht Harbours became Hamble Point Marina, now part of the Pon Group of Companies of Amersfoort, Holland.

I spent some time with Robin Pitt discussing the aims of the new company and what M. Pon was planning. He was very positive about Mijndert Pon's aims and said that the Dutch would spend a considerable sum making the marina up to the standard of their marinas in Holland. This was very encouraging as many of my ideas over the past few years had to put on the back burner due to lack of funds.

Mijndert was concerned about the morale of the company personnel so he organised a three-day trip for nearly everybody in Fairey Yacht Harbours to fly to Amsterdam from Southampton, go to the Amsterdam Boat Show, spend the first night in Amsterdam, travel up in a coach to see the land reclamation works on the Polders, up north over the sea wall between the North Sea and the Ijssel Meer to Pon's group of marinas in Friesland. Everyone was accommodated in local villages and there was a great gathering in the hall at Hindeloopen where the main marine was situated. After a considerable amount of booze and food, the Dutch put on a show of national dancing and certain visitors, including myself, had to take part. I find simple foxtrots, etc. difficult enough, but the Dutch dances were out of my reach. However, it is amazing what a few glasses of Bols Dutch gin can do!

Everyone from Hamble had an excellent time and after a trip round the Amsterdam Boat Show, we all climbed into the Fokker *Friendship* and flew back to Southampton. The whole trip was a success and helped enormously to build up the confidence of the marina personnel.

Over the months, I made many trips to Holland and the Dutch directors came to England to Board meetings and discussions about the provision of facilities, etc. to be built into the new marina. True to his word, Mijndert Pon did not stint – the best of everything had to be provided. The whole boat and car parking area, amounting to several acres, was levelled and 2 metre square, reinforced concrete slabs were laid. A substantial workshop and paint shop building, embodying a chandlery, workshop, offices, etc., was built. The doors were sufficiently high to enable the 'travel hoist' to be used for moving boats in for repairs and painting and out at the end of the job, etc. A substantial two-storey, prefabricated office block was imported from Sweden in sections, housing some 30 offices, marina male and female toilets, showers, etc. and a brokerage office for the marina broker.

When the building sections had been on the site a few days only, the fabricating company, who also had been contracted to assemble the building, went into voluntary liquidation in Sweden.

We took drastic action and took on the assembly, appointing a local firm, guided by our architect, to carry on with the job. It obviously took longer and as winter had set in, the assembly of the structural members, which had to be mounted on concrete piles, were often delayed by frost. The building was very Swedish in appearance and fitted in well with the surrounding features.

I then had to start letting the available offices to keep cash flow going. We had a very varied bunch of tenants. We tried to get boat orientated people to take them, but many enquiries came from a variety of trades. This went well and we were over 50% occupied within 18 months.

Meanwhile, the marina berths and pontoons were becoming available and to our delight, these filled up steadily and after 12 months we were half full. At the start we kept the berthing fees below those of other Hamble River marinas. We had a substantial HQ building, housing a chandlery, snack bar and bar, piermasters offices, etc.

I had my offices with a small staff of 4, dealing with berthing accounts, catering and general sales of office space, boat storage, and so on.

The Hamble Point Marina ran well and in a few years we had waiting lists for berthing and storage. The better offices were all taken and only a few smaller ones were available. We had gradually increased the rates until the marina was showing a healthy return. Our Dutch owners seemed satisfied, but always wanted more.

I was married to Heather at this time and we lived in a nearby village, Titchfield. We decided that it was better not to be on call in Hamble, as boat owners are "ruthless" about finding out about their boats or reporting problems at all hours of the day, or night. Quite by chance, the house in Titchfield was in the adjoining telephone book, being to the east of the Hamble River and consequently, everyone thought I was ex-directory!! We had a very nice house in the village with a large enough garden and laid back from the village street.

The Hamble Point Marina continued going well. We were gradually adding new features to the site, and equipment, and the turnover and profit increased considerably. This happy existence was not to last, unfortunately. The first blow was my wife, Heather, developing breast cancer. This was a real set back and the rapid development was distressing to say the least. The second shock was an offer to Pon in Holland of a substantial amount to purchase Hamble Point! This was an offer which Pon could not refuse and after negotiations, the sale went through. I was over 65 years by now and quite understandably, the new company wanted to put their own manager in. After a very short handover, I packed up my things, I think "cleared my desk" is the term. My "regular" term of work was finally over and I did not look forward to a life of no responsibilities. However, I quickly found some work which was in my field. A friend, Vic Simmonds, had started a small company, making marina pontoons and general steel work connected with the marina industry. This involved travelling the country, looking at marina sites and quoting for additional berths, etc., following up enquiries for boat cradles, dredging work, in fact, anything which Vic and his chaps could handle. I had plenty of time off for travelling, but enough work to keep me motivated.

In early 1996 I was asked to join a "Gathering of Eagles" in Montgomery, Alabama USA. This is an association of aviators from all over the world who have been involved in aerial exploits of widely different natures.

Jane and I were flown over to Atlanta via Germany and Lufthansa and on down to Alabama. Davd McFarland organises the people involved. This year it included such people as Chuck Yeager, first to exceed Mach 1, Richard Knoblock, pilot in Doolittle's Raid on Tokyo from a US carrier, Sabina Gokeen, Turkish lady fighter pilot from the 30s, and so on. Eighteen in all.

We stopped en route to Montgomery to be kitted out in blazers etc., green (!) with tie to match. Part of "The Duty" was for each Eagle to sign his name on a splendid print, 30" × 28", showing pictures of each person and the aircraft they flew. We had 1,000 prints to sign! No escape!

A video was made of each person answering questions about their exploits which later was shown to the audience from the USAF Air Command and Staff College and to the other Eagles. Each Eagle sat on the stage and after the video answered questions from the audience. A six-day event and three very relaxed days on the Gulf coast in a house lent by the Novosel Family, both father and son great helicopter pilots. Father an Eagle well-decorated for his bravery in Vietnam rescuing wounded troops.

A great adventure made even better by the kindness of the Americans involved.

At about this time, Jane, my future partner, gave me a birthday present of "A Trial Flight in a Glider". There had been a gap of some 25 years in my flying life. I was thrilled to get in the air again and had three flights with Brenda Pridal, a good friend from Hamble. Brenda and her husband, a BAA captain on Jumbos, gave me lots of encouragement. I joined the Gliding Club at Lasham, had come instruction and having gone solo on my third flight, was away doing as much as I could afford.

I found the whole scene very exhilarating and, apart from reaching instinctively for the throttle when undershooting on the approach, became acclimatised very soon. The experience of flying silently, manoeuvring about to stay in thermals and to climb effortlessly, was magic.

I progressed steadily and did my air experience instructors course which gave me a lot of flying at minimum expense, taking all sorts of people flying and letting them handle the glider, hoping they might get the "bug" and join the club. Only one in fifty were of the type who showed signs of wanting to continue flying. The majority had been given a flight as a birthday or Christmas present. Nearly all thoroughly enjoyed the experience.

Once I had climbed the ladder of experience a little, I enjoyed attempting cross-country trips and visiting other gliding sites in different parts of the UK. The most thrilling were trips to Aboyne in Scotland where we were flying in the mountains and experiencing "wave" flying. This is quite unique. Having been aero towed up through an area of extreme rough air, known as "rota", all is suddenly smooth and quiet and the rate of climb increases steadily and, with luck, a rate of climb of 2,000-3,000 feet per minute can be maintained (more in some instances). The experience is just like going up in a fast lift, silent and rock steady. This may keep going until tens of thousands of feet are below you. But not always.

I made many trips to Scotland, searching for wave but only had less than half a dozen successes – I was able to obtain my "Gold" badge which is a gain of 3,000 metres or 9,834 feet. This involves using oxygen and wrapping up thoroughly, as the only form of heating is from your own body!

One feature of high flying which can be disturbing is the misting up of the cockpit canopy on descent. The whole aircraft gets very cold with temperatures of minus 40 degrees and lower. This low temperature soaks into all parts of the glider and having descended into relatively moist, warm air, the whole screen is covered by a thin layer of ice. The small 4" X 4" clear view panel on the side of the canopy is all you can see for a reference of the ground and it seems to take for ever for the windscreen to thaw and clear.

Cross-country flying is exciting but can be very hard work depending on the thermal activity, the wind, the height of the cloud base, and so on. I was not an expert in finding thermals and staying in them to gain the maximum of height in a reasonably short length of time. If there is some wind, all the time you are circling in the thermal, the glider is blown along and, unless the wind is in the right direction, a lot of ground can be lost. The experts tend to do half or one full circle in the thermal and swing back on to track, picking up another thermal en route, achieving cross-country speeds of 100 kms per hour and more. Those days may come for me perhaps!

Another feature of cross-country flying, which everyone has to face up to, is "landing out". If one is unable to sustain a reasonable height, a landing must be made. All the time one is flying, it is important to keep a possible landing site in mind, if not in view. I am addicted to airfields. These areas are safe with good approaches and probably with someone on the ground to assist if required, with the added advantage that it is usually possible to get an air tow back to base, saving a long tow for the crew and trailer and having to unrig the glider and reassemble back at base. However, these are by no means always at hand. I have landed in many fields, gallops, etc., etc. All very interesting but very time wasting. Farmers are usually helpful, but not always!

My last gliding experience was very exciting and although a bit expensive, was "once in a lifetime". A party of eight Lasham members, including myself, flew out to Nevada, USA with hopes that we might get the wave from the Sierra Mountains. We went through the necessary formalities with the US Flying Authorities as we only had British Gliding Authority Licences. This was soon done with some very co-operative officials at Reno Airport. We then had site familiarity flight checks with the gliding clubs at Minden Airbase, about 60 miles south of Reno. Having familiarised ourselves on the various types, we did local soaring, climbing regularly to 20,000 feet in the excellent thermals. Still no wave but on day 6, the weather looked promising and I went off, armed with a signed and sealed barograph and oxygen in a Grob 102 Glider. The temperature on the ground was in the 80's. However, it was necessary to wear warm clothing, gloves, extra socks, etc. Wave had been reported, so off I went, being towed up to 6,000-7,000 feet by the powered tug. When the rate of climb exceeded 1,000 feet per minute, I released the tow rope and then dipped the glider down to establish a "notch" on the barometer trace, indicating that the attempted climb had started.

The aim of the flight was to establish a gain in height from the release point, in excess of 16,500 feet, which would entitle me to improve my Gold badge, achieved in Scotland, to a Diamond. I climbed to 17,500 feet steadily, keeping as far as possible in the same area in order to stay in the wave. The local air traffic rules were that 18,000 feet was the limit, unless the local air traffic control opened a "gate" to allow one to climb above this height. I called Reno to report my position and requested clearance above 18,000 feet. They soon replied and approved my climb, I proceeded up to 23,000 feet, still climbing in dead smooth airand going up as though I was in a lift. Magic, I broke off the climb at 23,500 feet and circled to establish my position and started a slow descent. When I broke through scattered cloud, I was about 30 miles south of Minden and there was a large accumulation of very black clouds to the north. I descended as rapidly as possible and landed at Minden with a total flight time of 50 minutes. A rapid flight and successful. My Diamond flight was approved by the US authorities.

Everyone in the flying fraternity in the US was very helpful and the spirit and comradeship among the members of Minden "High Country Soaring" Club, was wonderful.

Now I am back in the village of Titchfield with my partner of 10 years, Jane, who "kickstarted" my gliding experience with the birthday present of a flight from Lasham, and dreaming about going to Nevada again to do my other legs of Gold or Diamond cross-country flights in the wonderful conditions prevailing. Time and the Bank Manager permitting!

Those words were written in 1999 and since then that edition has sold out and I have written an extra chapter about my wartime years, primarily as a navy flyer, which starts overleaf.

MY WARTIME YEARS

L.P. Twiss Naval Airman 2nd Class 1939-1944

I had a fairly normal transition from flying training to joining an operational squadron but a few incidents spring to mind after all these years.

My first experience of war, apart from being on the receiving end of many air raids in London, Southampton and Yeovil Somerset, was an opportunity to 'have a go', to fight back. I was, at this time, at the Naval Fighter School at Yeovilton, Somerset – 759 Squadron, 11th October 1940.

The fighter school had Gloster Gladiators for training purposes, some of which were kept armed and could be used against the Luftwaffe, if the opportunity arose. One day when the 'red alert' was on, meaning there was a possible air raid in the offing, we heard the unmistakable drone of German aircraft which were on their way to bomb Yeovil/Sherborne, five miles away.

I climbed into one of the Gladiators, taxied out and took off, not having a clue what was happening or where! I took the aircraft up to the west in the general direction of Yeovil and continued to climb, putting on my oxygen mask at 10,000 feet. There was no sign of any aircraft and no information over the R/T. At about 15,000 feet I had still not seen anything when suddenly two RAF Spitfires flew past at great speed, looking at my aircraft. I then realised I was fortunate not to have been shot at! Deciding that I was probably more of an embarrassment than an asset, I turned around and flew back to Yeovilton.

When I landed I was told there had been a major air raid on Yeovil and Sherborne. Later I learned that some Italian CR42s had been among the raiders near Southampton and that I was perhaps lucky, as the two Spitfires I encountered could easily have mistaken me for the very similar CR42 Italian biplanes. Lucky me.

Later I met up with some friends in Sherborne, which had suffered serious damage during the raid, who suggested that the bombing could have been the Luftwaffe aircraft jettisoning their bombs when the Spitfires had attacked them.

My first operational sortie was not a great success, but it had taught me a good lesson. At least Gladiator N5540 had got me safely back to Yeovilton.

Posted to RN Air Station Hatston 771 Squadron:
The Far and Frozen North

There was a requirement for twin-engine trained pilots to join 771 Squadron at RNAS Hatston in the Orkney Islands.

Sub-Lieutenant Harris and myself were sent to RAF Andover, to the School of Army Cooperation, to do a conversion onto twin-engine Blenheims. We went there in November 1940 where, after a few hours of dual, we were let loose on a Blenheim to get twin-engine experience.

Inevitably, we visited Yeovilton by air to show off the Blenheim. After a steady low pass over the airfield by myself, S/Lt Harris, my co-pilot, said he would like to have a go and took over. His idea of a low pass was *very* low, so much so that as we approached the hangars we were below the height of them. I shouted at him and took over by pulling back on the control column. Most of us missed the hangar but we heard an ugly thump and realised that we had in fact hit the corner of it!

On the way back to Andover, we decided a heavy landing was called for, which Harris just about managed. We pulled up at the end of the landing run, stopped the engines in the middle of the grass airfield and got out to see the worst. The tail wheel was missing, no doubt having been deposited on the corner of the Yeovilton hangar.

We reported a heavy landing to the staff at Andover and apart from some remarks from pilots at Yeovilton to us, this was the last we heard of it. Things could not have been too bad with the damaged Blenheim, as I note in my log book that we flew the same aircraft later in the day.

On one occasion, 22nd May 1940, sadly not with me aboard, a Hatston Maryland, piloted by Captain Fancourt, carried out a remarkable recce flight over the North Sea to Bergen to find the *Bismarck* had sailed. The British fleet was alerted and the story of the damage done to our fleet well told, but eventually the German battleship was sunk.

Flying with 771 Squadron was very varied and interesting. One task was to provide 'target' for the fleet lying in Scapa Flow and in the surrounding seas. Target aircraft were varied – Blackburn Skuas, Rocs and Hawker Henleys, and we always carried a navigator or air gunner to assist with the radio if required.

We also had a regular commitment to do a met flight every day and pass temperatures, cloud type, etc. up to 12,000 feet to Met HQ in the UK. This was an unpleasant job at times, particularly in the winter months when it involved a dark take-off and climb to altitude (12,000 ft) and usually icing

on the climb and descent. Radio aids were limited. The Fairey Swordfish
was, in many ways, an ideal aircraft for the job because, although slow, it
was safe. The RAF used Gladiators for the same job – a much better
proposition.

The flying from Hatston was very challenging as, being on latitude 60°
north the daylight was almost 22 hours in summer and 7/8 hours in winter
with wet and windy weather. The airfield had narrow runways and there
was trouble if you let a wheel run off the runway, as it was boggy and the
Rocs and Skuas would tip on their noses if you strayed off for only a few
feet. Both aircraft were 'nose heavy'. The land/seascape was very wild but
I found it was easy to navigate with all the islands and lakes.

Leave was not very forthcoming but there were many places to visit on
the islands. The locals were very friendly, although communication was not
easy, as their local brogue was very strong!

If granted, leave to the UK was possible using the regular ferry aircraft,
a De Havilland DH 86, when space was available. This flew down to
Donibristle, near Edinburgh, from where trains to the south were good but
very full, usually standing and sleeping in the corridors, for the whole trip.

I enjoyed the countryside as I was very interested in the wildlife, in
particular the vast range of sea birds around the coasts, a fascination I have
maintained throughout my life.

I was later posted to Belfast to join 804 Squadron, flying Fulmars and
Hurricanes to provide a pool of pilots for the catapult ships, known as
Camships.

The following is an entry in my log book, 10th August 1941.

"Getting lift as passenger on leave from Aldergrove NI to UK.
Engine failure en route. Pilot, Captain Alexander (ferry pilot)
misjudged his landing at Jurby, Isle of Man, 60 miles from NI,
ending up in small field with stone walls! I was in rear of aircraft and
cut my head. I went off to get treatment on the island in a place full
of foreigners from various countries." [The Isle of Man was used as
a 'secure' base for the thousands of non-Brits living in the UK at that
time.]

"Stayed overnight and then by boat to Liverpool. Train to
Salisbury! Leave with headache! At the Livery, Winterslow, after. I
enjoyed leave but, after a week or so, back to Northern Ireland and
then off to Gibraltar to 804A flight on HMS *Audacity*, a small a/c
carrier with a squadron of F4F Grumman Martlets, escorting a large
convoy heading to the Far East. Probably 8/10 knot convoy. Plenty
of sub activity. The Martlets were launched a few times to scare off
German four-engine Condor recce aircraft reporting position of our

convoy to German sub fleets. One German Condor was fired at and damaged. A number of merchant ships were torpedoed during the 10 day trip. Once out of range of France, there was no more trouble from aerial spotting."

We disembarked to the North Front, Gibraltar and formed 804A Squadron where we lived in Nissen huts to start with and used the larger Nissen-type building as officers' mess and ward room.

Our main task was to provide gunnery practice for ships at Gibraltar and the guns on the Rock, using Hawker Hurricanes, to carry out dummy attacks on RN ships in harbour and around the Rock to keep gun crews in practice on ships such as *Ark Royal*, *Malaya* and *Argus*.

In addition we made sorties up the Spanish coast, in the Gulf of Cadiz, to check on incoming aircraft flying out from the UK, some of which had indicated shortage of fuel or other problems. Aircraft flying out to Gibraltar from the UK would have to avoid flying too close to the French coast in the Bay of Biscay to ensure they did not meet up with German aircraft patrolling the area. As a result the UK to Gib flight was likely to be over 1,500 miles from a take-off in Cornwall to Gibraltar and be 10 hours flying, nearing max endurance at cruising conditions and not allowing much for take-off and climb.

We would alert nearby naval patrol ships in the Straits (of Gibraltar) that their presence might be required. One such sortie was to locate a Swordfish which had crash-landed on the North African coast, crew unharmed. We sent a signal to Gibraltar giving their position, and later saw a high speed launch locate the spot and give aid to the crew.

By this time my new squadron, 807 Squadron, based on the aircraft carrier HMS *Argus* or ashore at the North Front Gibraltar were doing regular reconnaissance flights from the North Front to the North African north-west coast to check the position of the French battleship *Jean Bart*, which had escaped from France on the German occupation and moved to North Africa. She was a formidable ship, which could do untold damage to UK convoys, and had to be regularly spotted. We would take a Fulmar and fly round the north-west point of Africa, Cap Spartel near Tangier and fly south, approximately 150 miles, to the harbour of Casablanca where the battleship was lying.

We would climb to 8-10,000 feet, 10 miles offshore, locate the target, take a number of photographs (assuming it was there) and beat a hasty retreat. On a number of occasions French fighter aircraft were observed and anti-aircraft bursts could be seen well clear of us, the target. But when the ship was spotted in the harbour it was back to Gibraltar with the photos showing the battleship and a report, which gave some relief to the naval authorities. The round trip in the Fulmar was over three hours. It was May with clear skies and uncomfortably high temperatures, particularly at low altitudes.

A few weeks after this we had what was nicknamed the 'club run', escorting Spitfires to Malta. HMS *Argus* had too short a flight deck for flying these Spitfires off, with their large (180 + gallons) overload tanks, so we provided additional fighter escort for the larger carriers carrying the Spitfires and Force 'H' cruisers and destroyers. Often US carriers were used for the Spitfires with their long decks and 25-30 knot speed range.

The usual routine was to fly off the Spitfires approximately 350/400 miles from Malta. They would use up the fuel in the long-range tanks first and be in a position to jettison them if enemy aircraft were encountered, so as to get rid of the extra drag as soon as the fuel had been used.

The fleet would turn westwards, south of Sardinia, to avoid the Italian and German bombers, such as SM79s or JU88s. The small fighter force of Fulmars and Hurricanes with the fleet were usually kept busy until the British fleet was north and east of Algiers, approximately 500 miles from Gibraltar. The naval escort were occupied with Italian and German U-boats. The squadron Fulmars were also on call to fend off Italian bombers from Sardinia and elsewhere.

On one of the early runs, we attempted to fly off Fairey Albacores to Malta. These were to reinforce the hard-pressed Swordfish, which night after night would attack German shipping, which was taking supplies from Italy to North Africa. Unfortunately, the Albacores had not been used in the Mediterranean climate. This caused the engine oil temperatures to soar to unacceptable levels and the aircraft had to be recovered for modifications at Gibraltar.

On 14th June 1942 we embarked on HMS *Eagle*. 807 Squadron provided fighter cover and escort for a mixed convoy including the US aircraft carrier *Eagle* bound for Malta, Operation Harpoon. There were a number of merchant ships with vital supplies for Malta and two or three carriers with destroyer escorts. The speed of the convoy was limited to the maximum speed of the slowest merchant ship, probably 12-14 knots. As soon as the leading ships got within range of the Sardinia-based aircraft, Italian or German (approx 50 miles SSW of Sardinia) Italian Savoia bombers, accompanied by CR42 fighters, appeared over the convoy.

The CO, Fraser Harris, and I intercepted the fighters and a dogfight ensued. I was turning as tight as the Fulmar allowed and taking shots whenever possible. Both CR42s were badly damaged and one Italian pilot baled out. Luckily we suffered no damage. There was no doubt that a Fulmar on its own would have been in trouble. However, the Italians did not press their attack – fortunately for us. We claimed two aircraft destroyed (from 355ª Squadriglia) and retired to HMS *Argus* for fuel and more ammunition. During this operation three of 807 Squadron pilots were all shot down in their Fulmars.

Later on in the day, an Italian BR20 was snooping around the fleet. I had a small speed advantage and attacked from astern. However, his rear gunner was active. He managed to place a bullet in my Fulmar's propeller mechanism, which showered quantities of engine oil all over the windscreen and me. This meant that I had to open the hood to maintain visibility. I broke off my attack and worked my way towards the centre of the fleet. I had to fly low; even so, the escort destroyer took a pot at me, which fortunately missed.

I warned the carrier of my lack of clear vision. *Argus* turned into wind to receive me and it was a very oily Peter Twiss who arrived on deck to be taken down to the MO to have oil removed from his eyes!

During the brief engagement, I managed to damage the ailerons of the BR20, but lack of visibility prevented my knowing if there was any other damage suffered. My observer on both claims was Pty Off (A) R. Holroyd.

Commander R. Mike Crosley, DSC, RN, wrote in his book *They Gave Me a Seafire*:

> "That same evening, the dusk patrol – Lieutenant Fraser Harris and Sub-Lieutenant Peter Twiss (who later became Chief Test Pilot of the Fairey Aviation Company) – came on board in their Fairey Fulmars. They were the CO and Senior Pilot of 807 Squadron in *Argus*. Pete's aircraft had a cannon shell hole in its airscrew spinner and the whole of the oil in the constant speed unit had blown back and covered his windscreen. He managed to see the deck by hanging his head out to one side. Even then, his goggles were covered in the stuff and were almost impossible to see through. Yet when he landed, he did not bother to tell any of us about it."

The next day, while on patrol, I spotted two SM79 torpedo bombers up at around 7,000 feet. They split up and made off away from our fleet. The one I chased was nearly as fast as the Fulmar and I followed it in and out of clouds but it eventually evaded me. By this time I was some distance from the fleet and getting low on fuel. I was unable to raise a call for a bearing to the ship and used valuable and rapidly diminishing fuel searching for *Eagle* or *Argus*. So by now I was contemplating ditching procedures.

The welcome sight of one of the small convoy escort vessels was a great relief. However, he didn't seem to think the same and loosed off some anti-aircraft fire at me. My crew, Leading Air Gunner Philip, fired off some Very cartridges, which were the colours for the day, and which stopped the

firing. In a few minutes I was joining *Eagle* for a landing and was relieved
to land first time with the fuel gauge now showing zero. What a joy to feel
the hook catch an arrester wire!

The navigator or air gunner we carried in our aircraft did not have a
machine gun and consequently often felt inadequate. However, they had
W/T radio and could keep in touch with the fleet when radio silence could
be broken.

We often gave them a tommy gun, which gave some moral support, and
from the pilot's point of view they could be very helpful, as long as they
remembered to open the hatch before firing! They could also assist with
spotting aircraft and shipping and gave the pilot advice on 'friend or foe',
where a second pair of eyes are always beneficial. The CO would have a
commissioned navigator for leading the squadron on any sortie involving
four or six aircraft.

This was the last operation 807 Squadron carried out before returning
with the Fulmars to the UK. We flew off as a squadron to Abbotsinch
(Scotland) and on south to Yeovilton and Lee-on-Solent to hand over the
well-worn Fulmars to be re-equipped with Seafires, the navalised Spitfire,
becoming the first Naval Spitfire Squadron in July 1942.

The Spitfire Era
In autumn 1941 the powers that decided these things allowed the FAA to
obtain 400 Spitfires, MkVBs and VCs. The Seafires in the early days were
Spitfires with arrester hooks, folding wings, reinforcing for additional
structural loads for the arrester hook, and wing fold slinging points.

A trial Spit, Mark VB, was therefore fitted with an arrester hook and
slinging points for initial trials on HMS *Illustrious*. The trials showed that
the project was worth proceeding with and after further trials on HMS
Victorious in April 1942, which were successful, the name Seafire was
adopted.

The Seafire 807 Squadron moved from Lee-on-Solent to Yeovilton
during the early part of July 1942, where we started flying practice on our
new Seafire IICs, accumulating experience in slow flying formation,
aerobatics and general manoeuvring. We also tried take-offs to simulate
low wind conditions on the carrier. Although the Seafire had flaps, they
were intended for use when landing to provide drag on the very clean
configuration of the aircraft, which often resulted in 'float' and an excessive
run. We were more concerned with shortening the take-off from the carrier
deck. To this end we wanted to use the flaps to provide additional lift, and
to enable this to happen, use the existing flaps by lowering them to
approximately one-third of their travel, thus giving positive lift. We made
up lightweight wooden chocks to fit under the wings and on to which the

flaps would be allowed to retract. These were held in position by ground crew until the retracted flaps held them firmly. As soon as the aircraft was airborne, the pilot would select 'flaps down' very briefly and the chocks would fall away. This worked well and consistently shorter take-off runs were achieved. On board ship they would fall onto the forward part of the flight deck or onto the ship's foredeck and were usually recovered to be used again.

Practice flying continued at Yeovilton for some weeks, involving firing tests over the sea using the 20mm cannons and towed targets operating from Exeter, formation flying and, finally, towards the end of August the squadron set off in formation to Machrihanish on the Mull of Kintyre on the west coast of Scotland.

We carried out a series of ADDLs or Aircraft Dummy Deck Landings using a batsman on the runway in use, to familiarise us with the optimum approach technique for deck landings. This was very important to do prior to actually landing on the carrier deck. It all seemed so easy!

Our carrier, HMS *Furious* was operating in the Firth of Clyde and the north channel, about 30 miles south of Machrihanish, off the north-east coast of Ireland.

My first attempt to land on the carrier, on 4th September, resulted in a prang! I had made a classical mistake of touching down with some slight drift on. I had followed the deck officer's signals right through but, as I got his 'cut' signal, I left a small amount of 'crab' which I had used on the final stages of the approach to keep the batsman clearly in view past the long nose of the aircraft. Easy to do, but with a Seafire's undercarriage, not good news. The undercarriage collapsed and the wooden propeller was damaged. I was flown ashore in an Albacore to Machrihanish where I did a succession of ADDLs to cure me of this habit of continuing to yaw the Seafire after passing the batsman on deck. Once grasped, no trouble in the future. It reminded me that the Seafire could not be treated like the old rugged Fulmar!

Next day, success. I landed on deck OK.

HMS *Furious* was an old ship originally built for a South American country and sold back to the UK between the wars. She was fast, 32 knots, and lightly armed. She carried two squadrons of fighters, in our time Seafires, and two squadrons of Albacores or Swordfish. Rather antiquated quarters for the aircrew, slightly better for the ship's officers.

We stayed in the area onboard *Furious* and at Hatston for a few days flying exercises and finally embarked the squadron aircraft for departure to Gibraltar in mid October 1942; we were lucky to have a small fast convoy running at 20 knots until within range of the North Front, Gibraltar's air strip, 25th October 1942. There was one E – W runway with the sea at either end. I had spent some time here in 804 Squadron while disembarked from HMS *Furious* and *Argus*.

Having been ashore for a week, sleeping in bell tents, we were launched into Operation Torch. This was to be part of the reclaiming of North Africa from the French.

The convoy which entered the Mediterranean was huge, with a capital H. One of our jobs was to act as fighter escort to deal with the French fighters and other opposing aircraft, to enable the British and American invasion force to take control. The French had a small but efficient fighter, the Dewoitine 520, which was fast and well armed and the French fighter pilots were, contrary to some reports, well trained and determined. Our part of the total naval fighter force was quite small as there were several British carriers, each with at least one fighter squadron.

On 7th November 1942 our first task was to carry out a recce over the local airfield, La Senia, and report any troop movements. I flew my Seafire escorted by five others from my squadron to recce the airfield. Before we reached La Senia I spotted a flight of six or seven French Dewoitines diving down to engage my escort. I left the escort to deal with the French and dived down to check troop movements at La Senia and any other hostile activities. I saw some tank movements, which I reported back to HMS *Furious*. At the same time, I noted an American group of tanks approaching the airfield. I could not communicate by radio to report the possible clash, so I decided to land near the US armoured column to warn them of the situation.

I landed on what just seemed to be a runway-like surface and, leaving my engine ticking over, jumped out kicking a small stone in front of each wheel and rushed to speak to the Americans. They were very pleased at the warning and asked a few questions about other local activities, which would help their next move.

I remounted my Seafire and took off on a further recce reporting other tank movements two to three miles ahead. I was now short of fuel and dusk was approaching so I decided to stop for the night at Tafaroui and seek some fuel.

There were two RAF Spitfires which had been landed in the vicinity and two or three RAF personnel carrying out some repairs to them. They were part of a flight which had flown in from Gibraltar and been slightly damaged. They still had quite a reasonable amount of fuel aboard. I explained my position to them, that I had insufficient fuel to return to the carrier and could they help me to refuel my Seafire. They were very helpful, so I left them for a while to find a soft spot to have a kip as I had been up since 3.30am. I had no difficulty in dropping off despite the fact that the ground was as hard as iron. Before I did, I looked around and in one of the huts, now abandoned by the local French, I found a double-barrelled shotgun which I 'borrowed' as at least some form of defence, also a tin of baked beans which I devoured.

I woke up several times during the night imagining scorpions and such like but soon dropped off again. At first light I found the French and the airforce mechanics had managed to extract enough fuel almost to fill the main tank of my Seafire.

When I left Tafaroui to fly back to the ship, I tied the shotgun securely in the fuselage and eventually took it back home to our farm at Winterslow. When I next had some leave I thought I would try the gun on some of the many rabbits there were in the woods. When I walked into the wood and paused to load the gun, I was horrified to find that the 12-bore cartridge dropped into the breech and was a very sloppy fit. The gun was a 10-bore!! It took me some weeks to find a gunsmith who stocked 10-bore cartridges. When I finally did locate some, the gun was a great success having considerably more killing power than my old 12-bore, and was better for duck and geese.

Having left the salt lake, I flew a few miles to Tafaroui airfield but the French Dewoitine pilots were again strafing the airfield and I decided to return to *Furious*. As soon as I had climbed to 2,000 feet I could talk to *Furious* and report my movements and was given a position to rendezvous. Forty-five minutes later I was in the carrier's circuit and landed on deck, glad to be back.

A few days later I set off to air test the Seafire and was horrified to feel a severe restriction of movement on the rudder bar. I contacted the ship and explained my predicament and asked for a landing slot asap.

I made an approach trying to minimise use of the rudder – quite difficult in a Seafire as any slight change of power setting involved some slight rudder movement. I made as good a landing as circumstances would allow. We found, after landing, that the Very pistol was loose from its mounting and had partially restricted the rudder control circuit making it impossible to correct a slight swing on landing, although the arrester wire kept us on deck. The swing resulted in damage to the propeller tip on two blades. Bad news!

It was not my week. Two days later, returning from a one and a half hour patrol, the flap selector was faulty and I had to do a landing without flaps. Rather fast and difficult to keep the batting officer in view.

During these last three fighter patrols, no hostile aircraft were reported and the squadron disembarked to North Front Gibraltar. We were again sleeping in bell tents with salt water for washing and showers.

We had a few days flying practice from North Front. On one flight I must have strayed too near the Spanish coast as they fired a few rounds of ack-ack. It was nice to be able to do some aerobatics and generally fly for fun. Landing at North Front could be quite exciting if the wind was strong. One would approach the runway in use (either east or west). If there was a strong wind from SE or SW the mass of the Rock would result in a total obstruction to the wind, resulting in very rough conditions on the early part of the approach. Then suddenly, the wind speed dropped to nil leaving you with a lot of excess speed to lose in order not to overshoot the runway. This phenomenon resulted in a large number of accidents, in particular to aircraft being flown out from the UK. The crew would be tired after an eight to ten hour flight (or more). Most of the accidents were caused by overshooting the runway, which was about 1,100 yards. I had one more month at Gibraltar based at North Front and then, in February 1943, we returned to the UK in *Furious* to an entirely new world.

Night Fighting

I had been selected to do night fighting, which was something I wanted to do. So, off I went to Hinstock Instrument Flying School (IFS).

The first step was to do an intensive Instrument Flying Course on twin-engine Oxford aircraft and a lot of Link trainer time. This was a complete change from the squadron flying on board ship. However, night fighting involves a high proportion of instrument flying.

From this course I went to Drem in Scotland with 784 Squadron, which gave one a fairly intensive insight into night interceptions and the use of radar and night fighter tactics.

We lived in a beautiful house, which had been offered to the services for the duration by its owners, as quarters for the officers. This was on the edge of a golf course and well into the countryside near North Berwick with views of the sea, in particular the Bass Rock, the home to thousands of sea birds and one of the largest gannet colonies in the world.

We lived in luxury! We were only about five miles from the airfield and close to the A1 main road giving easy access to Edinburgh and our night flying from Drem.

Classroom work on the radar was intense, so that when we put this into actual flying interceptions, there was minimum time wasted. Airborne radar was still in its infancy and we had a lot to learn. The normal routine was for two crews in two Fairey Fulmars to take off together, one being the target aircraft. Having contacted ground control, they would carry out interceptions in turn on each other. The ground control radar would take over at the start and vector the 'fighter' onto the 'target' until the fighter had obtained a signal on its own radar of the target. This usually occurred when the fighter was three to four miles from the target, depending on the skill of the fighter's operator. Once contact had been established, it was up to the fighter's operator to direct his pilot to make an interception. This being at night, it was important for the fighter pilot to keep a *good* lookout for their target and follow the instructions of his radar operator carefully and promptly.

The display the operator had was on a tube showing the radar 'blip' representing the aircraft target above or below the fighter and to port or starboard. Also, the distance that the target was ahead. All this he had to pass to his pilot in a series of instructions, eg "Target to port, below us, at approximately three and a half miles. We are closing slowly. Turn gently port and descend 500 feet" and so on. Violent changes of height or direction had to be avoided to ensure the target was not lost.

So this series of manoeuvres went on until the operator suggested to the pilot that a visual of the target should be possible. As soon as the pilot spotted the target he would report to the ground control radar that contact had been made. It was always better to approach from below to try and silhouette the outline of the target and to avoid being spotted. Once the interception had been made it was usual practice to change around target and fighter.

In these early days of interceptions, the target would fly straight and level to allow maximum advantage to the fighter. As we became more experienced the target would weave about, as would be the case operationally.

The type of radar we were using at this stage was fairly basic as airborne radar was, in the early days, still in its infancy. Even in the very early days of night flying it was important to keep night adapted and having contacted your target, it was vital to keep it in view.

This type of exercise went on for a few weeks until almost 100% interception resulted from the initial contact of the target by the ground control station. Of course the weather was always a big factor and also the state of the moon.

We started off with the target using his navigation lights for safety's sake, but as we became more proficient and knowing that the ground control staff had an overall picture of the local skies, we were able to douse these lights until interception had been established.

Another aspect of interceptions was the height at which both aircraft were above the ground. The radar operator had to be able to differentiate easily between ground returns on his AI set and a clear signal of the target aircraft. A much clearer signal was available away from the ground returns, say 500-1,000 feet.

Night adaptation was all important, (ie no unnecessary white lights in view and to use torches with red screens, etc). Also, we had to keep cockpit lighting as dim as possible. Having contacted your target it was vital to keep it in view. The navigator/radar operator, having made it possible for the pilot to get a visual on the target was not himself night adapted, having been staring into his cathode-ray tube. It would be 60 seconds *minimum* before he would be sufficiently night adapted to see the target. So, it was vital for one or other always to keep the target in view. Should it be necessary for the operator to revert to the radar, the pilot had to maintain the visual contact; often very difficult, as he had to keep in touch with the ground control by R/T which often involved switching R/T channels and, of course, the blind flying instruments should one enter cloud even briefly.

So I finished the naval night fighter course with 784 Squadron at Drem on 16th May 1943. They gave me an 'above average' assessment as a night fighter pilot with no experience of actually meeting the enemy at night! However, it was an excellent grounding of the subject and I looked forward to putting the theory into practice and operationally.

My posting was to 746 Squadron at Ford on the south coast near Arundel, Sussex. The CO of the squadron, Major Skeets Harris, Royal Marines, was an experienced fighter pilot with much time on day time fighter work on carriers and shore stations in the Mediterranean and on Cyprus. His wife, Diana, was the daughter of a RN Admiral Talbot and she was a motorcycle dispatch rider based in the Portsmouth area.

746 Naval Squadron was attached to the RAF unit, the Fighter Interception Unit (FIU), which conducted trials under operational conditions based at Ford airfield. Their CO was Group Captain Chris Hartley.

The two units, RN and RAF, worked as one, carrying out trials, which involved RAF and RN, plus operations against the German night fighters. These trials often resulted in actual operations over France and the continent. There were a number of successes intruding and in anti-buzzbomb operations.

Our base was at RAF Ford, with a very comfortable mess shared by both units, and Tortington Hall, a girls' school, taken over for the duration. The notices above the beds, RING TWICE FOR A MISTRESS, caused much amusement, but no results!

RAF Ford was a very happy station and sadly, when the invasion of Europe became imminent, we were moved up to West Wittering near Peterborough to make room for fighter squadrons, who were taking part in the invasion of Europe and giving fighter cover to the invasion fleet.

However, during my time with the Night Fighter Interception Squadron (NFIU) at Ford and Wittering, we had opportunities to take part in various operations.

Night Intruding
The Fighter Interception Unit, in order to extend its experience of the MkVIII radar and recommend tactics for using it best, was given clearance to take the equipment over the Channel to the continent.

Our bomber fleets were regularly bombing a number of targets deep into Europe and were being beset by German night fighters operating from many enemy airfields in France, Holland, Belgium and Germany.

The FIU got the brief to send two Mosquitoes per night to patrol airfields, which were known to operate night fighters returning from harassing our bombers going back to the UK after their raid. Our FIU crews had a thorough briefing two to three hours before take-off being given various information such as:

- Details of the RAF bomber targets for the night and as much as was known about the likely airfields the Germans would use and any other aerial operation likely to be on the track of, or in the vicinity of, the target.
- The 'colours of the night', ie which colour cartridges were needed to reply to a challenge from air or ground, and the areas known to have strong anti-aircraft fire.
- Known operations being carried out by US or UK aerial forces which should be avoided. Diversionary UK airfields with suitable aids in case of bad weather, etc, etc.

The aircraft to be used were picked out and prepared during the afternoon, filled with fuel, ammo for the 20mm cannons, radar and radio checks, and a loaded camera gun.

Briefing for the crews either took place at home base, Wittering or Ford, or at an airfield with briefing facilities en route for the coast – often Manston in Kent or Coltishall (near Wroxham, Norfolk).

During the dress up for the trip, we had to empty our pockets to ensure every piece of evidence which might give a German interrogator confirmation of where we started from in the event of our being shot down, was left behind. The special pack, which we all took on overseas ops, and included escape aids, maps, money (correct for country) and a compass, was handed over to each crew member to include on his person while dressing for the flight. It was hidden as best as possible, but often unfortunately discovered while being searched! The special compasses might be undiscovered during the initial search and get through to a POW camp where they would be useful.

There were two secret devices that I remember – a collar stud which would reveal a magnetic needle if the paint was scraped from the base and a metal fly button which could be balanced on another, giving a rough compass bearing. I am still not sure how we managed with no fly buttons! While dressing it was important to include a small sharp knife and a torch with a red filter.

These details would be completed in good time for take-off, the crews would board the aircraft and avoiding radio chatter, taxi out to the duty runway, and carry out essential cockpit checks. Take-off would go something like this: flash Air Traffic Control with the period 'letter' and switch off the navigation lights when lined up on the runway. Then, after a final cockpit check, open up gently to avoid a swing, getting the tail up as soon as possible for maximum control and ease the aircraft into the air and select wheels up. When safely airborne, ensure throttle clamped fully open, change hands with right hand on stick. When safe single engine speed reached, about 175 knots, ease back to best climbing rpm and turn out of circuit.

At an early stage, while near airfield, turn onto the Pole star, (approx north) and check compass, cloud permitting. Carry out mutual crew checks, oxygen OK. Turn onto first course. The navigator would be doing his checks on radar, Gee and reporting to the pilot his estimate of time for crossing the English coast. As you reached this point, you would reduce height to approximately 500 feet above sea or ground level to avoid enemy radar and adjust course to ensure you were crossing the enemy coast at a point known to be reasonably free from intense anti-aircraft fire and searchlights.

During the early part of the trip it was important to check wind speed and direction for navigation purposes. Height would be gradually reduced to approximately 200-300 feet above sea level. A few minutes before the estimate for crossing the enemy coast, we would open up to maximum continuous power and climb to avoid small arms fire and finally cross in at a speed to confuse anti-aircraft fire – probably 240-250 mph. Having crossed the coast, height would be reduced to 500 feet until enemy radar was passed, map reading was done as soon as time permitted and we generally remained at 500 feet or less (terrain permitting) until safely through the coastal belt. The German radar interfered with the VHF when 2-3 miles distant. We would then climb to 3-4,000 feet and switch on our radar, all the time keeping a watch for any activities near airfields and noting where searchlights were active. A note of these positions was taken back to base for recording during future briefings.

My navigator, Dennis Lake, was ideal; calm, even when other aerial activity was present, he did not get excited, carrying on doing his job using radar and checking our position with Gee. While flying at about 200 mph, we would weave about to check that our tail was clear, ie that there was no sign of any other aircraft astern. Dennis concentrated on the radar, particularly when close to known airfields.

At frequent intervals he would check our position on Gee while keeping a weather eye on our radar. It was often found better to be clear of an airfield circuit to avoid anti-aircraft crews reporting noise from the Mosquito and passing a position to the searchlights or gun crews. All our aircraft would be on a common VHF frequency. Near airfields I found that keeping a good visual look-out often resulted in a contact which could be followed up by the radar.

On 15th June 1944, we were close to the circuit of an airfield near Lâon, which was our target. There was some activity. Every now and again the airfield runway lights would be switched on briefly, indicating that some German aircraft had managed to land. They had probably crept in at low altitude, too low for our radar to pick them up and switched off their lights as soon as a landing was made. The timing was about right for enemy night fighters to be returning to their base, to be refuelled and rearmed having had some contact with our bomber fleet, and they would be looking forward to some supper and a rest. The anti-aircraft fire from the airfield defence system was strong and it was not worth stirring it up unless a Jerry could be identified clear of the airfield.

Sure enough we spotted and identified a JU88 joining the circuit at 3-4,000 feet. From below we had a good silhouette of the aircraft turning towards the airfield. It was important to move quickly, as once the crew was aware of us they would take immediate avoiding action.

We had a mutual arrangement that, after spotting an aircraft and following it visually, if there was any doubt about identification, I would say on VHF, "If you are a British Mosquito, waggle your wings." The reaction on all Mosquitoes in a wide area was immediate, leaving one with no doubts, usually accompanied with a sharp comment on VHF and a violent wing wobble! One could imagine every Mossie within 50 miles plus, waggling as we all used a common VHF frequency while on these sorties.

If there was no reaction to the VHF warning, it was time to take action. Double check with Dennis his estimate of range from the enemy aircraft and compare with our radar. We had to be quick to avoid being spotted by the crew of the JU88 who would have taken violent avoiding action and might soon be warned by German ground radar from Lâon. We opened up the engines to close the gap between us and to position ourselves to be well below and astern.

We could now see a lot of detail of the aircraft and there was still no sign of them spotting us. We double-checked gunsight and guns and closed in gradually until we were 400 feet from the JU88 and ready to open fire. At 300 feet we fired the four 20mm cannons. The noise in the cockpit was *very* loud and everything shook. We had aimed at the port inner wing root and gave a 10-second burst. The noise, after hours of virtual silence, was shattering. There were a lot of strikes on the JU88's inner wing section and port engine.

The reaction from the German crew was not apparent. It seems certain that the pilot(s) were hit. The aircraft went into a port turn and lost height with signs of smoke from the port engine. The JU88 increased its loss of height and the dive to port and crashed near the airfield with flames and smoke. We took this as a kill and the anti-aircraft fire from around the airfield increased. We then turned away from the airfield in the direction of some cloud, which would give some cover from further anti-aircraft fire and German fighters.

As we had limited ammo and fuel in hand, we turned onto a westerly direction to aim for home and headed towards some cloud cover, which we thought might prove to be helpful. No other aircraft were seen. We had been airborne for just over three hours so decided to call it a night and look around for a train or land target on the way home. Occasionally a lapse in household blackout resulted in a door being open for a short period but rapidly shut, no doubt when the householder heard our Mosquito!

During our return, we spotted a train loaded with gear but not much passenger accommodation. It was worth a dive down from 2,500 feet to 300 feet for a short burst. No great success, no doubt a very frightened driver and stoker but not worth another go, so we resumed our homeward course.

The small amount of cloud cover was comforting. We opened up to a fast cruise speed, crossing the coast to the west of Dover. En route we saw a number of V1 buzzbombs winging their way over the Channel to the UK but not near enough to catch. Not that the normal Mosquito had the legs to overtake a V1 in level flight. One might be lucky to be in a position to dive on one for a fleeting shot. Later modifications to the Merlins produced enough power to overtake the V1s.

Being unmanned, the V1 seemed impregnable. From a few hundred feet astern, the throb from the engine seemed unstoppable but with a burst of 20mm in the right spot, silence suddenly prevailed and it was time to peel off.

Every V1 that escaped, however, probably resulted in a large loss of life from the ground below, particularly in a built-up area. Nevertheless, the risk of receiving damage from an exploding V1 was considerable and it paid not to approach too close.

We landed at Ford where we knew the night-flying supper was good and with mushrooms off the airfield. After supper and refuelling we flew back to Wittering, taking 40 minutes, and so to bed.

During the next two or three weeks we managed ten more intruder flights with one JU88 destroyed, on 7th August at Melun, and numerous ineffective attacks on buzzbombs! Always very tempting to try but a waste of fuel.

I see from my log book that the squadron, ie NFIU and FIU, went off in our Wellington III on 15th July with eight bodies, to the wedding of Slim Holme, one of our naval pilots. We flew into Ford from Wittering. A good party but, as Duty Pilot, I had to remain on 'top limb' for return to Ford the next day. Particularly as I had an op on 16th July with Flying Officer Lake on an anti-Diver ('Diver' was the code-word for V1) patrol, 3 hours 15 mins, but with no success. No doubt I felt a lot better than some of Slim's guests.

I carried on doing as many intruder operations as possible with the Fighter Interception Unit. Overall I did seventeen sorties to a variety of areas, wherever possible, with Dennis Lake. Sadly, while I was in the USA Dennis was killed in an unfortunate and needless accident in a Mosquito. He was flying with one of the FIU pilots on a local exercise and at the end of the sortie the pilot decided to do some aerobatics around the airfield at Ford, which resulted in a crash in which both pilot and Dennis were killed. What a waste. Both had top notch skills and were first rate people.

These were the last of my intruder ops as I was sent over to the USA for some more night flying trials on the new radar the RN was buying, and after that to the Empire Test Pilots' School at Boscombe Down.

Visit to the USA
In the summer of 1944 the RN was close to forming a night fighter squadron to be carrier based and equipped with a mixture of aircraft; the Fairey Firefly, a two-seater and the Grumman Hellcat or S6F, single-seater fighters both equipped with an American radar ASH. It was very satisfying having a good pilot or observer operator radar set, which had good performance and was simple to use. The US marines preferred to use theirs in single seaters, pilot operated. The Brits of course stuck to their observer-operated system for some years to come!

Skeets Harris was involved in forming a detachment from 746 at Ford/Wittering to go to the USA to learn about US naval carrier-based night fighter units. He was to form the squadron and gather together RN and Royal Marine pilots and observers who had some knowledge of radar operation, night flying, etc, etc. He picked a small group of two pilots and two observers (radar operators) and himself. I was included in the unit.

Skeets and myself had been working with NFIU at RAF Ford and RAF Wittering, flying all the RAF types such as Mosquitoes and Beaufighters, and using RN and RAF radar operators and all of us had been on night intruder operations in Beaufighters and Mosquitoes. The Firefly was unsuitable for this type of operation due to lack of performance against the German JU88 and ME 110s.

However, the RN had on order some Grumman F6Fs and Chance Vought Corsairs, which would form the nucleus of ship-borne night fighter units in the future.

We had received some of the Grumman F6Fs (Hellcats) already equipped with the radar. We also had the loan of a twin-engine Beechcraft Expeditor similarly equipped with radar, and four seats to enable the navigators to familiarise themselves with the equipment.

We travelled over in style, on the *Queen Mary*, joining ship on the Clyde with 20,000 others. They were mostly US service personnel being redrafted to the Far East. The ship was so full that we shared the bunks, having 12 hours in and then out – known as hot bunking! We had two meals a day with a good standard of grub but not many spaces to sit down to eat.

The *Queen Mary* set off at 30 knots plus and soon outdistanced our escort, a cruiser and two destroyers, which could not keep up in the open sea. Speed was of the essence to avoid U-boats, which had little chance of a hit. Thank God! She was an amazing vessel, which made countless trips like this to all parts, never having a problem evading the enemy.

We were to go to the States as the guests of the US Navy and Marine Corps to work with them, learn about the equipment and how to use it operationally and devise tactics which the RN squadrons would use when the equipment was fitted to US and British carrier-borne fighters which the RN was purchasing from the US.

All very exciting and interesting.

Our party duly arrived in New York and after a couple of nights moved up country to a US naval air station, Quonset Point, near Providence, Rhode Island – an hour's flying from New York. We were all given a US Navy briefing and welcome. We had been allocated two F6F Fighters and a Beechcraft Expeditor, a twin-engine trainer with four or five seats.

These were to be equipped with the radar equipment ASH that the Brits had ordered for the RN Night Fighter Squadrons to be fitted in the UK. We had plenty of good training on the equipment on the ground and in the air from the radar company's representative, Dave Manheimer.

We concentrated on flying the Expeditor with the radar and held off using the equipment in the single-seat F6Fs due to safety reasons. The pilot should be aware of other aircraft flying and not have his head buried in his cockpit, especially flying in the USA with all the air traffic.

I was diverted for some other duties after a week or so and went down to Washington to meet up with the British Navy Office including Captain Dennis Campbell, who had some other duties he wanted me to do. Dennis was a very well known Fleet Air Arm pilot with a mass of experience and he required me to visit a number of places to fly and report on projects that

Top left: A Fulmar undergoing an Airfield Dummy Deck Landing (ADDL) at Yeovilton, 1941. *(With thanks to the FAA, Yeovilton for some of the photos in this section.)*

Top right: Author with 807 Sqn Co Fraser Harris on board HMS *Furious*.

Bottom left: Drawing by Michael Scott, a pilot in 804 Sqn, of a rocket-launch Fulmar. This device would be used from a convoy ship if an FW Condor was sighted. The captain of the ship – non-aviation minded! – controlled the launching button.

Bottom right: Montage of 807 Sqn characters. Nicknames written by the author and pasted in his log book.

Top: Another page from the author's log book with the CR42 claim entered and approved.

Middle left: A couple of Italian BR20s, the type damaged by the author in June 1942.

Middle right: Operation Harpoon, June 1942. The convoy gets through despite an almighty battering as shown in this amazing photograph. *Argus* is in the foreground.

Bottom: 807 Squadron at Yeovilton, summer 1942, with the first Seafires. The author is at extreme left.

Top left: The Squadron's Seafire IICs aboard *Furious* in advance of the North African landings in late 1942.

Top right: Author 'hovers' above *Furious*, in his Seafire, November 1942.

Middle: Whirlwind at Yeovilton, 1943.

Bottom left: The devastating fire of the Mosquito night fighter, as demonstrated in the butts.

Bottom right: The author's 'office' in the Mossie. Pilot's control column on left, AI MK VIII radar display unit in front of navigator's seat on right.

Inset, top right: In the USA. Conference at Patuxent River with, left to right, Don Callingham, Dickie Law, ? Read, Dennis Campbell, ? Clarkson and author.

Top: Author wins Lympne Air Race in Firefly IV, 31st August 1947.

Bottom left: In a Tipsy Junior over *Ark Royal* on his birthday, 23rd July 1957.

Bottom right: With Raymond Baxter and Neville Duke at Eastleigh in 1986.

might have been of interest to our FAA.

I started by going off down to join our small unit at Patuxent River, a US Naval Test Centre about 60 miles from Washington. You could describe it as the US equivalent to Boscombe Down. It was a huge, recently built airfield on the river which runs into Chesapeake Bay, about 40 miles from Washington DC.

There were a lot of prototype aircraft being tested by the US Navy pilots; radio and armament trials of all sorts. Being on the river, there was a sea plane, and flying boat facility. All forms of flying took place and, as ever, all very hush, hush.

The resident RN pilot, Commander Don Callingham, put me in touch with various departments and arranged flying in projects that Washington were interested in.

During this time (October/November 1944) the UK had sent out a Supermarine Seafire for the Patuxent Test Centre, and others, to fly. I had the job of test flying it after assembly and also briefing a number of pilots to fly it. Without exception all were *amazed* at the small size of this fighter, which had been the backbone of the Battle of Britain. They all loved its flying characteristics, but wondered if it was beefy enough in its operations. Its performance over the years and many theatres of war, spoke for itself.

I found that it was a good trading partner because in exchange for a flight, I managed to get in the cockpit of a number of American aircraft I was keen to fly.

Towards the end of 1944, while I was still working with the Sperry Company, who were responsible for the AI equipment destined for the British F6Fs, I flew into La Guardia, New York frequently. I was able to garage the Seafire from time to time and they helped inspect and fuel the aircraft. One item caused some bother; this was the engine starting, which used a cartridge starter. As ever, we ran out of cartridges not available in the US!

The lads in New York were able to rig up a bungee system using a leather glove to fit one propeller tip and two lengths of heavy bungee cord to tension out in the direction of propeller rotation. The pilot would get all set for starting, prime the engine, check chocks were firm, get two men on each bungee cord to tighten up and the man on the propeller to stand by to swing the prop. At the 'Go', with switches on, full tension on the bungees and a sharp swing of the prop, almost without fail the engine started – much to the surprise of the onlookers! It was not always easy to find volunteers at out of the way airfields so to my great relief replacement cartridges came from the UK in due course.

I was able to fly the Seafire up to Grumman's on Long Island. As manufacturers who made most of their aircraft for naval use, they were very interested in the Seafire. A number of their pilots flew it and were truly impressed, despite the fact that the Spit looked minute standing beside their F6F Hellcat fighter in which we were trying the new radar at Quonset Point.

Later the same week I flew the Seafire into Chance Vought's airfield. This was the centre of Corsair manufacturing. They were major suppliers to the US Navy and the Marine Corps and the UK also had some in the British Fleet Air Arm.

Like Grumman's, the Chance Vought workforce and pilots were astounded at the small size of the Seafire. Nevertheless, their pilots were keen to fly the Seafire so, having given them cockpit checks, I left them to get on with it.

I came back the next day to find their engineers and draftsmen had removed a number of hatches to see inside. This was fine but, when one of their pilots flew the aircraft, a large panel broke away which had not been replaced correctly. By the time I arrived, they had made and fitted a replacement hatch. The pilots carried on flying and were all equally impressed with the Seafire's performance and manoeuvrability. I collected the aircraft the following day and returned to La Guardia.

The next task I was presented with, by the British Naval Office in Washington, was to fly a British Westland Whirlwind, which had been sent over for the US pilots to fly. They wanted it taken from Norfolk VA to a fighter conference at Eglin Field in Florida, an airforce/navy test centre on the Gulf of Mexico.

This was a first for me, so I spent half a day going over the 'plane with the US Navy engineer who had been looking after it. This would be the first time it would fly since it was dispatched from Yeovil! There was a set of pilot's notes, which I studied carefully. The range of this aircraft was approximately 250 miles (safe). Norfolk to Eglin was around 1,000 miles and this would involve at least three stops for fuel. Having made sure that I knew the fuelling points and had tools for access, I set off to fly southwards. The radio equipment was only suitable for VHF communication on a limited number of frequencies and there were no navigation aids suitable to be used in the USA. I'm sure the US personnel at Air Traffic Norfolk were glad to see the back of Whirlwind Aircraft number 6994 and Twiss!

The route I chose was from Norfolk – Cherry Point – Charleston – Savannah –Tallahassee – Eglin Field, ie down the Atlantic coast to Savannah and then inland to Tallahassee. All went well for the first two stops. On the flight from Savannah I ran into very low cloud and rain and was flying at 300-500 feet, map reading. Conditions were rough and I had a nasty shock when I looked at the compass and found that the needle had jumped off its bearing, meaning the compass was unserviceable. Very nerve-racking. I noted a rail line running in approximately the heading I had been steering and latched onto it in desperation, thinking the railway must go to a town, which might have an airport.

My luck was in as the railway ran into Tallahassee and one low level circuit revealed an airfield. My relief was considerable. I landed and explained my problem to the airfield staff who were very understanding. They gave me a lift into town and I went to a sports shop and bought a small hiker's compass to see me through the last few hundred miles.

I stayed at Eglin for a few days flying some interesting aircraft including the Republic Thunderbolt, an American fighter – the XP 63 – and a bomber version of the Mosquito, which had flown down from Canada. One amusing incident happened when I arrived at the accommodation block. I was booked in and unpacked when the staff rushed in and said there was some mistake, could I repack, and go to a much smaller room nearby, which was quite adequate. I then found that the reason for the move was to make a nice room available for Charles Lindbergh who had turned up unexpectedly. I know my place!

There was a sad ending to the Whirlwind story though, as spare parts were needed before the aircraft could be flown again, but these were not available in the USA.

The commandant of the station, a keen power boat owner, took over the Whirlwind and removed the Peregrine engines, which he modified and fitted to his motor yacht! With that sort of h.p. the motor yacht should have had a good turn of speed but I never saw it.

I flew back to Washington, Patuxent River and New York to continue with trials on the new airborne radar set destined for the Royal Navy.

I had one more trip while in the US which was to fly the P61 Black Widow on the west coast. This aircraft was to be the "be all and end all" of night fighters for the US airforce. It was a large (about the size of a Beaufighter), twin-engined, two-place aircraft with the latest radar available at that time. The pilot's cockpit was huge to my standard, full of instruments. However, it had a poor layout and at night the reflections on all the pilot's panels made it difficult to get night adapted. It was an easy aircraft to fly but lacked performance. The British were not impressed and I do not know if it saw operational service with the US Army. A nice trip but rather a waste of time. Nearly 2,500 miles each way and by DC3 Dakota!!! Very slow!

I did a few more weeks in the USA flying trials at Patuxent River. During this time I did a conversion experience onto helicopters. I say 'conversion' as it was not on a course, but doing a series of flights with Don Callingham in a helicopter (R.4B) and being let loose for a solo and very alarming flight on Idlewild airfield, which was in the middle of construction. It took me the length of the main runway to land – probably 2,500 yards! Don followed behind in his Jeep and took over, thank God!

So, my holiday in the USA was over. Very interesting and what a pleasure to work with such a dedicated bunch of pilots and engineers, many of whom would be off to the Pacific where things were happening.

The war was really underway and there were losses of pilots on both sides in the fierce battles for overcoming the Japs. I felt that the war we had against the German fighters, although intense at times, did not compare in intensity with the fight against the Japanese, whose backs were to the wall.

After the USA, I was posted as a student onto No. 3 Course of the Empire Test Pilots' Course at Boscombe Down on 8th March 1945.

The Empire Test Pilots' School
This posting suited me as I had hopes of taking up test flying as a career after I was demobbed from the navy and had been involved with this type of flying for some time.

My wife and I travelled to the UK on a recently US-built aircraft carrier. However, we were very much segregated and only managed to meet briefly. During the passage, the ship rolled an alarming amount. So much so, that a number of the new US-built aircraft we had on board for British FAA squadrons, broke adrift resulting in considerable damage. My wife, not the best of sailors, was very poorly. We landed from the carrier at Greenock and caught a train to the south. We managed to get a nice flat in a village near Boscombe Down and I started at the ETPS in early March 1945.

No. 3 Course was the first of the courses with more than 10/12 pilots. Back to school started straight-away! We had an exceptional team of instructors on the theoretical side and two to three seasoned pilots for aerial instruction. The CO, Group Captain Willy Wilson, a very experienced test pilot and well known figure in the flying world, and his team of pilots, spanned the knowledge on all the types of service aircraft we had in our fleet. The chief ground instructor was very well known, experienced in a wide range of test flying activities and theoretical sides to aerodynamics.

We were all interviewed to gauge the types of aircraft we had been flying. The instructors deliberately started us off in aircraft with which we had minimum previous experience. I was destined for the Avro Lancaster! I was set a programme of general flying with an observer to help take notes of my observations.

Very interesting! And I thoroughly enjoyed the experience. In those days there was no concrete runway at Boscombe Down. There were acres of undulating grass, quite hilly in places, but plenty of room. Long grass runways and good approaches. Surrounded by Salisbury Plain, a substantial area of grass downland, 20 to 30 square miles of rolling downs, it was ideal for a test flying centre, away from any built-up areas.

RAF Boscombe Down was an airfield from the 1914-18 war and had considerable hangarage and facilities, being two miles from Amesbury, the nearest town and seven miles from Salisbury.

The school consisted of a series of newish huts, which were the classrooms and offices for the commanding officer and admin staff of the school. Meals had to be taken in the officers' mess on the far side of the airfield. A car was almost essential if one wanted a meal and be back in time for the next flight or lesson.

The aim of the ETPS was to teach pilots to fly and assess new types of aircraft to a standard of stability and handling, which would satisfy the military or civilian operators.

Apart from the flying, we had some fascinating visits to aircraft and engine companies who, apart from explaining their products, made sure we had an interesting time with plenty of entertainment. We regularly went up to London or Birmingham to shows and ate in some excellent restaurants.

We met pilots and engineers from a wide variety of areas of the industry who later in our careers were good contacts and helpful in our jobs.

On my course, we had pilots from the RAF and Royal Navy, the US Air Force and Navy, and Canada, France, Holland, Belgium, Italy, China, New Zealand, Australia, and more. The two Chinese pilots, who obviously had language problems, did two courses one after the other and did very well.

The ETPS set a high standard of competence in the flying and testing of aircraft and a small number of pilots, who were struggling to keep up with the rest, were returned to their units without completing the course.

There was some interchange of pilots, for example between the UK and the USA. After about six months, the whole course and staff was moved to Cranfield, then on to Farnborough where it stayed for several years. However, the school returned to Boscombe Down in the 1990s and is still there.

In the early days the pool of pilots provided a source from which firms were able to borrow a pilot if the company had a peak in production or one of their pilots was sick.

Nowadays, though, the range of aircraft is considerable and a separate section has been started for the rotary wing pilots. In 2005 the school was still very active and holds regular social functions which I attend from time to time at which one can meet test pilots from the past, and up and coming test pilots still on course.

APPENDIX I

Extract from *"The Fairey Delta 2"*, by R. L. Lickley, B.Sc., F.R.Ae.S., and L. P. Twiss, read before the Royal Aeronautical Society on 14th February, 1957.

DESIGN AND CONSTRUCTION OF FAIREY DELTA 2

INTRODUCTION

The development of manned supersonic aircraft in this country suffered a setback at the end of the 1939-45 War, when it was decided that the use of manned aircraft would be too dangerous; however, more realistic views soon prevailed and, as a result, the ordering of such manned aircraft was considered in 1947 by the Ministry of Supply and in our submissions to M.o.S. in 1949, we described the aircraft as having as its primary function "Research Flying at Transonic and Supersonic speeds up to Mach 1.5."

The background which led up to this submission is of interest, as it shows a logical line of development within the Company.

In 1947, the Company was developing the F.D.I. at Stockport and scale models of it at Heston, in order to conduct vertical take-off experiments. The models were of advanced design, powered by a rocket motor with twin combustion chambers, controlled in pitch and yaw respectively by an automatic pilot. Information of behaviour in flight was telemetered to the ground.

In September 1947 the Company was asked if it could further develop the vertical take-off models to fly transonically after ground launching as part of the experimental programme. After consideration it became clear that, although the technique and experience of the V.T.O. models would be of great value, the experiments themselves would be of little use unless they were aimed at obtaining specific information on a layout representative of a typical possible piloted supersonic aeroplane. We. therefore, began a design study of such a piloted aircraft as a preliminary to the design of the pilotless models. Our first efforts resulted in a design of high sweepback on both leading and trailing edges, all-moving tip ailerons, conventional tailplane and twin engines in the fuselage fed from a nose intake (P.1 type layout).

This design was not proceeded with, but in February 1949, we were approached by P.D.S.R. (A) (then Sir Harry Garner), and asked to consider an alternative design for a further supersonic research aircraft, preferably based on a single engine. We had, of course, by this time considerable background in the problems of designing such an aeroplane. We had developed the necessary new techniques of drag and performance estimation and had collected together what slender information there was on the stability and control characteristics of various configurations. We decided to begin our considerations afresh and by the end of the year (December 1949) had come to a firm proposal which differed very little from the aeroplane as it is flying at present, although pressure from various sources to make changes was at times very strong.

The design which evolved was a delta-wing plan form of aspect ratio 2, having a Rolls-Royce R.A.5 engine in the body, with wing root intakes, with frontal areas cut to a minimum and all possible excrescences removed. The main reasons behind our choice of a delta plan are summarised elsewhere. The major target and guiding principle in the whole design period was to get an aeroplane of minimum weight, with the smallest frontal and surface areas, while still remaining a straightforward aeroplane to handle in the air and on the ground, and yet at the same time large enough to house the R.A.5 engine and sufficient fuel to enable worthwhile flights to be made. As an indication of the design problems raised by this approach, the *maximum* clearance between engine and fuselage skin is less than 6in. and, within this space, room had to be found for the main frames to which the wing is bolted.

Although the aerodynamic form was decided at an early period, the contract to build two aircraft was not placed until October 1950: lack of money, priorities and other problems caused this hold up and almost immediately after the placing of the contract, "super-priority" intervened, and the need at Fairey's to concentrate on the Gannet meant that a fully effective start was not made on the design work until the summer of 1952, and manufacture effectively began about the end of that year.

Little or no priority was given to the aircraft and, because of the demand on wind tunnel capacity for tests of service types under development, only very meagre and belated high speed tunnel tests had been undertaken before the aircraft flew. In fact, some supersonic tests were only analysed after the aircraft had flown supersonically.

With that introduction, we can now consider the main features of the design.

AERODYNAMIC DESIGN
(1) Moderate Wing Loading
This was chosen to give good high altitude performance, medium landing speeds and good performance from normal length runways.

(2) t/c Ratio
This, at 4 per cent, is still one of the lowest flying and, at the design date (1949), was the lowest known.

(3) Tailless
The advantages of this layout were held to outweigh the reputed disadvantages and, when one considers the various tail layouts to be seen today, and the established need for fully-variable tailplanes, the choice seems to have been the correct one, possibly more than anything else, because of the aerodynamic simplification produced.

(4) Intakes
Side intakes were decided on, as it was felt that the structural simplicity and saving in weight, compared with a nose intake, were worth more to the design than the possible aerodynamic difficulties introduced. At various times the intakes were the subject of strong criticism, both from the aerodynamic aspects and from the possible bad effects on compressor flow, but they have remained substantially as initially conceived, and have proved satisfactory up to the highest Mach numbers reached.

(5) Large Chord Controls
Much discussion has ranged round trim drag and the penalties it applies to delta

aircraft. Our thinking led us to believe that much of the drag could be avoided by careful design and, in particular, by the use of large chord controls which would keep the angular movements reasonable. So far, our only problem with these controls has been lack of jack effort in certain flight cases; as predicted, the effects of trim drag have not been serious.

(6) Aerofoils
Mathematically defined forms were used for aerofoils and fuselage, to enable high accuracy of contour to be attained in the final manufactured product.

(7) Dive Brakes
These, of petal form, at the rear of the fuselage, were designed to give minimum change of trim, etc., and in flight at sub or supersonic speeds have given no pitch or lift changes and more than adequate deceleration.

(8) Body Form
Considerable work was done on this and it might be described as an early approach to area rule – the short intake fairings (inspired by Küchemann) combined with a cylindrical body to the trailing edge and the swept-fin mainly behind the trailing edge.

These, briefly, were the aerodynamic fundamentals of the design and the results obtained in the flying have shown them to have been soundly chosen. Some of the flight results will be discussed later.

STRUCTURAL DESIGN
The use of a very thin wing, combined with a fuselage almost full of engine, presented many difficult structural problems.

The thin wing (4 per cent) set the major problems and it was decided to use a form of construction in which the spars were perpendicular to the fuselage, with ribs or stringers parallel to the fuselage centre line. This shortened the length of the spars and greatly simplified the joints to the fuselage frames. The wing root bending moment, due to the small thickness, requires a number of spars, situated aft on the wing. Each spar is attached to machined fuselage frames which, to ease manufacture, were made in three pieces, and this had the additional advantages of making the frame statically determinate.

The wing consists essentially of two torsion boxes, one at the leading edge and one, the major torsion box, between the chassis and the control surfaces which are cantilevered off the trailing edge of this box. The skins of this aft torsion box are of thick light alloy, the thickness being dictated by requirements of torsional stiffness. Except at the root, the wing skins carry practically all the wing bending loads, but at the side of the fuselage the loads in the skin diffuse out into the three main spars.

The fin is attached at leading and trailing spars in a manner similar to the wing. The main bending attachment was made integral at the root with a cross member, so that once the critical narrow base attachment had been made the introduction of backlash on the fin base through fin removal was rendered less likely, as the detachable attachments were on a wide base. The main fin skin thickness was determined by stiffness requirements for the avoidance of flutter.

The rear fuselage forward to the break joint is of monocoque construction and has the petal brakes mounted on it. The problems of mounting the petals have the feature which is reproduced many times on this aircraft, i.e. the difficulty of incorporating into a small space mechanism dealing with large loads.

The centre fuselage consists of heavy frames connected by longeron members; the frames take the wing loads and support the engine.

The cockpit, which droops to provide improved view for landing, provided another difficult problem as almost the entire top of the cockpit has to be open to provide for seat ejection, etc. This problem was dealt with by building the relatively open cockpit onto a complete box forward of the forward bulkhead of the cockpit. The cockpit, when in the up position, is attached to the front fuselage by a conventional set of latch pins.

The control surfaces are constructed with a heavy leading edge torsion box designed by stiffness, and a light trailing edge designed by strength considerations. Provision was made for mass balancing, but this has not been needed.

A point of interest is that the structure weight was one per cent less than the weight estimated in 1949.

FLUTTER
Very full and careful flutter investigations were made and only a summary can be given here.

Calculations made early in the design stage showed that with the expected impedance of the hydraulic jacks actuating the control surfaces, the addition of mass balance made little difference to the flutter speed of the wing-aileron combination.

Later calculations by the Multhopp-Garner theory confirmed this view and showed that the addition of mass balance could bring in a low flutter speed if it caused the control surface natural frequency to be reduced to two-thirds of its value with no mass balance.

In view of these results and the fact that mass balancing would add considerable weight to the aeroplane, it was decided to eliminate it from the aircraft.

This has helped in the avoidance of transonic control surface buzz and single-degree of freedom flutter by keeping the natural frequency of the controls as high as possible. Other favourable factors are the very small trailing edge angle and the large chord of the control surfaces. It has not been found necessary, so far, to fit hydraulic velocity dampers to increase the control surface damping in the transonic region.

Very full flight testing has confirmed this approach, stick tapping having been carried out throughout the full flight range. The responses obtained from stick tapping appear to be sufficiently accurate to confirm the policy of flight vibration testing by this method and, since the taps have been capable of exciting nodes at 35 cycles/sec., it was felt that it was not necessary to use other methods. The use of this method has meant that a large number of records have been obtained in a comparatively short period. The analysis of the results indicate only slight variation of damping with Mach number.

GENERAL DESIGN CONSIDERATIONS
The thin wings and small fuselage, already referred to, provided the over-riding design factors, but a further point was kept well to the forefront and that was, so to design the aircraft that easy maintenance and straightforward servicing were provided. This approach has paid high dividends, giving what has been described as "airline reliability" and permitting up to six flights per day.

Design matters of interest are:

(1) The Drooping Nose
With the need to keep the height of the windscreen to a minimum and yet give the pilot adequate view at the high angles of incidence at landing, various schemes such as retractable seats, etc., were studied, but the final, and the simplest solution was that of

drooping the nose portion containing the pressure cabin. This is hinged on the bottom longerons and is operated by a hydraulic jack. It is a light and straightforward means of giving the pilot better view and has been reliable in operation. It did, however, set us some problems connected with the jettisoning of the hood. To ensure that the hood would jettison correctly, it was desired that it should pivot about an aft hinge on release. This pivot point, however, could not be earthed on to the fuselage, due to the drooping of the nose including the hood. This was overcome by having two "Barrow handles" carrying the aft pivot points, tipping with the droop nose and lying flush in troughs in the main fuselage in the nose-up position. To keep the drag to a minimum, the hood was designed with very small clearance from the pilot's head and is kept flush with the surrounding structure by having hinges on one side, thus avoiding sliding mechanisms which would increase the difficulties of pressure sealing.

(2) The Main Undercarriage

This was a geometric, as well as a mechanical, problem. It was found that levered suspension was the most satisfactory manner of absorbing the required energy with the short length of leg at our disposal and that this would also most easily fit the very limited area and thickness available in the wing housing.

The wheel, when housed, lies in a plane parallel to the inner surface of the upper wing skin. To rotate the wheel into this position the top of the leg is attached by means of a universal joint to an inclined rotating eyebolt, while a side bracing member forms a secondary hinge and controls the path of the wheel during retraction, and telescopic fore-and-aft member takes the drag. The eyebolt is mounted on a boss on the spar forging.

(3) General Servicing

In line with the policy mentioned earlier this had considerable study and, along the fuselage, a top deck was provided to carry all control rods, electrics, hydraulics, filters, etc., and this has proved invaluable for easy servicing.

Access to the research equipment carried was through the nose wheel bay and here also was carried the recording equipment required by the F.A.I. during the World record attempt.

(4) Engine Installation

The engine is a Rolls-Royce R.A. series engine with reheat. The basic engine is standard, some small external changes being made to enable it to fit our fuselage.

With the exception of reheat problems in the early stages, there has been little trouble with the power plant, in spite of tight clearances, and the general reliability has been high.

The engine is fitted or removed by breaking down the rear fuselage near the fin, and sliding the engine out on rails onto special ground equipment. This has enabled engine changes to be made easily and without breaking any services other than to dive brakes and rudder.

(5) Hydraulics and Power Controls

These have been left till last in the description of the design, although great care and forethought were devoted to them, and throughout the whole period of flying they have given every satisfaction.

It was decided in the early days to use power controls of Fairey manufacture, as we were just beginning to manufacture these in quantity and felt that our equipment had many advantages over anything currently available elsewhere. The further decision was taken to duplicate fully the control system and to do without manual reversion. As a result, the aeroplane has fully-powered fully-duplicated controls, with Fairey valves and hydroboosters. To eliminate flutter tendencies as far as possible the jacks are attached to solid structure and the valves operated by push-pull rods, to keep break-out forces to a minimum.

There are two hydraulic pumps driven by the engine, one of which feeds a main accumulator which powers the flying controls. The second pump feeds a second accumulator which supplies power not only to the flying controls, but also to the main and nose undercarriage retraction mechanism, the droop nose, and the air brakes. In addition to these accumulators, there is an emergency accumulator which can be selected to power either flying controls or the other services and there is also a brake accumulator.

In the event of an engine or hydraulic pump failure, an emergency air-driven turbine pump feeding the second system can be lowered into the air stream.

The air brakes are also operated by similar methods and the four petals are synchronised to ensure even opening. Another problem here was to operate the petals without excrescences and this was achieved by a system of floating links, giving a good moment arm, but remaining flush when closed.

MANUFACTURING PROBLEMS

This aircraft was our first attempt at building from solid without any transitional experience of similar types of construction. As a result many detail problems arose in the manufacture but, by careful jigging and making full use of the solid frames and spars, we consider that the wing profile was made to a measured accuracy of ± 0.005 in. relative to the mathematical form laid down. In addition, the wings are attached to the fuselage by ten close tolerance fixing points and full interchangeability of wing to fuselage was provided.

Integral fuel tanks occupy most of the wing and their development was closely studied. It was finally decided to assemble the wing as a dry structure, designed and manufactured to be as fuel tight as possible in this state and subsequently scaled by slushing. This system has worked out very well in practice.

In spite of the major machining problems of the spars and frames from rough forgings, and the assembly difficulties of the thin wings and fin, the aircraft flew about twenty months from the start of construction. It is worth noting that the last three months were mainly involved in inspection, testing of systems, impedance testing and general preflight work, an indication of the complexity of the systems.

Finally, with all these problems behind us, the aircraft made its first flight at Boscombe Down on 6th October, 1954.

APPENDIX II

REGULATIONS FOR ABSOLUTE
WORLD SPEED RECORD ATTEMPT

SPEED OVER A 15-25 KM COURSE AT
NON-RESTRICTED ALTITUDE

CLASSES C, E AND H

Course

The records must be attempted in a straight line over a course of 15-25 kilometres previously approved by the N.A.C. of the Country where the attempt is to be made.

The course must be prolonged at each of its extremities by an approach of either 5,000 metres or 7,500 metres.

The method of marking out the course is left to the discretion of the N.A.C. concerned but must be approved by the F.A.I.

Flying Altitude

The altitude of flight over the course is unlimited.

Nevertheless, the competitor must maintain level flight with a tolerance of 100 metres at the entry to the course and over the course. Moreover, the altitude at which the approaches to the course are entered in the two directions must be the same subject to a tolerance of 100 metres.

The altitudes shall be verified by barographs or by any other suitable method which, however, the F.A.I. is free to reject if it deems it to be inadequate.

Barographs must be carried in the record aircraft and must be sealed; they should be removed by a steward and the charts duly verified by the steward must be included in the record file.

From the time of take-off or release of the aircraft until the flight over the course has been completed, the aircraft must not fly at an altitude exceeding the mean of the altitudes at which the approaches to the course are entered, by more than 500 metres when an approach length of 5,000 metres is used, or alternatively by more than 750 metres when an approach length of 7,500 metres is used.

Measurement of Distance

The distance to be considered in the calculation of the speed shall be based on the arc of the great circle, but at the altitude at which the record attempt is accomplished.

Measurement of Speed

The aircraft shall fly over the course once in each direction, and the speed adopted shall be the average of the two speeds, calculated to the nearest kmh, below the actual figure recorded.

If more than one run in each direction is made during the course of the same flight, any two consecutive runs may be selected for submission to the F.A.I. on condition that they shall have been accomplished in opposite directions.

The two runs selected must have been achieved within a maximum lapse of time of thirty minutes. No landing shall be permitted during the record attempt.

Accuracy of Measures

The overall margin of error allowed for the determination of the speed must not exceed 0.25 per cent.

Difference Between Two Consecutive Records

A new record must be at least 1 per cent higher than the preceding one.

Special Conditions

If the record aircraft is fitted with special devices, these must be jettisoned before the first run over the entrance to the course.

Composition of the Record File

Besides other documents listed elsewhere, the record file must include the following:

(a) The name and location of the course which must have been approved by the N.A.C.

(b) A report on the flying altitude of the record aircraft during the attempt. The report shall contain all the necessary information concerning the methods employed for measuring the altitude as well as a certificate of the exactness of the measurements.

(c) Reports on the timing of the record aircraft on each of its flights over the course. These reports must indicate the direction in which the course was covered.

(d) If necessary, a certificate by the steward, of the jettisoning of any special apparatus.

(e) A report by the steward, on the method of starting used by the record aircraft.

(f) Detailed report drawn up or certified by an approved Scientific Body on the methods of time keeping and on the apparatus used, with particulars of the degree of accuracy obtained.

APPENDIX III

SUMMARY OF RECORD ATTEMPT

An attempt was made on 10th March, 1956, to establish a new world air speed record at unrestricted altitude over a 15-25 Km. course. The attempt was made by a Fairey Delta 2 aeroplane, registration WG.774, powered by a Rolls-Royce Avon jet engine with reheat, and piloted by Mr. Peter Twiss, over a course recently established near Ford and Chichester, Sussex, in South England, at a height of approximately 38,000 ft.

The attempt was timed by a team of engineers from the Royal Aircraft Establishment, acting on behalf of the Royal Aero Club, and the resulting speed was later confirmed as a world record.

Method of Timing
The record attempt was timed by the camera-chronometer method which in principle consists of photographing the aeroplane, on each timed run, at the beginning and again at the end of the course by two cameras which have been set so as to define two parallel and approximately vertical planes in the sky. The time interval between the two photographs is recorded by an electric chronometer.

The Course & Survey
The course between Chichester and Ford was surveyed by Colonel R. C. A. Edge of the Ordnance Survey Dept. The accuracy achieved was 1 in 20,000. The distance overall was 15,564.0 ± 0.5 metres.

The Record was made on the 10th March, 1956. The aircraft took off from R.A.F. Boscombe Down at 1122 and flew over the measured course first in an Easterly direction and then in a Westerly direction before returning to its base at Boscombe Down at 1145.

The speeds achieved are set out in the table below.

Flight Direction	Distance in Metres	Time Secs.	Speed K.P.H.	Speed Stat. M.P.H.
W-E	15473	30.971	1798.5	1117.6
E-W	15669	30.563	1845.7	1146.9
Mean			**1822.1**	**1132.2**

The Measurement of Height
Before the attempt. In order that the altitude could be measured accurately, it was essential that the static position error be measured over the Mach number range to be flown by the aeroplane. The measurement was made using a calibrated Venom aircraft from A&AEE Boscombe Down by flying the F.D.2 past in a series of runs.

The Venom or Datum aircraft flew at 38,000 ft. straight and level at Mach 0.75; as the F.D.2 flew past the Datum auto-observer records were taken in both aircraft, and a photograph of the F.D.2 taken from the Venom in order that the physical difference in height could be measured. A light fitted in the side of the fuselage of the F.D.2 wired to the auto-observer switch enabled a synchronisation of the records between F.D.2 and Venom.

The actual flight results covered the speed range M = 0.75 to M = 1.7.

The airspeed and altimeter system of the F.D.2 were given a thorough test for leaks before the Position Error Tests; this was repeated before and after every record attempt.

The following procedure was adopted and carried out by A&AEE Boscombe Down before each record attempt.

1. The Hussenot recorders were calibrated through the speed and height range required.

2. The recorders were loaded and sealed and then fitted into place and sealed into the aircraft by Royal Aero Club Observers.

3. The whole aircraft system was then checked for leaks.

4. The recorders were switched on before take off and off after landing.

5. When the aircraft was airborne, the pilot and Royal Aero Club Observer put an event marker on the Hussenot records both before and after the runs, so that the times at which the aircraft passed over the cameras could be identified on those records, and the gate positions deduced from the recorded and corrected aircraft indicated airspeed.

6. After landing the aircraft pitot-static system was again checked for leaks.

7. The recorders were removed under the supervision of the Observers of the Royal Aero Club.

8. The recorders were recalibrated.

9. The records were developed, certified and sent to the R.A.E. Farnborough for analysis.

The summarized height results were as follows:

1. The difference in height between gates 1 and 2 was 98 ft.

2. The mean height at these gates was 37,799 ft.

3. The maximum height attained during the flight was 38,647 ft.

4. The difference in height between the mean height at the two entry gates and the max. height attained was 848 ft.

5. The aircraft climbed from the entry gate to the end of each run.

Acknowledgements

The R.A.E. team engaged in timing operations at Ford and Chichester on the 10th March were W. J. Cox, J. E. Craig, M. A. Fisher, G. R. W. Labrum. W. J. Norman, C. R. Hunt and J. A. Maskell assisted with star calibrations at a later date.

The calibration and installation of the Hussenot recording equipment at Boscombe Down was supervised by G. McLaren Humphries and E. H. Goody.

The reduction of the height data was carried out by a team of computers led by Miss G. J. Griffith of R.A.E. Farnborough.

The data reduction for analysis of height was carried out by T. H. Kerr of Aero Flight R.A.E. Bedford.

The timing and preparation of the report for submission to the Federation Aeronautique International was done by N. E. G. Hill, W. Goldsmith and T. H. Kerr.

FAIREY DELTA 2

PERFORMANCE DIAGRAMS

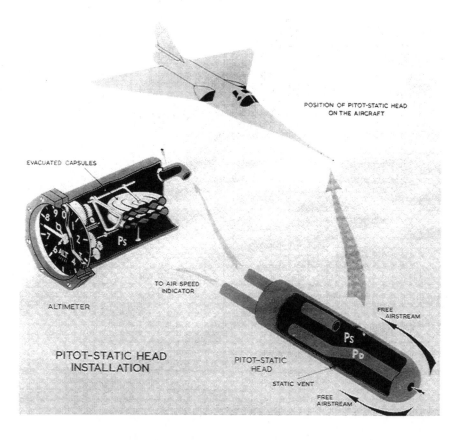

Main components of pitot-static head installations (see p. 183).

COCKPIT RAISED

COCKPIT LOWERED

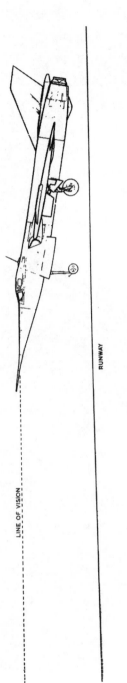

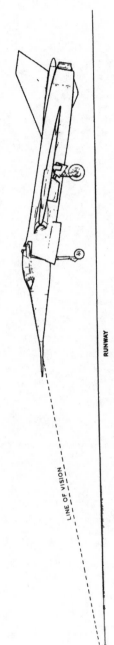

View from cockpit with drooping nose in raised and lowered positions (see p. 177).

View of FD 2 passing the camera site at beginning of one run and end of next.
Taken by the timing camera during record runs in 1956.

INDEX

Aeroplane, The, 34
Aitken, Max, 162
Andover, 68
Appleton, Leslie, 13
Appendix I, 174
Appendix, II, 180
Appendix III, 182
Avro 707, 131

Battle of Britain, 68
Beachy Head, 64, 74
Blackburn Roc, 68
  Skua, 68
Boscombe Down, 12, 13-15, 25, 49, 62, 76, 87, 90, 100, 134, 142, 144
Boulton Paul P-111, 131
Bowyer, Edward, 153
Bristol Aircraft Corporation, 150
  Blenheim, 68
  Fighter, 113
Bristol-Siddeley, 154
Bull, General, 147
Burma, 20
Burnard, Alan, 159
Butlin, Billy, 158

Calshot, 56
Catapult Armed Merchantman, 68
Cazaux, 136-144
Chaplin, Charles, 13
Chemical Warfare Division, 61
Chichester, 65
Child, Maurice, 17, 26, 43, 46, 59, 102, 103, 134, 135
Clarke, Roger, 163
Clegg, R., 118
Connery, Sean, 160-161
Convair XF-92A, 131

County Hotel, Salisbury, 87
Currey, C., 158, 159, 161

Daily Express, 162
Daily Express Offshore Power Boat Race, 162
Daily Mail, 122
Daily Sketch, 119, 120
Daily Telegraph, The, 121
De Havilland Mosquito, 56
   Rapide, 13
   Tiger Moth, 67
   Venom, 76, 98
De Plant, P., 140
Dimbleby, Richard, 113
Douglas Skyray, 131
Du Cane, Peter, 159
Duke, Neville, 115

Eastleigh, 68

Fairey Air Surveys, 164
Fairey Aviation Company, 29, 34, 105, 119, 123, 127, 129; sold to Westland
   Aircraft, 149, 150, 152, 154
   Battle, 67
Fairey Huntress, 159
Fairey Huntsman, 28, 160
Fairey Yacht Harbours, 167
F.D.1, 131, 144
F.D.2 Delta, 12, 13, 14; first flight, 13, 23; 'droop-snoot', 13; test flying, 13;
   flutter tests, 14, 45; emergency landing, 14-17; supersonic flight, 19;
   speed record preliminaries, 34-38; re-heat trials, 44-50; tracking troubles,
   50-52; operation 'Metrical', 59; smoke trails, 61; the record course, 62;
   timing the record, 72-84; making contrails, 78; camera problems, 80;
   first runs, 89 ; failures, 83-91; final run, 95; record run, 98-101;
   camera error, 102; the record ratified, 110; faster than the sun, 111;
   flying in France, 138; insurance trouble, 138; French insured, 140;
   visibility troubles, 143; controls, 144; flying in Norway, 146, 149
Fairey, Richard, 28, 39, 40, 157
Fairey, Sir Richard, 28, 29, 31, 43, 164
   Firefly, 156
   Fulmar, 69, 70
   Gannet, 31, 35, 43, 72, 124, 129
   Rotodyne, 125, 129
   Swordfish, 68
Fairey Marine, 156, 163, 164
Fawley Oil Refinery, 64
Fleet Air Arm, 67
From Russia with Love, the film, 160-161

Gagarin, Yuri, 62
Gathering of Eagles, 170
Gellatly, R., 155
General Post Office, 65
Gibraltar, 69
Gliding, 171-173
Gloster Meteor, 78, 83, 90, 97
Gokeen, Sabrina, 170
Green, Leslie, 91, 118
Guardian, 121
Guinea Pig, The, 40

Hall, G.W., 35, 122
Hallet, Colin, 163
Hamble, 156, 163, 169
Harding, Gilbert, 124
Harrison, Rex, 160
Hawker Henley, 68
    Hurricane, 68
Hawker Siddeley Aviation, 153
Hayling Island, 158
Haynes, Colonel H., 24, 45, 73, 122
Head, Lord and Lady, 159
Hill, N. E. G., 81
Hinchingbrooke, Viscount, 123
H.M.S. *Argus*, 69
H.M.S. *Ark Royal*, 69
Hunting Aircraft, 150

Indian Ocean, 21
Inglesby, Mr., 77

Kelly, Barbara, 124
Knoblock, Richard, 170

Lacanau-Ocean, 145
Lewis, Merrick, 162
Libya, 165-167
Lickley, Robert, 13, 36, 43
Lindfield, 20
Lindfield House, 20
Lithgow, Mike, 115

Malaya, 20
Mandalay, 21
Marcel Dassault, 136, 140
Martin Maryland, 68
Mathews Squadron Leader J. O., 148

McFarland, Dave, 170
Ministry of Supply, 24, 28, 34, 123, 125, 137, 146
Moulton, Alex, 163

Naval Air Station Ford, 64, 70, 72, 99
Netheravon, 67
Newbury, 16
North American F-100C Super Sabre, 25
Novosel family, 170

'Ogee'wing, 149, 150
Operation Torch, 70

Parker, E, 61
Parkfield, 32, 42
Paul, D. M., 118
Payne, Air Commodore L. G. S., 121
Pitt, Robin, 167-168
Pon, Mijndert, 167-168
Portsdown Hill, 53, 118, 164
Portsmouth, 64
Portsmouth Evening News, 118
Purvis, Group Captain Brian, 77

Queen's Commendation, 20

R.A.E. Farnborough, 46, 63, 68, 81, 105, 108, 136
Rolls-Royce Avon, 24, 97
Royal Aero Club, 60, 63, 108

Sandhurst, 55
Schneider Trophy, 56
Shaw, R. A., 36
Shuttleworth Trust, 145
Simmonds, Alan, 167
Slade, Gordon, 24, 26, 43, 72, 74, 89, 97, 98, 99, 110, 115, 136
Society of British Aircraft Constructors, 153
Southampton Water, 64
Sopwith Pup, 114
Sopwith, Tommy, 114
Stainforth, O. H., 56
Stevens, James Hay, 131
Stockbridge, 29
Strode, Warren Chetham, 40
Stubbington, 55
Supermarine S.6B, 56
   Seafire, 59, 70
   Spitfire, 56, 68
Swordfish, Vospers, 159

Tangier, 69
Thompson, E. W., 39
Thompson, Squadron Leader T., 50, 98
Thompson, T. E, 122
Thorney Island, 99
Thurgood, D., 114, 117, 119
Times, The, 122
Tunnicliffe, Nigel, 159
Twiss, Paul, 21, 32, 55
Twiss, Peter: birthday, 20; parents, 20; grandparents, 20; early days, 20;
   F.D.2 first flight, supersonic, 23; thoughts on speed record, 24, 29;
   with Brooke Bond Tea Co., 31, 57; at Sherborne School, 32, 39-42;
   early school days, 32; 'boxing party', 41; record plans, 43-54;
   F.D.2 re-heat trials, 44-45; tracking problems, 46-47; brother's death, 56;
   mother remarries, 56; joins Fleet Air Arm, 57, 67-71; operation 'Metrical', 59;
   smoke trails, 61; planning the record course, 62; operational service, 67-71;
   joins H.M.S.*Ark Royal*, 69; awarded D.S.C., 70; to America, 70;
   timing the record, 72-84; making contrails, 78; camera problems, 79;
   faster than the sun, 111, 125-126; aftermath, 112-114; press reaction, 115-124;
   salary, 125-128; flying in France, 137-146; insurance troubles, 139;
   French insured, 140; visibility problems, 142; flying in Norway, 147-148;
   end of career as test pilot, 147-151; joins Fairey Marine, 156; remarries, 157;
   the Fairey boats, 157

Westland Aircraft Company, 29, 105
White Waltham, 12, 13, 25, 134
Whittington, 21

Yeager, Chuck, 170
Yeovilton, 68

INDEX TO 'MY WARTIME YEARS', PP 174-197

355ª Squadriglia, 179
746 Squadron, 186, 191
759 Squadron, 174
771 Squadron, 175
784 Squadron, 184, 186
804 Squadron, 176, 182
804A Squadron, 177
807 Squadron, 177, 178, 179, 180
Aircraft Dummy Deck Landings
   (ADDLs),181
Albacores, 178
Argus, 177, 178, 179, 182
Ark Royal, 177
Audacity, 176
Avro Lancaster, 196

Battle of Britain, 193
Beechcraft Expeditor, 192
Bismarck, 175
Blackburn Skuas, 175
Blenheim, 175
Boscombe Down, 196, 197
BR 20, 179
British Westland Whirlwind, 194

Callingham, Commander Don, 193,
   195
Campbell, Captain Dennis, 192
Camships, 176
Cap Spartel, 177
Chance Vought Corsair, 192, 194

CR 42, 174, 178
Crosley, Commander R Mike, 179

DC3, 195
De Havilland, 176
Dewoitine 520, 182, 183

Eagle, 178, 180
Empire Test Pilots' School, 196, 197

Fairey, Firefly, 191
  Fulmar 176, 177, 178, 179, 180, 184
  Swordfish, 176
Furious, 181, 182, 183

Gladiator N5540, 175
Gloster Gladiator, 174, 176
Grumman Hellcat, (F6F), 191, 192, 194
  Martlets, 176

Harris, Fraser, 175, 178, 179
Harris, Major Skeets, 186, 191
Hartley, Group Captain, 186
Hatston, 175, 176
Hawker, Henleys, 175
Hinstock Instrument Flying School
  (IFS), 184
Holme, Slim, 191
Holroyd, Pty Off A R, 179
Hurricane, 176, 177

Illustrious, 180

Jean Bart, 177
JU 88, 178, 189, 190

La Senia, 182
Lake, Dennis, 188
Lindbergh, Charles, 195

Malaya, 177
Mosquitoes, 187, 189, 190

Naval Fighter School, 174
Naval Spitfire Squadron, 180
Night Fighter Inception Squadron
  (NFIU), 186, 191
Night Fighting, 184-185
Night Intruding, 187

Operation Harpoon, 178

P 61 Black Widow, 195
Philip, Leading Air Gunner, 179

Queen Mary, 192

RAF Ford, 186, 187, 190
Republic Thunderbolt, 195

Scapa Flow, 175
Seafire, 182, 183, 193
SM 79, 178, 179
Sperry Company, 193

Tafaroui, 183

V1, 190
Victorious, 180

Wellington, 191
Wilson, Group Captain Willy, 196

XP 63, 195

Yeovilton, 174, 175